To Kathy
May the paths you travel
lead to happiness!

Lew Gottfried
Fran Gottfried

TRAVELING UNCHARTED PATHS

The Tale Of Two Retirees And The Peace Corps

BY LEW AND FRAN GOTTFRIED

Fairway Press
Lima, Ohio

TRAVELING UNCHARTED PATHS

FIRST EDITION
Copyright © 1992 by
Lew and Fran Gottfried

7910 / ISBN 1-55673-455-7   PRINTED IN U.S.A.

We dedicate this book to all Peace Corps Volunteers who have traveled uncharted paths to find a better road for people in the third world to travel.

Acknowledgements

We wish to acknowledge the help of free-lance writer Pat Tubbs, Cincinnati, Ohio. She not only encouraged us, she organized the material and gave us her professional help in writing this book.

We also wish to acknowledge Bill and Gloria Fraley of Heritage Computer Service, Tiffin, Ohio, who took responsibility of our manuscript while the final changes were made.

We also wish to express our special thanks to Emily Wilson and Stanley Schmidt for their editorial advice and to Carol and Bill Mason and Jean Tom for their technical assistance.

Table Of Contents

Introduction

Fran and I were both born and raised on small farms in northwest Ohio. We first met in the sixth grade, and our immediate attraction to each other has never ended.

We married immediately after high school, in the small rural Lutheran Church where we both worshiped regularly. I then joined the U.S. Navy and served two years in the Pacific during World War II, while Fran worked as a welder in a machine shop. After the war we took over my family farm and spent the next 25 years of our lives developing a highly successful herd of registered Holstein dairy cattle, and raising our family of three children, one daughter, Gloria, and two sons, Stephan and Ron.

Our interest in other countries developed during those years, beginning by serving as family hosts for youth visiting America from the Netherlands, Denmark, France, Israel and Nepal through the International Foreign Youth Exchange program. It was these young boys and girls who first sparked a love in us for people with backgrounds different from ours.

At the age of 50 we became restless. With our children grown and starting their own lives we found ourselves wanting to see more of the world with our own eyes. We also had a desire to, in some way, to say thank you to God for our many blessings through the years.

The Peace Corps emerged as the way to meet both our needs. At that time it was just beginning to expand the role of its good will ambassadors, to looking for individuals who could provide technical assistance to developing nations. Our background in farming, business and cooperatives made us just the kind of volunteers needed for this task. We spent two years in the Dominican Republic, working among the poorest of the poor in places we have never dreamed existed.

It was not until several years after our Peace Corps experience that we decided to write this book, when, after our parents' death, we found all the letters we had written to them from the Dominican Republic — they had saved them all. Seeing our words again, we realized how much they revealed. More than just a diary of our daily activities, recorded here were our innermost thoughts, feelings, joys

7

and frustrations. We read them over and over again, and each time, our eyes became misty as we realized how much we had gained by taking a risk in order to serve others.

It doesn't matter how old you are, you have the opportunity to do the same. May this book challenge and inspire you to take your own trip "Traveling Uncharted Paths Together."

Fran and Lew Gottfried

Part 1

Departure

Chapter 1
The Journey Begins

We were at the airport in Miami, waiting for our connecting flight to Puerto Rico, the first stop on our Peace Corps journey.

"Here are two seats, Fran, they should make a good place to rest," I said.

"Great," she said, sitting down with a big sigh. I organized our bags around us and sat down next to her with an even bigger sigh. We had been traveling five hours and had at least three hours to go before our plane left for San Juan. But right then, neither of us seemed to mind.

"The way I feel right now," Fran said, "I could sit here for ten hours."

"That's good," I replied, pointing to our bags, "because with all this around us there's not much we can do but sit here." Our two large suitcases, two regular ones, and two flight bags seemed like a lot now, but they held all the clothes, personal items and equipment we thought we'd need for the next two years of our lives.

Fran looked at our luggage. "I hope we have everything," she said, as I started counting the bags she added, "I meant, do we have everything **inside** them?"

I looked again at the bags. We'd packed in two days — who knew if we had everything? It had only been two months since I had taken our Peace Corps acceptance letter out of the mailbox at our farm in Ohio. Then we had figured it would take about a year before we left, but here we were at the airport, staring at our luggage.

Packing was only a small part of getting ready to go — we also had to sell 60 head of dairy cows and 40 head of young cattle. Even though we had found good buyers, it was still hard to see a lifetime breeding program go rolling out the lane on four cattle trucks. Selling our farm machinery and equipment proved to be even a greater sacrifice; we had lost a lot of money on that part of the sale. I was beginning to wonder about our wisdom in making this decision!

Fran interrupted my thinking. "You know, I don't think it was not until the last two weeks that I really realized that we were leaving home, when different groups started to have farewell parties for us."

"I know," I said, "everyone made me feel like we were going away forever."

We started to laugh, remembering the different reactions our friends and relatives had to our decision to join the Peace Corps. My cousin had asked, "Why are you leaving — don't you like us anymore?" In response to a routine check by the F.B.I. our neighbor first told the agent he lived next door to us his entire life, but went on to say he didn't know a thing about us. In a way, maybe, he was right. He certainly did not know the part of us that was on its way to Puerto Rico. Right then, I wasn't sure if we totally knew us either.

We sat in silence for awhile, watching the mass of people rushing by in all directions.

"It sure would be interesting to know just where everyone was going and what they were going to do when they got there," Fran said, turning from the crowd to me.

"Are we sure we know where we are going and what we are going to do?" I asked.

There was another pause, this one longer than the last. "I guess we have a little of the same feeling our great-great grandparents must have had," I said at last, "sitting at the harbor among their trunks waiting to sail to America, worrying about whether or not they had made the right decision and if they had everything. I can feel the butterflies they must have had in their stomachs."

Fran nodded her head, but said nothing. There was a long, last pause as we sat there thinking. Finally she reached for my hand and softly asked, "Lew, what do you honestly think? Did we make the right decision?"

This time neither of us broke the silence. All we knew for sure was that we were about to find out.

11

Chapter 2
Entering The Heat

Our final destination in Puerto Rico was Ponce, the second largest city in the country. It was located on the opposite side of the island from San Juan and was relatively unspoiled; you had to cross the mountains to get to it, and most tourists never got that far. As a result, the Spanish culture was very much alive here, making it a good place to train volunteers as well.

Fran was the first to disembark from the plane. Unexpectedly, she paused in the doorway and I bumped into her from behind.

"What's the problem?" I asked.

"Whew, feel the heat!"

I joined her at the doorway. "You're right. It was never like this in Ohio!"

"Do you think it will be like this all the time?"

"It's probably just been a hot day." I answered, hurrying along with wishful thinking, but the heat steaming up from the concrete into our faces made me wonder.

We followed the crowd over to get our luggage, but we only felt worse when we got there.

"Oh, no," Fran exclaimed when she spotted our bags, "what a mess!" The lid had been totally torn off one of her suitcases and tied back on haphazardly, leaving clothes hanging out on all sides.

"That's the one that had my good things in it!" she said.

I tried to be cheerful. "It looks like they're all still there," I said, "even if they're not in the same shape as when they left home." But the bag did look a little pitiful, and actually, the more I looked at it, the more I thought it looked like us — a little tired, a little tattered, and a lot shaken up.

We were saved by Charlie, a young Peace Corps representative who had appeared to meet us and take us to the Peace

Corps training center. He made us feel better by laughing at our experience with the luggage, but more importantly by being a friendly face.

Charlie explained lots of things to us as we drove along, including the fact that he was taking us to the training center, which was formerly a convent for Catholic nuns. "This will be a good stepping stone from your U.S. lifestyle to your new one," he said as we pulled up to the gate.

"Is this where we stay?" I asked.

"No, just your luggage. We are going to leave it here in our storage room."

He got out and lifted the bags off the truck. "Just take what you need for tonight. We have a place for you in town. Tomorrow morning, you will return here and sort out your things that you will need for the next two months of training. The rest will be locked up in safe storage here until you are ready to go in-country."

Our flight bags held enough for an overnight stay, so we grabbed them and climbed back into the truck. We drove only a short distance before Charlie pulled up to a building and said, "This is where I leave you. See you in the morning."

I looked around — it couldn't be what it looked like, but I had to ask anyway.

"You mean we are to stay in a bar all night?"

"There are a couple of rooms in the back. The manager knows you are coming. He will take care of you."

"Is this the best hotel in town?" Fran asked.

"The Peace Corps does not have money for the hotels," he replied, driving off, leaving us on the street.

We just stood there, unsure of what to do until we were spotted by the manager of the bar, a short Puerto Rican man with a "cookie duster" mustache. He came out to greet us and then took us through the bar to our room.

"Many new Peace Corps volunteers spend their first night here," he said, opening the door with a smile, "When you are ready, come out. I will give you both a free drink!"

He left, and we looked around us. The room was hot and noisy with Latin music and loud chatter in the bar. It had three bare walls. The fourth wall had a window that was too high to see through, but that was just as well, since it looked out on another bare wall — which we later found out was the back of the restroom for the bar. We found that out when we discovered that the bar's restroom was our restroom, too.

The only furniture was the bed, so we sat down together; it had been a long day and this was not the kind of ending we had anticipated. We sat there for awhile saying nothing. Finally Fran burst into tears, sobbing, "Lew, what did we get ourselves into?"

I put my arms around her and said the only thing I could say — "I don't know, I just don't know."

Chapter 3
Knocking On Doors

The next morning, we walked over to the training center to meet other volunteers, who, like us, were brand new to the program. The sun was shining as we entered the gates and heard the laughter, enthusiasm and friendliness of young people; there was even a volleyball game going on.

After our first day, it was all a welcome relief, even though we knew from the start that there would still be many differences between us and the rest of our training group, primarily due to our age. Originally, the Peace Corps was designed to gain goodwill and understanding between nations through the efforts of young people. But now the host countries were demanding more and more from the volunteers. They wanted to drill new water wells and initiate agricultural, educational and health programs and more, which called for technically experienced, older volunteers like Fran and me. We were one of the first older, married couples to be accepted into a program which normally attracted students fresh out of high school or college. It would be easier for them to change and learn new things, especially a new language, but we were the kind of pioneers the program needed. Could we make the necessary adjustments? Could the Peace Corps adjust to us? I could only hope that together we would find the answers.

We made it through our first few days quickly, developing friendships with the younger volunteers who helped make us feel more at home. We actually began to feel a little better about our decision, until the head teacher called us all together at the end of the week for an important announcement.

"Our budget is very tight," he began, "and there is no money to pay for housing while you are here. So we are asking all of you to go out in the different barrios (communities) near here and find a home to live in."

There was a short silence, then a lot of long questions from the volunteers and a lot of short answers from the director.

"Do we just go anywhere?"

"We have divided the city and have a hand-out indicating your territory."

"Are all the territories close enough to walk to class?"

"No, some are not."

"How much do we pay them?"

"You make your own deals."

"What sections do the rich Americans live in?"

"Sorry, there are none, and besides, you must find a home that speaks Spanish."

"Since I'm paying my own way, can I stay in a hotel?"

"Absolutely not! Finding a home is part of your training. When you go in-country for service, you will need to do things much more humbling than this."

"Can we go in pairs?"

"Postively not. Most homes are too small, and besides, you would speak English to each other. That is a no-no."

Fran and I asked if that meant us, too. The younger volunteers found this humorous.

"Here's your chance, Dad," one said.

"I hear Puerto Rican women love old men," said another.

"Let him go, Mom, you can always have me!" a third added.

The teacher tried to re-gain control. "Okay class, let's leave "Mom and Dad" to settle their own problems," he said. And that was it.

The next morning, we found ourselves out early, walking the streets in search of a house. We stopped at each corner and looked up and down the blocks.

"Let's choose a nice house," Fran said, heading down one of the better looking streets. "Those look like really nice homes over there."

They were nice homes. And they all gave us a really nice turn-down. After the last "no," we decided to try a new strategy — knocking on every door on the street.

We had reached the next house by this time, so I turned to Fran and said, "Your turn."

Fran knocked. The door opened. The lady smiled. The door closed.

"At least she smiled," said Fran. "Your turn."

"This hardly seems fair," I said. "You get the smiles and get the **no** answers."

After a couple of hours of trying with no luck, we finally sat down to rest. "This is humiliating and embarrassing," Fran said, then stopped when she saw that I was smiling at her. "And, okay, I guess, a little fun."

I laughed, "We are making a few friends. We have a fan club already." I pointed down the street at four dogs who had been following us for over an hour.

Fran shook her head, "I think they are looking for a home to stay in just like we are. I hope they don't expect to stay with us!"

We had our first good luck at the next house. A sweet old lady greeted us and nodded her head up and down, saying, "si."

I held up two fingers and pointed at Fran and me. The lady said "si."

I walked into the house and Fran followed. The lady stood there and smiled and said, "si" then she pointed at two chairs. I said "si" and we sat down.

The lady left us alone for a little while and then returned with a small boy. The boy smiled.

"I speak little English," he said. "My mother no understand what you need."

We explained to the boy. The boy explained to his mother. This time the sweet little old lady did not say "si."

On the street again, I said, "Well, we learned something."
"What?"

"They don't understand us either!"

It was all very frustrating. We had had only one week of Spanish, so our vocabulary was *very* limited. All we could say was "Peace Corps" — "My name is Fran" — "I want house to sleep" — "Yes" and "No."

17

"They don't know if we are salesmen, comedians or selling apple butter." Fran said.

"Your turn!" I said.

We finally hit the jackpot at the next house. A jolly man answered in English and invited us to sit on his porch. He asked us all kinds of questions about ourselves and then told us all about himself before I finally got him back on the subject of sleeping and eating at his home.

"I would love to have you two nice people," he said, "but I have no extra bed. I only wanted to practice my English. Few people in this part of the city speak English."

We sighed, smiled and started to walk back toward the street. The man called after us. "Come back, that was not nice of me! You return tomorrow, maybe I can help you."

While we had our doubts, the jolly man proved true to his word. The next day, he told us that he had found a home for us that was about a 15 minute walk from the training center. It was not one of the nice ones we originally chose, but it was a place to stay, and we took it gratefully.

Our new home was a little frame one, with wooden floors and wooden walls. Our bedroom was so small that the bed filled the entire length of the room. We had to get up one at a time to get dressed, and walk through the bedroom of one of the family's sons to get to the bathroom.

It was also located right on the curve of a busy one-way street, with no lawn or trees in between the house and the traffic. By day, the heat from the street made it unbearably hot, and by night the noise made it almost impossible to sleep.

First came a lot of traffic and horn tooting. Later the drag-racing drivers came out with tires squealing, followed by the police with sirens going full blast. Then, when it was almost morning, the peddlers came along with their two-wheel carts, yelling very loudly to get the early risers to come out on the street and buy food for the day. Because of all this, Fran and I soon became early risers too. If I woke first, I would open one eye and say, "It sure is wonderful to finally have a home." Fran would then open one of her eyes and reply, "Sure is," but then she would open her other eye and add, "I can lie just as well as you do."

Though our first living arrangements were difficult, we were fortunate to have friendly and supportive neighbors on both sides of us. They genuinely seemed to like us just for who we were and we drew much comfort from them.

On our left lived Felix, a tall, thin elderly gentlemen. We could always count on finding him out on his front porch, smiling and rocking easily in an old wicker chair. The highlight of his day seemed to be when we came out our door and shared a little conversation with him.

As soon as we said our hellos, Felix would always say, "Muie calor hoy." (Very hot today.)

"Si," we would answer.

"Tu quirie vino?" (Would you like some wine?)

When we were on our way to school, we always said "no," of course. But it didn't take me long to figure out that it was a good idea to walk out on my porch just before I went to bed. There would be Felix, rocking in his chair and smiling, never failing to make a comment about the heat — and an offer of wine.

On the right side of our home lived Pedro and Carmen Serrant. They were our favorite Puerto Ricans and the two people most responsible for getting us through our first month of training. Like Felix, they also sat on their front porch each evening, smiling and waiting for the new neighbors to come out. We met when Carmen surprised Fran one night by catching her attention with a greeting of "Hi neighbor, welcome to Ponce!" in beautiful English.

They apologized for not coming over to visit us, but they couldn't do this since they were at odds with our housemother. The boys in our home were known for getting into all kinds of trouble, but when Pedro and Carmen had tried to help, the mother had resented their interference and forbid them from setting foot on her property.

"It's unfortunate that we can't be friends with your housemother, but we want you to know that you are always welcome here," said Carmen.

Pedro and Carmen shared many things with us that helped us begin to feel very welcome, introducing us to Puerto Rican foods, like fried bananas, and taking us to some of the most beautiful parts of the country. One special weekend, we drove to a rain forest in the heart of the island, where we shared a picnic lunch surrounded by a lush, clear waterfall, dense tropical trees and exotic birds. There, in that quiet and beautiful place, we began to reflect and to share some of our problems with our new friends, whom we had come to know and trust.

Our first three weeks had not been easy. Cramped in our small hot and noisy bedroom each night, we got little sleep, so we were always tired each morning as we went to our studies. Our classes were now taught entirely in Spanish, and we just weren't keeping up. We really hadn't broken our ties with home, and worried often about our children and our farm. It seemed that the less we understood in class, the more we thought of Ohio instead of our lessons.

On top of this, when we came home after a tough day, we were exposed to the problems of our housemother and her family. Pedro and Carmen were right; the boys in our home were in all kinds of trouble. One day we were shocked to see the older son chained hand and foot to his bed, which his mother told us was the boy's attempt to break himself free of a drug habit. It was pitiful to see him lying there, sweating and shaking.

"We're worried," I said at last. "We don't seem to be progressing fast enough at school and I guess we wonder if we're really cut out for this." Pedro and Carmen said nothing, just nodded and smiled reassuringly at us. I realized then how important they had become to our survival there. Like the beautiful cool restful place to which they had brought us, they had given us a break from all our worries. I reached across the table and grasped both of them by the hand.

"You know, the only reason we have been able to continue has been you and your friendship, doing things like bringing us here. Your kindness and thoughtfulness have meant a lot to us."

We had come to the Peace Corps to give, and here we were receiving. I hoped that we could one day do for others what Pedro and Carmen had done for us and wished with all my heart that we would find something to help us get through our studies.

A few days later, I received an answer to my wish. The Peace Corps staff had also realized that this wasn't an easy transition for us and assigned a special Spanish instructor to work with us individually for a week. His name was Alberto, and he was a Cuban who fled his country to be free. His wife had remained behind, but he still had hopes that she would one day join him.

We felt we had many things in common with this man who would be teaching us. We certainly understood his loneliness, for we too missed our family. But unlike us, he had no assurance he would ever see his family again. Hearing his story, we began to feel a little less sad about our situation.

Alberto proved to be just what we needed. Not only did he instruct us in the classroom, but he took us into the community to teach us the practical skills like shopping that we would also need to survive.

After our final lesson, Alberto closed his book, and smiled at us, complimenting us on how much we had progressed. He then told us that on Monday we were to report to the training director's office for new instructions.

We were a little puzzled. "Why does he want to see us?"

"I don't know. I am only your Spanish instructor," he said, "but don't worry."

Nevertheless, we did worry as we walked home that night.

"Do you think maybe we have flunked?" Fran asked.

"I don't think so." I said, putting my arm around her.

"Others have packed their bags and gone home, you know."

That was true enough. Over the past few days, it had become clear that some of the volunteers just weren't going to make it — they were disillusioned perhaps, or couldn't adjust, or maybe missed a boyfriend or girlfriend back home too much.

"I don't think they were ordered to go," I said, "I think they just realized this wasn't for them."

"But we don't know for sure," Fran said, still worried.

I shook my head, no, and suggested that we stop to buy some ice cream on the way home, something that always made us feel better. But this time even that didn't work. Despite our improvements under Alberto, and the help of Pedro and Carmen, we knew we were still far behind the other volunteers in being ready to go "in-country." There could only be one reason the director wanted to see us — we were failing to make the transition.

On Monday, the director greeted us with a friendly handshake and smile. He began by asking, "How are you doing and do you feel like continuing?" He had a pipe and he tapped it in his hand as he looked at us.

We looked at each other out of the corner of our eyes, unsure of how to respond.

"Well, we haven't asked to go home yet, have we?" Fran said, finally.

He folded his arms across his chest and looked at us again. "We have a conference once a week with the staff to evaluate everyone. We had a long talk about you two last week." He smiled, but hesitated before he continued.

"To be honest with you, we are very concerned. This is a tremendously big transition for you. You have already had some difficulty adapting to the ways of this country — there'll be even more of that once you're on your assignment. So we've decided to do something that we don't do for most volunteers. We are going to send you both to the Dominican Republic for three or four days to allow you to visit your site."

Our eyes lit up. This was not the surprise we had expected; instead, it was just the right thing to answer our doubts, and we told the director so.

"Good," he said. "When you return, we'll meet again to make a decision." He tapped his pipe again. "Any questions?"

"When do we leave?" asked Fran.

Two days later, the director again summoned us to his office to tell us that we were to fly to Santo Domingo at

8 a.m. the next morning for a three-day stay. He also informed us that Kathy, one of the younger volunteers, would be going with us. Just out of college, she was friendly and outgoing, and a very pretty blond. We had gotten to know her a little, but she hardly seemed like a guide for us.

"You mean you are going to send me alone with these two beautiful women?" I asked. The director laughed.

"I agree they're beautiful — but we think on this little trip, you might be able to help us as well. Kathy could use a little parental guidance, and we think you two are just the right people to give it to her."

Now we understood. The Peace Corps was doing us a favor by letting us get a sneak preview of our country, and we could help by using our influence on Kathy in return.

"We'll treat her like a daughter," Fran said.

"She might be very helpful to you as well," he said, reminding us that Kathy was a very advanced volunteer in Spanish.

He came forward and shook our hands. "I think you are going to find this to be a very, very interesting three days," he said.

Chapter 4
First Impressions Count

The next day, the three of us pressed our noses to the window of our plane as it lowered for landing in Santo Domingo, the capital of the Dominican Republic. It was a clear sunlit day, and the view was incredible with the ocean sparkling like diamonds, and the landscape green with trees. Had we been ordinary tourists, our thoughts might have stopped there. But our minds were full of questions — what lay beneath those beautiful palm trees? Will this be a place I can live for the next two years? What kind of people live here? Will they accept me?

Our small plane soon landed and we grabbed our overnight luggage and headed for the terminal. Everything was mass confusion, and we were glad for Kathy's knowledge of Spanish, as she helped us move quickly through customs. We were also glad to find a P.C. volunteer waiting for us to give us a ride to the capital. So far, everything had gone smoothly.

Our volunteer driver was friendly and greeted us in English. We loaded up our bags and piled in, immediately asking what seemed to be a thousand questions as the jeep bumped along the road. At first we focused on generalities — "What state are you from?" "How long have you been here?" "How did you come to be a volunteer?"

Finally, Fran asked the big question. "So, just what is it like to be a PCV here — what can we expect?"

This time the driver didn't answer. Instead, he honked his horn at a man riding a donkey down the middle of the road.

We reached the capital in about 20 minutes. There, the streets were crowded with more than donkeys — cars, bicycles, and people seemed to be everywhere. Periodically, our driver would blow the horn, stick his arm out the window, or yell — sometimes all at the same time.

"Where did you learn to drive?" Kathy asked.

"Here!" he replied, swinging the jeep around the corner, where he stopped it abruptly, apologizing for the ride. "We are in the old part of the city, and the streets were just not designed for modern traffic," he said.

"Why are we stopped here?" Kathy asked.

"This is your hotel."

"This?"

He had pulled us up to what I had assumed were storefronts. The buildings were all old and built right up to the sidewalk. A sign on the front of the one closest to us said, "La Victoria (The Victory)." I wondered about that one as we climbed out.

"PCVs don't stay at tourist hotels," the driver said, handing us our luggage, "but it's adequate. It has beds, water and toilets — it may not be private or comfortable, but you'll get along fine."

We stood there looking at him as he got back in the jeep and closed the door.

"Now what?" Kathy asked.

He gave us another smile, "Don't ask me. I was just your driver. Someone should know where you are and contact you in the morning."

"But where and when?" I asked. Being good Americans, we wanted a time and place.

"Don't worry about the details. Things will work out. They always do." We watched as he drove off down the street, honking, yelling and waving his arms.

"Well," I said after he had disappeared from sight, "if we're going to be PCVs, I guess we'll have to start looking after ourselves."

We picked up our bags and checked in, then sat down in the lobby until we began to freeze from the air conditioning.

"There's nothing to do here," Kathy said. "Let's go for a walk."

Kathy was wearing a very short dress, and Fran looked at her with a motherly eye.

"Shouldn't you change first?" she asked. "I'm thinking of our last week during culture class. Remember, Kathy? They said not to wear shorts or other suggestive clothing."

"This is all I have," Kathy answered impatiently. "I can always hang on tight to you and besides, Dad will look after both of us, right?" She stood up.

"Right," I said, joining her. Fran sighed and gave in and we ventured forth.

Outside, it was hot but not unpleasant. We walked leisurely for a few blocks, observing and comparing thoughts on the new and different culture. After a moment, it was clear that Kathy wasn't just checking out the shops and restaurants.

"Something's wrong," she said. "Our training just hasn't been right."

"What do you mean?" Fran asked.

"The men here — well, they haven't given me a second look. And remember how concerned you were about my dress?"

Fran watched a few men go by — Kathy was right, not a second look. "I guess you're right!"

"I get more attention than this back in Pittsburgh," Kathy sighed.

I had been eavesdropping on their conversation. Kathy's last comment gave me an idea. "Do you mind if I walk on the other side of the street for a minute?" I asked.

"Are you ashamed of us?" Fran said.

I laughed. "No, I just want to do a little observing of native culture."

I wandered to the opposite side, keeping a close watch on my little family. From this vantage point, I could see that our training was right after all. As the girls walked, the men passing the other way would look at the ground or stare in the other direction, or act unconcerned As soon as they had passed, however, it was a different story. From the back, all heads and eyes snapped up and stared in the direction of Kathy's hemline. I watched for awhile, and then came back to join them.

"Don't worry," I said, putting my arm around her shoulder, "you wouldn't get this much attention in Pittsburgh in a week!"

As the day grew hotter and we grew wearier, we decided to try our luck at hailing a "publico," the Dominican version of a taxi. Not knowing the custom, we stood by the side of the street and waved like we would in the United States.

Almost immediately, an empty car pulled up with a very friendly driver. He jumped out and opened the doors for everyone, insisting that Kathy sit next to him. Delighted with the attention, she smiled and climbed in, explaining to the driver who we were and why we were here.

"I know the PCVs here!" he said enthusiastically, "I love them all."

"Is that true of most Dominicans?" Kathy asked.

"Most," he said. "Some think you are rich gringos and some think you are CIA, but I love you all!" For emphasis he shouted the last words, then kissed his fingers and tossed the kiss into the air.

He took us to a restaurant owned by a friend of his. I thanked him and asked the cost, but he said, "Nothing for you, my friends. You are Peace Corps. But if you had been tourists — mucho, mucho, mucho!"

He left us in a good mood as we entered the restaurant and were seated at a sidewalk table in front of it. Our spirits quickly changed, however, once our food and drinks arrived, for then, little children appeared from everywhere to stare at us while we ate. We did our best to ignore them for awhile, until one very small and thin little boy came up right beside me, tapping me on the arm with a low pitiful sound as he begged for a scrap of food. Before I could do anything, the waiters came running out and chased the starving boy and the others away.

We sat there in silence, unable to finish our meals. Nothing in our training had prepared us for this. Just moments ago, we were laughing with a publico driver who loved all Americans, now we were dealing face to face with starving children in the streets. We had only been in the D.R. three hours, and already we had found joy and suffering. Was this a true sample of life on this beautiful island?

Part of our "training experience" in the Dominican Republic allowed for a brief visit to check out our proposed assignment. Our host was Mike Arnow, a PCV (Peace Corps Volunteer) who had been working with the same Dominican Foundation with which we would be working.

Mike was now in his last week of service and I took a good look at him when he arrived at our hotel to pick us up by jeep. He was well tanned, but very thin and even though he was much younger than us, his eyes had a tired look that matched his washed out shirt and trousers. As we shook hands, I wondered — would this be what I would look like two years from now?

Mike looked a little surprised to find that Fran was accompanying us, but he said nothing, so we both climbed aboard. As we left the capitol, Fran and I looked intently out the window at our first glimpse of the rolling, undeveloped rural area where we'd soon be working. Mike explained we were going far inland to find three head of cattle that were given to some compensenos (farmers) by the Heifer Project, an American charitable organization that gives different types of animals to the very poor rural people in developing nations such as the Dominican Republic.

Mike told us that no one had seen the cattle since they were delivered as they were grazing in areas where there were no roads to reach them. In addition, the farmers had no great desire to be found by representatives of any government after their experience with Trujillo, a former Dominican dictator. He would often take cattle from farmers to give to his army. Farmers that refused were sometimes shot. While Trujillo was no longer in power, the fear still lingered.

Up to this point, Mike had directed all his conversation to me, even though Fran was seated right next to him. At last he turned to her and asked, "And what are your plans for today?"

Fran looked surprised. "I thought you knew that. They told us that you would pick us up and be in charge of both of us!"

"Well," answered Mike, "that's news to me." Seeing Fran's reaction he added, "Don't worry, a surprise like this is no surprise after you've worked here awhile."

Fran looked around at the unfamiliar surroundings. "In that case, I'll go with you," she said.

Mike gave a big laugh and turned the jeep off the main road. "Hang on!" he yelled, speeding up, "We're going into the country. This could be an interesting day!"

For the next hour, we drove along on roads that became progressively small and bumpier. Despite the lack of good roads, Mike felt we had a good chance of finding the cattle — the Foundation had kept decent records and Mike had some directions to follow.

At last, we pulled over and stopped, leaving the jeep facing a large clearing. A ramshackle sort of house could be seen a short way off, with children playing outside. "I'm afraid this is as far as we can drive," he said, "From here we go by foot."

For the second time, Fran showed her doubtful concern about today's plans, "What do I do now?" she asked without much enthusiasm.

"You can wait at the jeep," answered Mike, "but I have a better idea. I parked here because I know the people who live in that farm house. They will watch the jeep for me, and the children can take you to a couple of homes to visit. You'll have fun!"

Fran looked at him as if fun was not the word she was thinking of to describe being left alone in the Dominican wilderness. While we were talking, one of the older Dominican girls had walked over to join us. Mike explained the situation to the girl, and before Fran knew it, she was out of the jeep and walking hand in hand with the girl toward the house. Halfway there they turned around and Fran gave me a farewell wave a doubtful expression still on her face. She continued on toward the house with the barefoot girl in the tattered dress, until an older woman with a friendly, toothless smile, came out and greeted Fran with a big hug. Then, the children

29

gathered around, and started to look at Fran, laughing and giggling — they seemed to be quite amused by this strange lady with white hair who had come to visit them.

Later, Fran told me that she wasn't even aware of the children's reaction. Instead, she was engrossed in her first close-up view of a rural Dominican home. It consisted of four poles stuck in the ground, with a thatched roof and sides, and a dirt floor. Mike had said it was a farm home, but this was like no farm she had ever seen. Instead of fields, there was lots of grass, a few scattered trees, and a mountain in the distance.

When Fran disappeared into the house, Mike and I turned and headed off into the other direction to search for the cattle. The sun was hot on our backs as we made our way down dusty paths. The air was quiet, allowing sounds to travel a long distance, sometimes echoing in the hills. Occasionally I heard the sounds of a radio playing very loudly, but saw no one. On a distant hillside there was a small clearing among the trees. I could hear the crack of a whip and a compeseno yelling at his oxen as he plowed the soil. At times I had the feeling of walking a trail in a national park, however, by the sounds, I knew people were all around me. Despite the heat, I found myself enjoying the day. We were now out in the rural areas, and it was nothing like my kind of country, I felt more in my element there than I had in the classroom or in the cities where our training had taken place up until now.

We continued walking, occasionally meeting other walkers on our way. Mike asked each of them for additional directions, which led us down paths less and less frequently traveled. The path took a refreshing turn downhill into a wooded area. At the bottom of the path was a cool stream with rocks set down as stepping stones. I was surprised to see a beautiful young girl seated on one of them, washing clothes.

I stood and watched while Mike approached her and spoke a few words. She smiled and kept on with her washing. She had a jug of cool fresh water she had dipped from the stream to take home for drinking water. She nodded her approval for Mike to have a drink.

I moved forward to join him — we had been walking a long time and I was parched — but Mike put his hand out to stop me. "Sorry, Lew, but this water isn't for you yet. After some time, your system might be adjusted, but not now."

I nodded my head. He was right, of course, but right then I felt like someone who had just been tossed out of paradise.

Meanwhile, Fran was experiencing another side of Dominican culture back at the house. She had been ushered inside and motioned to sit in the best chair, which was the only one with a seat.

While her Spanish had improved, it would be awhile before Fran could understand the rural dialects, so not much communication could take place beyond an understanding that the lady was busy, but Fran was welcome to sit and wait with her.

Fran decided this was her chance to write an eyewitness account home to her family. No one was watching, so she pulled over a small table and began to write:

Dear Ron, Gloria, and Steve,

Kids, you will never believe where I am now and what I am doing. I am alone in this rural home somewhere in the D.R. It's very hot outside but rather pleasant in here as a gentle breeze is now blowing.

It's quiet, as everyone seems to have left me alone here. I can see why they trust a total stranger in their home, because as I look around there is nothing but four walls and two chairs (and I'm sitting on one of those) and a table in the corner.

Oh yes, I have company now, a couple of chickens have just entered the front door. They seem to know what they are doing as they scratch in the dirt. I'll try to be a friendly visitor and not upset their daily routine. One of them is giving me a good look. Oh, oh, — here she comes — excuse me. Well here I am again, that old hen came under my table and pecked at my toes. I had to be unfriendly and ask her to leave the room.

You will never believe this, but I have some more company! Now, a couple of ducks have walked in. I can almost guess what is going to happen. I better not let anyone see me, because I think I'm going to have to be unfriendly with them also. Oh heavens, I'm too late, they just gave a couple of squawks, a squat and a squirt. I just yelled and they waddled out just like they waddled in. I hope I have not made enemies of the family or their animals!

While Fran was writing her letter, Mike and I were discussing our next move back at the stream.

"Ready to go on?" he asked.

"How much farther?" I asked him back.

"From my information, we should have reached them already. Oh well!" And with that we started out again.

After some winding around, we reached the crest of another hill. Here Mike stopped, noticing that I was beginning to lag behind.

"Do you think you will be able to walk back if we keep going?" he asked me.

"Not if we go much further," I answered, honestly.

Mike looked around at the hills. "I'm sure the cattle are in the next valley — but then I thought that three valleys ago."

"How about if we just stop and rest?"

"We don't have time to do that if we are to see the cattle and get back to the jeep before dark."

I had always prided myself on being in pretty good shape, but between the heat and lack of water, I really needed to rest. "I guess I'd better wait here, then," I said.

My decision made things a little awkward, since I was the one who could determine the health of the cows, but I told Mike as best I could what to look for — insect bites, the brightness of their eyes, signs of being beaten or improperly fed, and so on.

"Well, I can do that," said Mike, "wait here." And he headed off down into the next valley.

After he left, I looked around and spotted a nice large stone under a shady tree. It was evident that this must have been a resting place for many people, as the ground was well-worn around the stone. I decided that I liked that idea, too and stretched out and settled down, glad to be off my feet . . .

Back at the house, Fran was also getting hot and thirsty as she continued with her letter . . .

. . . This is a little later; the family returned and we went outside and sat under a shade made of four poles stuck in the ground, with a thatched roof over head and all four sides open . . . It makes a nice cool place to sit.

Another delay; I got thirsty. I turned down their offer for water and they seemed to understand. They sent one of the small boys to buy me a Coke. I don't know how far he went, but it took a long time.

Everyone was happy when he returned; however, they did not have a bottle opener, so a big brother took charge. He held the coke bottle over the back of a chair and hooked the cap on the edge and hit it hard with the heel of his hand. The cap flew off and the warm, bubbly coke foamed and flew over everyone. I managed to salvage a couple of swallows. The boy felt badly about it and offered to send his younger brother after another one. I simply said, "No, thanks it was sufficient."

Well, now the family said we will go to visit another neighbor. I'm sure I will never be able to keep up with my writing. Dad is walking somewhere in the hills hunting for cows. I know all of you thought we were a little crazy when we volunteered for this and when you read this letter, you still may think the same.

Love, peace —
Mother

At this point of course, I had given up hunting for cows. Instead, I had fallen asleep on the big shady rock. I don't know how long I slept, but when I woke, I was not alone. A burrow stood a few feet away from me. I looked slowly up from his hooves to his head and was startled when I saw a baldheaded shirtless rider staring down at me. His hand clutched a machete that hung from his belt, like he was ready for an attack. He looked larger than life and his scarred face made him look ugly and mean. He said nothing.

I had been sleeping very soundly, but this sight woke me up fast. My mind raced — should I run? Is this a friend or foe? Nothing in our Peace Corps training had prepared me for this kind of encounter.

I decided to look as friendly and unafraid as possible. I nodded my head, and smiled, acting as nonchalantly as my pounding heart would let me.

The rider did not return the smile. He continued to stare motionlessly at me, as if he were waiting for me to make the first move. Now this was something I was certain I shouldn't do, even though my legs were ready to go. A lifetime seemed to pass, before the rider took his hand off his machete, kicked his burro and started down the path. He glanced over his shoulder once, probably to make sure I was still sitting there. He didn't have to worry.

My breathing was about back to normal when Mike reappeared. He too had seen the rider and his burro — but more importantly, he had found the cattle and they were in good condition. We could now head back!

The rest of our walk home was uneventful. My shoes seemed very heavy and I lagged far behind Mike the whole way. It was nearly dusk by the time we arrived back at the farm house where we left Fran. We found her sitting on the fender of the jeep, waiting for us.

"How was your hike in the hills?" she asked.

"Very nice," said Mike. "Sorry you couldn't come along."

"I'm not," said Fran, "I had fun right here." She pulled out the letter she had written to our children and handed it to me. I smiled as I read about her experiences — until I reached the description of her encounter with the cola bottle. Suddenly I realized just how tired and thirsty I was.

"Let's go!" I said, thrusting the letter into my pocket and pushing us all into the jeep. "I feel 99 percent dehydrated!"

Mike left us off at our hotel. "See you in the morning!" he yelled as he disappeared in the traffic.

I stood still a moment with the most exhausted feeling I could ever remember. My knees were weak, my head aching, my entire body tingling. My mouth and throat were so dry, I could hardly murmur to Fran, "Let's go to the nearest bar for a beer."

Crawling on the stool, I asked the bartender for "Una Cervasa Grandee." I immediately clutched the oversized bottle of beer he handed me and drank the entire contents without stopping. My entire body seemed to absorb it like a dry sponge. I plunked the empty bottle down demanding "One more!"

I don't know what thoughts were going through the mind of the bartender, but I knew mine: this day was over, but there were many more ahead. This Peace Corps idea was going to be much different than we had envisioned it, with adventures we could never imagine.

Chapter 5
Final Commitment

Mike was late to pick us up at our hotel the next morning, so we sat down on a small blue bench to wait for him. The sun was already shining brightly, and although the day had barely started, after yesterday it felt great to rest.

Soon Mike came running up, and we greeted each other warmly. You would have thought it had been years instead of hours since we last saw each other, but after surviving yesterday, Fran and I were feeling more positive and so were anxious and enthusiastic about continuing.

Mike explained that today we were headed to Villa Mella, the village that would be our home during our two-year stay. Here we could look at some of the places we might live in and also drive over to the farm where I'd be working.

After he explained, I only had one question. "Will there be someplace to get something to drink?"

Mike laughed. "Oh yes, no problem today. In fact, you might even want to stay overnight in the village. Your plane doesn't leave for Puerto Rico until noon tomorrow."

We discussed it, and after a moment, Fran ran back into the hotel to pick up a couple of overnight items for us. While she was gone, Mike turned to me and said, "What do you think, Lew, will she make a PCV?"

I didn't answer right away. At this point I wasn't so sure about anything. But then, I thought back to our farm in Ohio, about all the rough times we'd made it through together. I thought about what it would be like to be down here without her. As Fran returned from the hotel, I turned to Mike and said, "No problem, amigo. Let's go."

Mike drove us through the capital, so that we could get to the only bridge that led across the river and out into the country. Beyond the bridge we turned a sharp curve and then drove up a small hill. As soon as we were over the top, a soldier surprised us by appearing quite suddenly. He walked over to stand in front of our car, holding his rifle in the air. Mike stopped the car and smiled, but he did not roll the window down. The soldier looked inside, then smiled at Fran and me and motioned us on.

"What was that all about?" Fran asked.

"Nothing to be alarmed about," Mike said. "The army has a small base right here and the soldier was on sentry duty."

"Does he stop everyone?"

"He sure does. If we were natives, he would probably have searched us very, very thoroughly before he would have allowed us to pass."

"What are they looking for?"

"Mostly guns and weapons. But don't worry. They seldom search Americans. They always smile and wave me on. They will do the same when they know you."

Fran turned around and watched the soldier out the rear window as he strode back to his post.

"Okay," she said, but very slowly. Somehow, soldiers on the street just weren't in our reckoning of life in the Peace Corps.

Villa Mella was only about eight miles outside the capital, but the ride was slow and very bumpy. We reached the village "downtown" very abruptly — Villa Mella was not large. Like most Spanish towns, there was a square, park-like area in the center of town. This one had a few trees, some concrete benches, and some ornamental bushes in need of trimming. On the east side, across the street, we saw a church and a school. On the other side were shops, bars, a police station, a post office and a few small homes. Behind these there were more homes and beyond those open country. As far as we could tell, that was the village, and we had seen it all without even leaving our car.

I made a comment about it to Mike who said, "Oh, there are a lot of homes you can't see from here," and waved at the distance. That seemed to make sense, for there were too many children running around to belong to just the few places we could see.

We parked and Mike said he would show us around the village. Just as we got out and started heading across the street, however, a small beat-up Datsun sedan came speeding up to us. The driver slammed on his brakes, parked the car, and came running back toward us with his arms out-stretched and a smile that revealed large white teeth. He had light brown-colored skin, was of medium build, and wore dark rimmed glasses. He seemed to be bubbling over with enthusiasm, and surprised Fran by running straight over to her and greeting her, by name, in very good English.

"Hello, Francisca," he said, "I think you are the new volunteer coming here."

"Why yes," said Fran, puzzled as to how he knew about her.

"I am Padre Miguel, the village priest," the man said, "you will be working with me."

Like so many other things in the D.R., meetings with people like the Padre just seemed to happen. I thought of the words of one of the first PCVs we encountered, who told us not to worry, the details will take care of themselves.

The padre was still excited and offered to show Fran the church and the village, while Mike and I went on to the farm.

I'll take good care of Fran," said the padre, leading her off. Again, she gave a farewell wave and headed off, and we were separated like yesterday. We were getting used to this!

Mike was very familiar with the farm and proved to be an excellent guide, informing me that it was a full 80 acres in size and had been used as a recreational and vacation home by the dictator Trujillo when he was in power. The main house was very large, with several guest rooms and a swimming pool. There was even a race track, with a finish line that passed directly behind the house so you could observe the winner from a balcony on the second floor.

After Trujillo had been assassinated, the farm had become the property of the newly formed democratic government. Now it was run by the Foundacion, a non-profit group that supervised and managed many different projects for the growth of the country.

The largest buildings on the grounds were the race horse barns, and as Mike and I walked by them he said, "The Foundacion's job isn't always that easy. After the dictator was executed, the people killed all of the animals and whole families moved into the stalls."

I looked at the huge house, and back to the tiny stalls. "They lived in here?" I asked.

"Some still do," Mike said, "and why not? They have a roof overhead, a concrete floor, free electricity, running water — and best of all, no rent! The Foundacion wants them out, however, so stalls can be used for livestock. And the kids also cause lots of problems."

"Perhaps you can help with this problem," Mike said, studying me with his hand on his chin. But I could only wonder.

The luxury of the big house did not compare with what Fran was seeing, of course, on her tour. Like Mike, Padre Miguel was turning out to be a good guide. He knew everyone and everyone knew him.

The first thing he showed Fran was the church, proudly saying, "It may not be as big as the church in the Capital, but it's very nice and sufficient for this village."

Fran wasn't so sure. Built of concrete, the church held 14 rows of wooden benches, which could seat about six people each. There could have been an aisle down the center, but since the benches were not fastened to the floor, everything was in disarray. The entrance doors on each side were open, which no doubt explained the origin of the two dogs Fran observed sleeping inside on the cool floor.

Next the padre took Fran to the public school. It, too, was made entirely of concrete and though not so large as the church, inside were several classrooms, each with chairs and a blackboard. The walls were dirty and had some writing on them.

"Before school starts the walls will be painted," the padre assured Fran. "It's a nice school, don't you think?"

He then led Fran around the school to an unpaved street. Here she saw many homes, all small, some with concrete floors, and others only with dirt. All were neat and clean and only a step from the street.

The padre stopped proudly at a small building and showed Fran four women who were working with pedal-powered sewing machines inside.

"These machines were donated for use by the Catholic Social Relief to help us make and repair clothes. The ladies are all volunteers." They looked up and smiled at Fran, but kept on working.

Now the padre took Fran by the arm and said, "There is a room behind this building where you may stay tonight if you wish." Ushering her around the corner, he showed her a neatly made cot, in a room with a dirt floor and no windows. There was no sign of running water or a toilet. A curtain covered the only door and around the corner of the building, Fran could see an open gutter full of stagnant water.

The padre was so enthusiastic that Fran felt badly about turning down his offer, but so far, Villa Mella made our Dominican hotel room look like a palace.

"Thank you, Father, but I'm not too sure we want to stay tonight," she said.

"Oh," said the padre, looking puzzled for the first time.

Meanwhile, Mike and I were continuing our farm tour. We were up to the milking parlor for the dairy. Like everything else, it was made of concrete. Inside were about 10 milking stations. In the corner I saw a Surge milking pail (a mechanical milking machine) gathering dust.

"It needs a few repairs," Mike said, "so for now they milk by hand. Maybe that is something else you can help us with." I had noticed a new trend in Mike's conversations with me. Yesterday, he had presented us information; today he kept pointing out ways that I could help. I wondered if Fran was experiencing the same with Padre Miguel. It looked more and more like we had our work cut out for us, for already I had two jobs — evicting squatters and being a repairman.

At this point, the padre had taken Fran into the post office, where he showed her a telephone on the counter. The phone lines didn't reach too many of the homes, he explained, so most people came here to make their calls. "You see?" he said, pointing to a couple of people standing in line nearby.

The next stop was the food store, where Fran hoped her waning interest would pick up. So far she had seen a deserted church, a dirty school, the line she would have to stand in to call home, and had been offered the chance to sleep in a room with a dirt floor. The store was her last hope, and while she had her doubts, she tried to be positive as they entered.

Inside, she found several bins of bulk rice and beans, and a large stalk of bananas hanging from the ceiling. The shelves held several unwrapped loaves of bread, some candles, bottles of Coca Cola and rum. Fran looked around, and then walked out. The padre followed, assuring her, "You can go to a modern supermarket in the capital and buy anything you want, of course."

"Thank you," she answered, but she doubted what she would be looking for would be found there or any place in the D.R.

The final stop on my farm tour with Mike took us to a baseball field. Even though it was all grass and weeds and had a solid six foot concrete wall around it, it was the first welcome sight to me, as I had always been a big softball player.

"Now this might be something that I can help you with, Mike," I said, and this time we both smiled.

Fran's final stop on her tour was the police station. A couple of soldiers with rifles stood outside, but the ever optimistic padre pointed out how friendly they were.

Fran was still sorting that out, when the padre whisked her off to show her some places that we might want to consider renting for our home when we moved here.

The first one he pointed out was a room above the bar. Like a good real estate agent, he pointed out all of the advantages.

41

"You'd be right at home here in the center of town, it is very safe and there is a balcony on the front, overlooking the street. Very nice for hot nights."

"How late does the noise and music last?" Fran asked, thinking of our first "hotel" room in the bar in Puerto Rico.

The padre shrugged, "I'm a priest, I do not spend my nights at the bar," but he sensed her lack of enthusiasm and quickly added, "come, we'll look at other places."

For the next few minutes, Fran tagged along after him as he showed her several places which might work, even though it was clear that he had little knowledge of whether they could be rented for sure. She found herself liking this bubbly little priest — he was friendly, courteous, and cooperative, and had certainly gone out of his way to please her. The village, however, had yet to win her over.

After they had exhausted all the possibilities, the Padre stopped and said, "Well, Fran, now you see the places we have for you to stay. And I think I understand that you do not like any of them. So I promise I will keep looking for something nice for you."

"Thank you, Padre," she answered, hoping that this nice man wouldn't hold it against her if she decided we just weren't ready to stay anywhere.

They walked slowly back to the car, each in his own thoughts. The padre opened the door to his Datsun and insisted over Fran's objections that she let him take her to the farm to join me and Mike.

"No problem," he said, "I am headed that direction anyway. I was on my way to give last rites to a very sick lady when I saw you and stopped."

Seeing Fran's face, the padre continued, "No, no — don't worry — the people here know I cannot be every place at the same time." And they drove off, with Fran feeling as puzzled as she did when we first arrived in Villa Mella.

Mike and I found Fran waiting for us at the gate when we returned. We greeted one another and then Mike surprised us both by informing us that he would be leaving us on our own at the farm for awhile.

**Padre proved to be a great friend —
later Fran hangs banner of Peace
during church service.**

"Don't worry, you can wait here in the house. I'll return later; the Foundacion is having a farewell party for me here tonight. I leave the country next week." He shook our hands and departed.

We wondered inside, where a maid approached. She was very courteous and brought us a couple of chairs and a table and some fresh orange juice to drink. We were both quiet, thinking, and after a minute Fran decided to put her thoughts into a letter home, just as she had the day before. This time she wrote to her mother.

Dear Mother,

Here we are in the D.R. It's about the end of our visit to get first-hand information on our assignment. The Peace Coprs has tried very hard to prepare us mentally for this.

They informed us this was one of the poorest countries in the Caribbean and the new democracy was a little unstable politically. However, yesterday and today proved to be a tremendous shock to us. We found our village of Villa Mella to be very poor.

Mother, I have actually seen some children running around naked. I saw naked babies sitting and playing in the dirt with snotty noses running down their dirty faces. Most homes were right next to the street. The houses were about 12 by 12 foot or 12 by 15 foot square. You could see in many of them from the street. Most have dirt floors and no electricity. They had no refrigeration, no stove and no TV. They had a bed, maybe a chair or two, a table and that was about it. Most people do not have a job. There are no government unemployment benefits. The pity of it all is that this is probably the most beautiful island that God created. The countryside is beautiful with abundant palm trees and wild fruit trees. The soil and climate is such that it would be possible to raise the largest variety of crops here than anywhere else in the world.

We are trying to find out what we can do here. We both wonder if we really can accomplish anything. Yesterday Lew walked all day in the mountains, just looking for a couple of cows. I stayed in a rural home. It was a shock for both of us.

Today was a shock also. We sit here now wondering, what can we do?

We are not sure. Maybe there is someplace else that we can do more. It looks hopeless for us here. Do not misunderstand, we want to help these people, but our question is . . . . CAN WE?

Sorry, I had to write you such a negative letter, but you always wanted me to be honest. Our health is good, but right now, our morale is low. Tomorrow we return to Puerto Rico. The training director wants a report on how we feel. I don't know Lew's inner feeling right now, but I think I'm ready to admit this Peace Corps idea was a mistake.

Love,
Your wandering daughter, Fran

Fran did not show me her letter at the time, but I would have only added one line — "This goes for me, too!"

Mike returned later to find us both asleep in our chairs. Perhaps it was the cool soft breeze coming in the windows, or maybe we just wanted to escape from our general low feeling.

"Wake up you two," Mike said, gently shaking our shoulders. "You are going to miss the party!"

We stood up and tried to straighten out our clothes, while Mike looked anxiously over to the education building where the party was to be held. "Most of the people are there already," he said.

We told him to go ahead, and we watched as he hurried off. After we made ourselves presentable, we followed him over.

The educational building was the former recreation hall for the dictator's parties. It had a smooth concrete floor and was large enough to handle 80 to 100 people, though there were not that many on hand now. There were six other PCVs who worked with Mike and about 10 people from the Foundacion office. All were drinking Coke, some mixed with rum. Although we were hungry and wanted to join in, we felt out of place. Everyone else seemed happy, drinking and reminiscing about their adventures — and ours hadn't even begun. We decided to wander over toward Mike, the one person we knew, but stopped before he saw us when we overheard what he was saying to a couple of other volunteers.

"The old man followed me up and down the hills all day," he was saying, "and I kept thinking to myself, what will I do if he collapses in the hills? But when I finished, he was still with me. He had to be tired, because I was!"

They all laughed and one volunteer asked, "What about his wife?" Mike answered, "I saw the village priest on the way out here and asked him how he got along with the new recruit today. He seemed quite concerned."

Another volunteer interrupted, "Did the priest take her for a walk into the mountains?"

Again laughter. "No," said Mike, "but he showed her some homes she might live in. Her big concern seemed to be the grocery store. I don't think he understood her reaction — when they came out she told him, 'All that the store had was rum bottles and beans!' " There was laughter from all of them at this time, then a third volunteer spoke up, while drawing an imaginary mark in the air. "Two more PCVs bite the dust!"

We decided two things at that point. First, not to move in and talk to this group. Second, we were not going to 'bite the dust' with these younger volunteers laughing at us. To this day we wonder what we would have decided if we hadn't accidentally overheard that conversation.

After the party, Mike dropped us off again at our hotel. Our goodbyes were sober and sincere, for despite his comments at the party, we had come to like one another, and we would likely never see each other again.

"I wish you the best of luck," he said. We wished him the same, and we all gripped our hands together tightly.

Many times through the next two years as PC volunteers, we were to feel this common experience of spending only a few days with some individuals, yet developing friendships that were at once very deep and unbreakable. The barriers of sex, race — and as we were to prove, even age — could all be overcome in the common experience of being Peace Corps volunteers.

Our plane took off on schedule the next morning. It was another beautiful sunny day, and we were again moved by the incredible view.

"Well, now we know a little more about what's below the palm trees," I said.

"And there's still so much we don't know," said Fran in return, speaking very softly.

The next morning it was up as usual and back to the training center. True to his word, the director was waiting for us.

He could hardly wait to ask the big question. "How was your trip and do you want to return as volunteers?"

We had been up all night talking about it, of course, stating every doubt we had and all the reasons we didn't think we could do it. But in the end, it was those comments of the other, younger volunteers that kept coming back to haunt me — "chalk up two more PCVs."

"Well," I said, "we actually made two decisions. The first was that we have seen enough; this is a tougher job than we realized."

The director looked a little unsure. "And the second?" he asked.

"That we want to go back again for two years."

His puzzled look turned to a broad grin. "And what changed your minds?"

"The people and the country need help. Although we have some questions about what exactly we can do, the village priest seems to want Fran to be there, and the farm has a few problems that Mike Arnow thought I could do something about."

"I see," said the director, "so you're returning because they need you and want you, is that right?"

I might have stopped there, but Fran urged me to tell the whole truth. So I went on to explain about the added "incentive" of the overheard conversation at Mike's party. "They

47

may be younger, with more energy and endurance," I said, "but we want to prove to them that we can walk side by side with them."

The director nodded and smiled, then motioned with his head toward the door. "Your class has already started — you had better hurry and join it."

Chapter 6
Casa Dulcie

Our training completed, we were again aboard a plane preparing to land in the Dominican Republic. Again we stared out the window at the blue water and green landscape. We now knew a little more of what was below, just enough to be sure that the next two years were not going to be easy. We reached over to tightly hold hands, silent, but knowing each other's thoughts, "This is it!"

When we landed a PC volunteer met and drove us to "La Victoria," the same "no frills" hotel where we had stayed during our trial visit. Early the next morning, we reported to the Peace Corps Center, which was located in a large, old Spanish-style home. It was built on a square plan with an open courtyard in the middle and was located far enough from the street to have a large yard with flowering trees, including a beautiful fan palm out front. Inside were two stories of offices, reception areas, a medical room, library and classrooms. But its best feature, as far as we were concerned, was that it was easy to reach from a number of routes traveled by publicos, the Dominican version of taxis and the only public transportation available. A very friendly Spanish-Dominican girl smiled at us as we approached the reception desk, greeting us by name and explaining that they'd been expecting us. "We have a lot of things for you to do in the next couple of days!" she said.

We were ushered upstairs to meet the country PC director, Frank Rey, a short well dressed man who spoke with a New England accent. He greeted us, and then officially made us volunteers by leading us in the Peace Corps oath. Very solemnly we raised our right hands and repeated after him:

"I do solemnly swear that I will support and defend the Constitution of the United States against all enemies, foreign and domestic; that I will bear true and faithful allegiance to the same; that I take this obligation freely, without any mental reservation or purpose of evasion; and that I will well and faithfully discharge the duties of the office of which I am about to enter. So help me God."

After we were sworn in, Mr. Rey sent us back to the main desk, where we found a stack of papers several inches thick waiting for us.

"What's this for?" I asked.

"It's the application for your driver's license. That's the next thing you need to do."

"All this for a driver's license?"

"Oh yes, I'm sorry, but there is a lot of red tape to get official documents here."

We frowned, but decided to give it our best shot. After what felt like hours, we returned to the desk with our completed project, only to have the receptionist tell us we weren't done yet. "Now, you will need 12 photographs of each of you," she said, handing us another piece of paper with an address on it. "If you go to this place, you will find a self photograph booth that takes the correct size. After you have your photos, take them to the U.S. Embassy along with your application." She then handed me back the papers I had just handed to her.

"All of this just to get a driver's license?" I asked for the second time.

She smiled and repeated her earlier statement, "Sorry, but there is a lot of red tape to get official documents around here."

It took us three hours and a lot of learning about the publico system — the photo booth was located across town — but we finally got our pictures taken and made our way to the embassy. There, we were given a permit and some additional forms which we added to our growing stack.

We returned to the center, where we had to wait for a gentleman named Max to sign our completed applications — apparently, he was the only one who could do so. He arrived in about an hour, scribbled his name on the top form and sent us to the receptionist once again.

"You're making excellent progress," she said. "All you need now are your passports for your next stop."

"Our next stop?"

"You also need an eye exam. It can only be given by a special doctor across town."

Fran and I looked at each other, sighed, and headed toward the door one more time. The receptionist called after us.

"There is a problem, however. The doctor is only there from 8 a.m. to 11 a.m. You'll have to wait until tomorrow to go."

Seeing our expressions, she again added a familiar statement. "Did I tell you? There's a lot of red tape to get official documents here."

The next morning, we got up early for our eye examination. After a long trip across town and even a longer wait in line at the office, it was finally our turn to see the "special doctor."

Our exams consisted of reading the top three letters on an eye chart while standing on a box and holding a piece of cardboard over one eye.

"You can both see good enough to drive," he said, signing our papers with an unreadable scratch.

From there, it was on to the embassy again, where we turned over our papers to a clerk who told us they would be sent to Washington to process and that we could expect to get our licenses in a few months.

It was nearly the end of the day by the time we finally returned to the center. This time, I knew just what to do. I walked up to the receptionist and said, "By the way, did anyone ever tell you that you have to go through a lot of red tape to get official documents around here?"

"You are learning fast!" she said with a smile. House hunting was next on our agenda. We got up early the next morning to hail a publico for the trip to Villa Mella, hoping for a driver who loved Americans to take us under his wing.

It appeared that we were going to be in luck, for within minutes an empty car pulled up. The driver jumped out and asked in broken English if he could be of service to us. From our training, we knew we not only needed to tell him where we wanted to go, but to ask the fee up front, before even getting into his car.

"Villa Mella?" he said. "Yes, my friends, I can take you there, and for you," — he shrugged his shoulders — "only $10."

Fran and I had a short discussion about that. His fee was much higher than the normal rates, but he seemed friendly and we were anxious, so we nodded and got ready to climb aboard.

"Okay, we go!" I said.

The driver was delighted. He practically ran to open the door for us.

"To Villa Mella!" he said, and wheeled the car into traffic. After only a few blocks of driving and some bad jokes, he asked, "Amigos, I was looking for a friend when I stopped to pick you up. Do you mind if I go to see him first?" Before either of us could answer, he made a sudden turn to the right and said, "You are very kind. I think he lives this way."

The driver had a piece of paper with this friend's address on it. Every few feet he would stop the car and wave the paper out the window at the passerby, asking how to get there.

After several attempts like this, I finally leaned over into the front seat and asked him if he knew where his friend lived.

"Oh yes, I know. But he moved and I've never been there."

He kept driving and asking questions, one minute taking us through lovely residential areas and the next into slums, where we bounced over chuck holes and around open sewers, stopping often for people and animals to get out of our way. On one particularly narrow street, he spotted a pretty girl on the sidewalk. This time he not only slowed down to talk to her, but stopped the car in the middle of the street and ran over to her.

After a few minutes, what was left of Fran's patience ran out. "Sure wish he could find his friend," she said.

"I think he's making progress," I answered, observing that the driver now had his hand on the girl's shoulder, and a big smile on his face. By now several cars had pulled up behind us and were starting to honk their horns at our car, which was blocking the street.

"I think we're not the only ones who are getting impatient," Fran said. "Don't you think we should do something?"

"You're right," I said. On the spur of the moment, I leaned forward over the front seat and began honking our publico's horn in return to the cars behind us.

Fran grabbed me by the belt of my pants and hauled me into my seat. "What do you think you're doing?" she asked.

"When in Rome, do as the Romans do," I said.

Fran glared at me as if she was now as perturbed at me as she was at everything else. "This could be a long two years!" she said.

My technique, however, seemed to work. Soon the driver came running back to the car, laughing and giving a friendly wave to the cars lined up in the street behind us.

"Did she know where your friend lived?" I asked.

"Oh no — she never even heard of the address."

"Then why did you take so long to talk to her?"

"It's my weakness. I cannot resist talking to pretty girls."

Now I was impatient, too, and Fran was still glaring at me. "I think it's time we forgot your friend and go to Villa Mella," I said.

"You are right," the driver agreed. "I apologize a thousand times. I'll forget about my friend now."

We gave a big sigh of relief and sank back into our seats, until, on the very next block, our driver suddenly pulled into a driveway and stopped the car.

"What now?" I asked.

"My friends, this is where I live. Excuse me a moment while I stop in to give my wife a big bug and have my morning cup of coffee." He ran off and into the house without waiting for any comment.

In the back seat, Fran and I sat gritting our teeth. Then, we looked at each other and started to laugh simultaneously, realizing that anger wasn't going to get us anywhere any faster.

"Where in America could you find so much entertainment for $10," I said. We were apparently going to have to be flexible and willing to see the humor in things to survive in Villa Mella — if we ever got there!

We were still wiping tears of laughter from our eyes when our driver returned to the car. His wife stood in the doorway and gave us a big smile, waving goodbye to us as we pulled away.

"My friends," he said, "I must apologize again. As you can see, my wife is very lovely and as I told you, I cannot resist such things. But now we go to Villa Mella!"

This time he kept his word. We rolled along at top speed until we reached our destination, our driver laughing and singing at the top of his lungs the whole way.

I told him to drop us off at the town square. "Shall I wait for you?" he asked.

"Oh no, we have transportation from here," I said quickly, ignoring Fran, who was giving me a "We do?" look.

"Okay, Amigo!" he said, sticking out his hand to shake mine. He held the grip longer than necessary, saying, "I don't like to ask this, but do you have a dollar? I need gas. We used all of mine up while looking for my friend."

"I suggest you tell your friend that when you see him," I said, removing my hand from his grasp and giving him a friendly wave. He shrugged his shoulders and drove off — still singing and playing his car radio very loudly.

We were left standing in the middle of an all but deserted street. "And just where is this transportation we have from here?" Fran asked me, rather pointedly.

I looked down at the ground. "For now," I said, "our feet! Anything's better than him." I started to move toward the buildings that lined one side of the square, but Fran did not budge.

"I already walked around the village with the padre when we were here before, remember? There's no place we can live in here."

Well, let's look again. Maybe we can find something if we lower our expectations."

"How low do you want to go?"

I was saved from responding by a young boy who came running up to us.

"Senor," he said, "the padre has been waiting all morning to see you. He is at the church. Follow me."

The boy led us to the padre's office, a small room behind the altar. The padre was smiling and happy to see us. "Hola! You are here to stay?"

We told him yes, and then explained that we were here to try to find a home one more time.

"Good," he said with an even broader grin. "Then I have great news! As promised, I looked for a nice place for you and I found one. Come, let me show you." We followed him outside to his car. "It will be necessary to drive," he said.

We climbed in, and the padre took off, driving fast and all over the road while tooting his horn a lot and waving at people. Like the publico driver, he seemed to have his mind more on talking than on the road.

After a little more than a mile, he pulled in a driveway and stopped. "There it is!" he said.

We opened the car doors and got out. Before us was a small, blue, one story home built of wood and concrete. A nice porch ran the full width of the front, with one step leading up to it, and a railing around it, high enough to sit on. The yard was large with many shade trees, and one side lined with a hedge of hibiscus.

"You like?" the padre asked. "It is empty now and the landlord will rent it to you for only $100 a month."

"Well, the price is right," I said.

Fran nodded. "It is close enough to see the cars and people on the road, but far enough away that we wouldn't be able to hear their conversations," she said. This was a real selling point to us after our street-side dwelling in Puerto Rico.

We walked up the path to take a closer look. "The house has electric and running water, too," said the padre. "How does that sound, Fran?"

"Good. Can we go inside?"

The padre ran ahead of us but stopped at the door a moment before letting us in. "The floor inside is piled high with sacks of feed for the dairy cows," he said, "but the landlord will clean this all out."

Inside, the padre showed us around like a good real estate agent. "Notice the nice concrete floors," he said, moving some of the sacks aside.

"I like the floors," said Fran. "It's the walls I'm not crazy about. There are no windows."

The padre walked over to one of the walls and pushed open a pair of wooden doors, opening up a hole about three feet square. "Windows!" he said.

"But there is no glass or screens."

You do not need screens here," explained, opening up another "window" on the opposite side. "Feel the nice cross ventilation?"

The light and the air helped remove some of the mustiness from the place. Fran looked satisfied and so far this was the only place we'd seen with a floor, electricity and water.

"How soon can it be ready?" I asked.

"In two days," said the padre, elated. "Should I tell the landlord, 'si'?"

"Si," we said. We had a home!

Despite the padre's promise, it was almost a week before we were able to complete all our assignments at the center and move in. We needed to have certain medical shots to prevent illness, and also received advice on what foods we could eat until our bodies became adjusted to the climate. In addition, we also visited several offices of the government and the Foundacion for whom I would be working. We wrapped up the week with a good session with Dwight Walker, the Country Peace Corps Farm Director, who would be in charge of my efforts, and ended the week with our favorite task — more paperwork.

The day of our move finally came. We began by waiting an hour for a truck that was supposed to pick us up first thing in the morning. When our transportation did show up, it was a small car instead of a truck. There was not enough room

'Casa Dulcie' — in front of our new home.

for us and our driver, let alone our luggage and supplies like
cots and medicines that we had picked up from the center. In
our newly adjusted way of looking at things, we decided to
take our suitcases out first while we had access to a car, and
then return to the center to wait for the truck to return. Another
volunteer had taken it into the country, but we were assured
it would be back that afternoon.

When we finally arrived after a bumpy, cramped ride, we
found the door to our new home open and the inside empty
of feed sacks. We had just put our suitcases down, when Fran
gave a startled "Oh." A young barefoot Dominican boy had
entered unnoticed behind us as he apparently had a message
to deliver.

"Fernando say this for you," he said, holding out a key
for me. I took it from him, saying, "Gracias," he smiled, but
his eyes gave us both the quick once over before he left as quietly as he entered.

The key fit the front door, so we locked up and headed
back to the center, arriving well before noon. Even though
it was close to lunch, we decided not to leave the building and
take the chance of missing the truck. We had our fill of "red
tape" and delays — we wanted to "go home," even if "home"
was a shack in the jungle!

Many thoughts went through our heads while we waited. We were both understandably anxious. Fran had been a homemaker for 30 years, and after months of living in hotels and in other people's homes, she wanted to do her own cooking and housekeeping. As for me, I was tired of PC training and going to school. I'd been a farmer all my life, a self-made one at that, used to setting my own goals and planning my own course of action. We were both ready to go to work!

On the other hand, our new home was not exactly a "10," when you compared it to the movie star resorts featured in the magazines, but a "9" compared to how our neighbors were living. We had lowered our standards a lot to take it, and the longer we waited to get there, the more we wondered how much lower we would have to go to make it a home and be truly happy in it. I began to reflect on how much different — and more difficult — this experience was going to be from what we had originally pictured. But I also thought about the many things Fran and I had accomplished in our lives by working together. Maybe we wouldn't achieve all of our goals in the D.R., but at least we would try and we did have each other.

As we should have guessed, the truck did not return as promised. For the first hour, we relaxed and thought and read magazines and books. Then, we alternated between reading and walking to the window to look for the truck. Finally, it was mostly walking. At last, at 5:30 the truck arrived.

It didn't take long to load up the truck — we had plenty of time to organize things in one pile — but convincing someone to drive us was another story. It was quitting time and no one was in a mood to go to Villa Mella.

"But our things are there!" said Fran, at last, after some "discussion" back and forth.

"Oh my," said a staff member on duty, "did you lock up good? I hope your things are still there!" and he ordered the driver to work overtime.

It was almost sundown by the time we arrived. The village and the road on which our home was located were quiet and deserted. If we had expected a band or a welcoming delegation, we would have been very disappointed.

The driver hurriedly helped us unload, then jumped back into his truck. "Have a nice evening!" he yelled, pulling out without looking back or hearing me tell him that it would be hard to do that with all our supplies on the porch and night falling.

Fran tried the lights and nothing worked. The padre had told us there was electricity, but we should have guessed that didn't necessarily mean it was working.

"We'd better act fast before it gets too dark," I said, gathering up the cots.

We moved quickly. Fran carried in the supplies while I set the cots up in the middle of our living room for the night. Tomorrow, in the daylight, we could move them to the back room — it had more privacy than the rest and would make the best bedroom. It was just about dark when I finished the job, and we both sat down on them with a big sigh.

"Does this ever feel good!" Fran said. "I must have walked a mile at the center waiting for the truck. I'm tired!"

"You're tired and I'm hungry," I said. "We should have eaten this noon at the capital."

"Oh — that reminds me," Fran said, smiling. "Have I got a surprise for you!" She rummaged in one of our suitcases and brought out some bananas. "I bought some fruit so we could have something for breakfast tomorrow," she explained.

We each grabbed one, eating them like they were manna from heaven as we sat on our cots in silence, the light fading around us. After a minute I started to laugh.

"What's so funny?" asked Fran. Apparently she could see no humor in sleeping on a beautiful World War I army cot in the middle of a strange house with no lights, in a country where we didn't know if we were surrounded by friends or enemies.

"Remember our first night in Ponce?" I said in answer at last. "We thought things were bad then because we were in the back room of a bar! At least we had a bed, electricity and a toilet!"

"I see. Since this is even worse than that, it must be funny. Well, ho-ho-ho," she said, sounding like a fainthearted imitation of Santa Claus.

After a pause, I heard her rummage around for something in the dark. At last she turned on a flashlight she'd found. "Well, since we're enjoying this so much, I'm going to shine this around the room to make sure we aren't missing anything to make this night even more fun," she said, swinging the beam out in a low arc around the room. Suddenly, she froze with the light focused on the base of the wall nearest us.

"Oh, my God, look at those!" she cried. In the light, we could see big, fat cockroaches crawling out of the wood. Quickly, we each pulled off our shoes and started to swat at them as they came near our cots. For awhile all you could hear was the crack of our shoes on the concrete.

"I keep missing!" said Fran. "How do you hit them?"

"Don't swat at where he is," I yelled above the smacking of our shoes, "swat where he is going!" After a few moments of shoe swatting, both our techniques improved enough that the enemy retreated back into the wood for what we hoped would be the rest of the night. When it looked safe, Fran got up off her cot, still holding the flashlight. "I'm going to check the back room," she said, "just in case."

"You do that," I said, exhausted. I laid back to stretch out on my cot at last — but in a minute Fran let out a horrifying screech. "Lew, come here quick!" she screamed.

From the sound of her voice, I knew there was more than a cockroach back there. The PC did not give us a gun, so I grabbed the most lethal weapon I could find — a shovel — and headed back to where Fran was.

She was standing at the door, the light in her hand and shaking a little as she pointed it at a spot in the center of the floor. Under the spotlight was a mammoth overgrown spider, the size of a dinner plate. It was a tarantula!

In training, we had been informed that tarantulas were the only known poisonous insect in the D.R. Though their bite was not necessarily fatal, it could make you very ill.

Bewildered by the light and Fran's scream, the tarantula was parked in the middle of the floor, unsure of which way to go. While Fran nervously held the light on our latest victim, I lifted the shovel high over my head and brought it down on the invader with as much strength as I had. The handle broke off at the base as I hit it and the tarantula splattered all over the room. We could see bits and pieces of it everywhere as we shone the light around, but we didn't see any other whole ones.

"That's a relief," said Fran.

"Maybe yes, maybe no. Where there is one of something, there are usually two."

Fran pointed the light from the wall to me. "So, what are you saying we should do?" she said.

I shrugged my shoulders. "Well, let's go to bed. If one crawls on you, remember what they told us in training, 'Lay still and it won't bite.' "

"Ho-ho-ho," said Fran.

We returned again to our cots, where we each ate another banana to calm our nerves. "Okay," said Fran, "I'm ready to lie down."

We both lay still for awhile, Fran clutching the flashlight, me the broken shovel handle. Then Fran spoke, "Lew, the next time we go overseas, let's be a little more picky about the places we stay." She shone the light around the room one more time, but no invaders were in sight.

She turned it off, but then a strange cry sounded. Both of us sat straight up in our cots.

"What was that?" Fran whispered, turning the flashlight on. It sounded again. We listened a bit, and then I realized what it was — a donkey! He must have been right outside our back door.

"I hope he doesn't do that all night," said Fran.

As if in answer, the donkey cried again, this time loud enough to wake up a rooster right outside our window.

"And we thought the Cubans were bad singers in Ponce," Fran said. "What a rotten duet these two make."

"He'd make a better Sunday dinner than a singer," I said. "What about the donkey?"

"You can have him. You know I like chicken."

"Good night," said Fran.

The next morning, we were both up at the break of dawn. As I opened our door and the wooden doors of our windows to let the day in, our friend the late night rooster crowed at me from under the trees. "If you keep that up," I cracked back at him, "you'll be crackling over a hot fire instead of crowing from that tree."

Fran heard me and laughed from the living room where she was busy opening suitcases, hunting for a knife to peel a pineapple for our breakfast. I turned to join her in the hunt when suddenly a man walked right into our home, startling both of us. He was carrying a pipe wrench and he walked past us into the room with a toilet. Fran and I looked at each other, puzzled and alarmed. I followed after him to investigate.

Though it was still too dark to see well, the man was banging away at the pipes in our bathroom. "What's the problem?" I asked.

"The water runs all the time. Fernando told me to fix it."

"I see. Tell Fernando the electric does not work either," I said.

The man kept banging at the pipes. "Okay, I'll tell him," he said. "No problem." He banged one more pipe. "That should be all right now," he said and left leaving the water running the same as before.

Fran came walking in from the other room, "What did he fix?" she asked.

"I really don't know," I said. "Did you know he was coming in the house?"

She shook her head. "I wonder if this is something we should expect," she said, as this was the second time someone had just walked right in our home without knocking.

A little later we had company again — this time the landlord himself, Fernando. It was the first time we had actually met or talked to him. He was short and a little on the stout side, with a round face, thinning brown hair and a well-trimmed mustache. Though he wore a western style gun belt, complete with a gun hanging from his right hip, he was very friendly.

He introduced himself with a big smile. "Good morning. How is everything?"

"Well," I began, wondering just how to describe the events of last night and this morning, but Fran interrupted.

"Fine, just fine," she said, "though we still need a few things. I would offer you some coffee, but we have no stove. And you would have nowhere to sit and enjoy it, since we have no furniture."

"Qua paina (what a pity)," said Fernando, shaking his head. "I think I can help you. I'll be right back."

In less than an hour, he returned with a small table top two burner stove, a tank of gas, some lumber and four men. They started to work at once. In a short time, they had built us a table about four feet wide and six feet long, which they placed against the wall under the window. With obvious pride, Fernando asked, "What else do you need?"

Fran and I conferred quietly for a few minutes. "What do you think?" she asked.

"I think he's in a good mood," I answered. "Ask for what you want — he can only say no."

Fran stood back and looked at the 10- by 10-foot room that was to be her kitchen — it had nothing in it but bare walls and a window. "How about a counter top this high, and about the entire length of the room on this side." She held her hands out about waist high and pointed to the wall under the window.

Now it was Fernando's turn to confer with his men. One stepped off the length, then nodded at Fernando. "We can do that," Fernando said, smiling.

Fran decide to go for broke. "And I would like it to have shelves below the entire length." The men conferred again, but once more, Fernando came back smiling. "We can do that too, but we need more wood. We will be right back."

Fernando and two of his workers left, while the other two stayed behind to install the tank for the gas stove outside below the kitchen window. For a while we heard nothing but the sounds of their work, but all of a sudden their voices became very excited. I ran out to check and they smiled at me and held up a big, dead tarantula. They had found the nest and destroyed them.

"Gracias," I said, "Muchas gracias."

In the meantime, Fernando and his other helpers had returned and true to their word, soon built Fran her made-to-order countertop.

"Senora, you now have the nicest kitchen in Villa Mella," Fernando said, again smiling proudly. Judging by what we'd glimpsed of our neighbors' homes so far, he was probably right. We thanked him and then he and his men left us to get organized.

A short time later, Fernando returned again, this time bringing with him his wife and their four children. "I want you to meet my family," he said.

Fernando's wife, Marie, was quite a contrast to him. She was very thin, had curly black hair, and was a foot taller than her husband. Marie was very shy until Fran offered to show her new kitchen. Once away from Fernando, she became very talkative. She was also very thrilled with what the men had done and offered to help us any way she could. Then she motioned her children in and introduced them to Fran one by one, ending by giving Fran a big Dominican hug herself.

Meanwhile, Fernando and I had been talking in the living room. He too, was very polite and courteous. We had been talking about his farm, which was located directly behind our house. The driveway past our house continued on back to a tenant home plus a dairy barn. He offered to take us on a tour and soon we were all headed out the door, the children running on ahead.

As we walked past the back of our home, I noticed a tree with breadfruit growing on it, a tropical fruit quite common on the islands. "Is this good to eat?" I asked.

"Oh yes," replied Marie. "Let me show you how to fix them."

We gathered up two or three of the fruit, which were a little larger than softballs. Fernando cut them open and cleaned out the seeds — they were the edible part and about the size of buckeyes — while Fran and Marie got a tin can and filled it with water. Then Marie placed the seeds in it and put the can on Fran's new stove. "Let it boil slowly while we walk back to the farm," she said.

The lane was dusty and well-used. It was wide enough for a pick-up truck and lined on both sides with pasture fields. The donkey that had awakened us the previous night was grazing on one of them and raised its ears and gave a loud "hee-haw" as we passed by.

The fields were beautiful, slightly rolling, with palm trees, wild orange trees and even a large avocado tree — all loaded with fruit. Fernando pointed out his cattle barn to us. It was at the end of the lane and four large, ferocious dogs were guarding it, each tied with what I hoped were strong chains. They barked loudly and continuously at us, frightening the children.

"I'll show you the cattle some other time," Fernando said. We all agreed that was a good idea.

The only thing remaining to see was a tenant house built of poles stuck into the ground. The walls and roof were made of palm fronds. Fernando explained that this was where the family which did his farm work lived.

By this time, Marie was getting anxious about the breadfruit we had left on the stove, so we headed back to our home. There, Marie poured cold water on the seeds and then showed Fran how to peel them open. We all gathered around our new table to try the new treat. To our surprise, they tasted much like boiled Idaho potatoes — though given what we'd eaten in the last 24 hours, Fran and I would have found them delicious no matter what they tasted like.

It was now late in the day and Fernando called for the children, who were playing outside. Marie pulled Fran aside and handed her something from the pocket of her dress, then patted her hand to indicate Fernando was not to know. Fran smiled back, keeping the secret.

We walked them to the door, waving goodbye. I turned to Fran, feeling enthusiastic for the first time.

"Well, not bad for our first day," I said. "We have a new table, a new kitchen, and a nice landlord and landlady who cooked dinner for us."

"Not only dinner, but breakfast," said Fran, holding up two oranges and two eggs — the items Marie had slipped to her She placed them on our new counter, and we both smiled, relaxed. I tilted my head toward the bedroom, where I had moved our two cots earlier that morning. "Now, all we need is a good night's sleep!"

Chapter 7
The Women At The Well

Our second morning, we were again up at dawn, this time awakened by another new sound. This one, however, was much different from Fernando's donkey or our friendly rooster. Echoing in the quiet of the early morning, was the unbelievably beautiful sound of a woman singing.

Fran rose first, going over to throw open the kitchen window to see if we could tell where it was coming from. I joined her and she pointed to our hibiscus hedge on the other side of our driveway. There were several homes over there, and we assumed it must be coming from one of them.

"I'll find out who that is before the day is over," Fran said, thinking it would give her something to do while I went on to my job at the farm. But no sooner had Fran spoken, than the sound came closer.

It belonged to a young Dominican girl — we guessed she was about 16. She was barefooted and wore a ragged, short dirty dress that hung from only one shoulder, leaving the other bare. She was carrying an empty three-gallon tin can and as we watched, she crawled through the hedge and headed toward the back corner of our house.

While I got dressed, Fran hurried out to meet our early morning visitor. There was a faucet at the back of our house, and the girl had filled her can with water from it. She was just placing it on her head as Fran arrived. "Hola, neighbor," she said, standing there with the can on her head and a smile on her face. Fran could now see a tall, slender girl with brown eyes and straight white teeth that complemented her pleasant smile. Fran was thinking, "What a beautiful young lady."

"I heard you singing," said Fran, "it was beautiful.

The girl laughed. "I sing for you," she said. "I sing a song of welcome. I make up my own words and music. This morning I sing, 'Welcome neighbor. I want to be your friend. ' "

Kiki — the barefoot girl in rags grew into someone beautiful and special for us.

Fran was deeply touched by the girl's friendliness and openness. "I want to be your friend, too," she said.

Fran found out the girl's name was Kiki. She said she had a lot of work to do, but she would return.

Fran came back in, and we enjoyed the breakfast of the eggs and oranges that Marie had donated to us. Then I left for the farm while Fran tidied up the kitchen.

Later, Fran told me that as she did her work, more women and girls came with different sizes of cans, to use the faucet behind our home. It was like a little parade, or even a game, for all the women were curious about their new neighbors, but they did not want to pry. So while they kept their heads straight, they kept their eyes sideways.

Fran watched them come and go, feeling it was a great way to meet the women, but wondering if Fernando knew our home was the local watering hole. She had a chance to ask him when his truck pulled in the driveway a short while later. "Is it okay for the women to get their water from our faucet?" she asked, flagging him down.

Fernando explained that the women had no water and would have to go to the creek to get it if they didn't come here. He didn't mind it unless they caused problems, since he had no water meter and paid the same amount of money no matter how much water they used.

With that question answered, Fran decided to go out and take advantage of this opportunity to meet and talk with the women. She hunted around her kitchen for something she could take outside with her to the water faucet. At last, she gathered our washing together in a basket and carried it outside to the faucet.

The women were all chatting when she came out. Fran held up her laundry to show them what she was up to. They laughed and then came over and laid their hands on her arm to show their approval. Two stopped to help her and show her the Dominican way to wash clothes, rubbing them between their knuckles or beating them hard on the concrete steps.

Fran thanked the ladies for their advice and help, as they, like Kiki, each headed off to do their own work, walking straight-backed with their cans of water on their heads. Only one woman remained, who instead of filling her can, picked it up and handed it to Fran.

"Here," she said, "you will need this." Then she turned her back, walking away without her water.

Alone on the steps, Fran was silent, her wash in one hand and the can in the other. The woman's kindness moved her deeply. She felt like she was in biblical times, meeting other women at the well. And she thought of the parable of the poor widow, who gave her last coin to another, even though it was only a mite. The lady who gave Fran her water can might well have given her all she had.

"Here I am with my own well right here at my door," she thought, with the people I came to help, helping me instead. Then she said softly, out loud to the countryside around her. "How lucky can I be — and what can I give in return?"

Women at the well chat with Fran.

Chapter 8
Beginning Problems

While Fran was meeting the women at the well, I was on my way to the "Finca" or farm, where I would be working.

The day before, while we were visiting with Fernando, a man from the farm had stopped by, driving a badly beat up pick-up truck. His name was Louie and he was the farm foreman. Louie was short in stature, with a short, black cookie duster mustache on his dark brown, friendly face. He was a very good natured, hard working man, which was necessary, because as foreman, he organized the farm workers in the absence of the manager, who lived in the capital.

Louie had said he'd be by to pick me up the next day, but after waiting for him for two hours, I ended up walking to the farm instead.

Louie was at the dairy barn when I arrived. He walked over to me, laughing very loudly, and said, "Amigo, we have many problems today — many problems! The truck won't start, the milker no work, a cow is sick, nothing but problems. Manana, I pick you up."

I spent the rest of the day looking around the farm, then walked home again. The next day (manana) came. I again waited on my porch, and again, there was no Louie. Again, I walked to the farm to see what the "problem — problem — problem" was this time.

Today, they were having problems with the Jersey bull. He had arthritis and looked very nasty and mean. He stood in a field, fenced in by a 31 foot high barb wire fence. All of the workers were afraid to go into the area where the bull was pawing and bellowing. They were very happy to see Lew, the American "expert."

"Americano," said Louie, removing his straw hat, "we need help. The cow is in heat and needs the bull. But no one will go into the field to get the bull. Do you know what to do?"

I looked at Louie, then at the bull, which was now putting on a furious little performance in the field, then looked back at Louie again. I could see why the men were afraid. "I know exactly what to do," I said. "Forget about the cow and leave the bull alone!"

Louie shrugged his shoulders. "But that's exactly what we are doing now."

"Then you're doing the right thing." I looked back at the bull. "Why do you keep such a dangerous animal here when you have no proper facilities to handle him?" I asked. "He could kill someone!"

Louie explained that although the manager and others knew the bull was dangerous, they couldn't get rid of him because he carried a $5,000 inventory value. Since no one would pay that much for the bull, they kept him to prevent a loss on the books.

I shook my head, and walked around the farm again. I saw many things, that while not quite as dangerous as the bull, were equally wrong. There was very little shade for the milk cows. The milking procedure was poor, done by men who slapped the cows, making them nervous and inhibiting their milk flow. No provision was made for proper timing for breeding, which could greatly affect their production. No matter what the amount of milk the cows produced, they were all fed the same amount of grain, instead of giving higher nutrients to those who produced more milk. Sanitation was also an obvious problem, from workers who failed to wash their hands, to not sterilizing the milker, to leaving each cow on the milker too long, any of which could cause bacteria to form.

In addition, even though there was a large house on the farm that could house the family of the foreman or manager comfortably, no one lived there, making supervision poor overall. A lot of problems could also be solved with better assigned manpower. And most importantly, the bull needed to be replaced with artificial insemination, no matter what the cost.

These were the kind of thoughts going through my mind, when late in the day, the farm manager drove in from the

My first reaction was to lean back and smile until I realized the problems were more serious than funny.

capital. He had made a special trip up here to meet me. He seemed pleased when I told him I had already made a few observations, even though I didn't give him any specifics.

"Good," he said. "The agency wants a complete written report from you about your opinion of our operation here."

I hesitated at this, even though I knew there were things to be corrected. "Are you sure I know enough to comment after only two days?" I asked.

"Take your time," he said, "and when you feel ready, write your report."

That night I told Fran about the manager's request and what I had observed. For what was supposed to be a model farm, there were many problems, especially when compared to operations back home. But how did I know that conditions weren't excellent as far as Dominican standards were concerned?

All the while I had been sharing my thoughts with Fran, she had said nothing, just listened steadily. Now she looked right at me and asked me simply, "Why are you here?"

"To help the Dominicans improve their agriculture."

"Will your suggestions do that?" I nodded. "Then what's wrong with writing them down?" she asked. "You're an experienced farmer and you're here to help them from your experience."

I wrote my report to the manager that night, and dropped it off the next day, thinking that my comments would help the Dominicans solve their problems. Little did I know that as a result, mine were just starting!

We didn't know that Fran was also about to have some problems of her own. That same night, Padre Miguel had come rolling in with his beat up Datsun. As always, he leapt from his car, smiling enthusiastically.

We chatted, just small talk for awhile and then he asked Fran if she was ready to start work.

"Tell me when," Fran said. She was feeling very confident, since making friends with a few ladies at our well.

The padre was pleased. "Why don't you come to the church tomorrow night and meet some of the ladies of the village."

"What time?"

Padre shrugged his shoulders. "Around 7 p.m., mas o minos (more or less)." This expression was a favorite Dominican way of setting time — because it did not hold them to an exact hour.

74

Fran was very excited. She spent all of the next day studying her Spanish and writing a little speech to give to them that night. I offered to go with her for moral support, and I found her waiting for me to go into town with her when I returned from work.

"Hurry Lew, I don't want to be late!" I looked at my watch — it was only 5:30, but I could see she was anxious to get there and no doubt worried that we might have to wait a while to get a publico into town.

"Okay," I said, "but let me get changed and clean up first — and by the way, what is there to eat?"

"Eat? I'm sorry — I was studying so hard, I forgot about eating. Guess I'm a little nervous."

"Well, that's one way to get me to hurry up," I said. "Let's go now, and then, I can get a few bananas for dinner at our tienda while we wait on a publico."

Our tienda was a little food store located right at the end of our lane. Small stores like this were located throughout the countryside. Most only had enough room for one person behind the counter and two persons to shop. Tiendas usually stocked native bananas, bulk rice and beans in open bins, a few shelves of Coca Cola and rum and hard crusted, unwrapped bread rolls. You could also find candles, rock salt and sugar, and even fresh eggs. Our tienda came in handy for us many times, especially on nights like this.

I ate my bananas and Fran practiced her speech as we stood by the roadside, waiting for a publico.

"Yo soy una voluntaria de cuerpo de paz. Vivo aqui con mi espouso, Lew. Yo quiero ayauda ustedes en su casa y otra cosas." (I live here with my husband, Lew. I want to help you in your homes and with other things.) She was speaking quietly and with the sounds of travelers on the road, I could not catch all the words.

"That sounds good," I said, "but you'll have to speak up or they won't be able to hear you."

"Padre is only inviting a few ladies, not a whole church!" she replied, but then looking nervous again, added, "I hope!"

The church doors were open when we arrived, so we strolled in. No other soul was around, so we took a seat in one of the back benches. It was nearly 7 p.m. and Fran asked, "I wonder where the padre is?"

We heard a noise and turned around, but it was only some small children playing what looked like hide and seek. About 7:30 a real visitor strolled in — a lean and hungry looking dog. I called to him but he only gave us a puzzled look, then rudely turned and walked out.

"I guess I didn't impress him," I said, trying to cheer Fran up.

She laughed. "No wonder, you spoke to him in English. I just hope you didn't chase away the only one who was coming tonight." Just then there was a sound of a car making a sudden stop by the church door, and the padre came bursting through the door.

"Hola! So nice to see you," he said, as if everything was just fine.

"Do we have the wrong night for the meeting?" Fran asked.

"No, my friend," he said, laughing, "but maybe no one will come. The ladies never have an evening meeting." He patted Fran's hand. "Don't worry, we'll schedule another. I will announce it in church this Sunday and urge the ladies to come."

"Not the whole church, Padre!"

"No problem, that will not happen."

The padre drove us home, getting us there in record time. He swung into the driveway at high speed and stopped the car just short of the porch. Without waiting to be invited in, he was the first person out of the car, saying, "This is nice out here in the country. We were so lucky to get this for you."

"Would you like some coffee?" Fran offered.

The padre nodded. "Maybe I can help Lew with something?" he asked.

I laughed. Judging by the padre's driving and meeting-planning capabilities, I was not sure I wanted him to play "Mr. Fix-it" at our home. I picked something I didn't think he could fix.

76

"Everything's okay unless you're an electrician. The light on our porch doesn't work."

"No problem," he said. "Here, a priest must be able to do everything. Do you have something I can stand on and some tools?"

Fran went into get the coffee, while I scrounged around and came up with a chair, screwdriver, a flashlight and a boy-scout knife. I handed them to the padre with reservation. "Are you sure you want to do this?" I asked.

With a smile, he jumped on the chair and started to take the light fixture apart.

I became alarmed. "Be careful! The electric is not turned off. You could get hurt."

"I tell my people to trust in the Lord. I must do the same," he said, busily working. He needed both hands to work, so I tried to hold the light for him, but it seemed like the padre always had his hands or body in the wrong place. A couple of times, I had to catch him before he tumbled off the chair. Finally some electric sparks flew and then suddenly the light came on.

"Let there be light!" he shouted triumphantly.

Then he jumped down and ran off to his car, saying good-night along the way. He was pulling out of the driveway when Fran came out of the door with his coffee.

"Not exactly like our pastor back home, is he?" I said. We toasted the padre with our coffee, but all that was left of him was a cloud of dust in our driveway.

The padre had set another date for Fran to meet with the ladies. This time, he told Fran, he would pick us up so that we didn't have to wait for him. He told us he would be there at 6 p.m. (mas o minos) a week from tonight.

The day of the meeting came and went without any sign of the padre. Finally, two days later, his car came bouncing into our driveway. "Hola! amigos," he yelled, "I apologize for the meeting but my car broke down. We will schedule another."

Fran sighed, "Would you like some coffee" she asked. The padre was already out of his car.

The padre scheduled the third meeting for a Sunday afternoon. This time he was "mas o minos" on time to pick us up. As we passed ladies on the road to town, he would stop and slow down and invite them to the meeting.

When we arrived at the church, two ladies were there. The padre took one look around and said, "Excuse me, I'll be right back." He then walked out into the village and, presumably, contacted every lady he could find, urging them to come.

In the end, about 20 ladies gathered to hear Fran. I squeezed her hand for good luck as she got up to give her little speech, now quite well-rehearsed.

Though they listened politely, the ladies had no questions for Fran, and none of them rushed up to her afterwards to ask for help. Her little meeting, so long in the making, was soon over. We were all so down-hearted afterwards that the padre didn't even stay for coffee when he dropped us off.

Our disappointment continued the day after Fran's meeting, when I received a note at the farm from Dwight Walker, the agricultural representative on the Peace Corps staff. He had been very friendly when we met him during our orientation period, but his note left me uneasy. It said, "Please come into the Peace Corps Center to see me at your earliest convenience."

I knew Fran was feeling low after the meeting, so I went home to get her first before going into the capital. She was glad for the trip out. While she got ready, I told her about the note from the PC Center. "I hope it's good news," she said. "We could use a little!"

We were in good spirits when we arrived at the center. The publico we had traveled in was full inside and out. There were five or six live turkeys tied by their feet on the top of the car, and a small, live pig with its feet tied together on the floor by my feet. We were laughing about traveling on "The Livestock and People Express" as we headed up the path to the center.

Fran accompanied me to Mr. Walker's office. "You came to my meeting for moral support, I'll go to yours," she said.

It turned out that I needed it. Mr. Walker was sitting in his office when we arrived and wasted no time in telling me there was a problem with my report.

"I'm afraid I'm the bearer of bad news," he said, handing a copy of my original report and a lengthy written reply by the Foundacion. Each had been translated into both English and Spanish.

Mr. Walker was silent as Fran and I carefully read the report, slowly sinking into our chairs with each page. The Foundacion had made a very careful and pointed effort to answer all my suggestions by insinuating that the "new volunteer's" comments were not to be taken seriously since I had no knowledge or understanding of the farm situation. Not one of my recommendations was recognized as an actual, true appraisal of the situation. They even said that the Jersey bull was obviously no threat to anyone because of its arthritis and that I was recommending they get rid of a valuable bloodline.

Finally I laid the papers down. "Every opinion I stated was from my best judgment based on my actual farming experience. I don't understand why they were so defensive."

Dwight was sympathetic. "You're the first volunteer they've had with any real farming experience. Obviously, they weren't prepared for your report to criticize their efficiency."

"But what did they expect?" Fran asked.

"You must understand that the Foundacion is supported by grants of money from the government, American agencies and large corporations. They want that money to continue. Your report makes it sound like they should be doing a better job than they are — which could jeopardize their funding. So, they had to discredit you."

I felt terrible. In my desire to help, I had accidentally destroyed my chance of doing the very thing I came here to do. "I guess I should have shown you the report first," I said.

Dwight continued to be understanding. "And I could have discussed the situation with you first, too. And I would have, had I known they were going to ask you for a report like this on your first week!"

I took a deep breath. "So now what?"

He shook his head. "It's not good. Since they went to such great length to discredit you, they can't exactly turn around now and follow your suggestions." I nodded my head. He thought a little, then said, "There are a couple of things we can do, however. For one, we can switch countries."

I shook my head at that — we had invested too much into the D.R. to move now.

"Or we can give you another job here," he added.

"Like what?"

"There's a farm on the other side of the island requesting help from a volunteer. It's unprofitable and run down and they need a good manager."

"What would I accomplish going there?"

"If you can make the farm profitable, it can employ 10 or 12 more people." I thought about it, then shook my head at this idea as well. "No good," I said. "It might run well while I was there to manage it, but the minute I left, it would go back to where it is now. I gave up too much to come here to just manage a farm for 2 years."

Discouraged, we stood up to leave. "Well, let me think about it," I said at last.

Mr. Walker agreed. "Come back in a few days," he said. "We'll talk again."

We left the center in far worse spirits than when we had arrived. Our day in the capital was ruined, and we went directly home, not saying much to each other on the way there.

We went into our bedroom and sat down on our cots. It was the only room where we never opened the windows and so the most private place in our home.

I took Fran's hand. "We have a lot of serious thinking to do."

She looked straight ahead. "This is the most frustrating thing that has happened so far," she said. "First my meeting — when Padre had to drag those ladies there. Now, your report. It's obvious, they don't need or want our help here."

I nodded, staring ahead in the same fashion. "We may have been able to force ourselves to change to survive here, but I guess we can't force the people here to change their lives if they don't want to."

There was a short silence and finally Fran spoke. Her voice was very low. "I don't like to say this, Lew, but maybe we should admit we are failures as PCVs and return home where we are loved and wanted."

I sighed. Admitting defeat was not easy for me. I was an active player of sports from baseball to golf, and I always played to win. But this time, it looked like we had failed. Why waste any more of our time and the Peace Corps money, trying to convince ourselves we hadn't?

Chapter 9
A Turning Point

Despite a night's sleep and a willing attitude, neither of us felt any better about things the next day.

"Well," said Fran, "shall we go in today and tell Mr. Walker our decision, or wait a day or two?"

I didn't answer her right away. By now the first rays of sun were beginning to creep through the cracks in our house. I watched them as I thought about how far we had come — and all we had sacrificed to get here.

"Let's wait," I said. "We will probably never have the opportunity to live in a place like this again in our lives. Let's take a few days and enjoy ourselves here before we throw in the towel."

Fran agreed and we set off after breakfast to explore the area. We were now in good spirits. Making the decision to go home had taken the pressure off and we found it easy to relax and enjoy ourselves.

We began with a walking tour of our own immediate area first. We took our camera along, thinking we would be recording our last few days on the island for our memories.

We started toward Villa Mella — there were many homes along the way, and we spoke and waved to everyone we saw. We felt a little like politicians out campaigning for votes, but everyone seemed to appreciate our greetings and returned them with a smile.

We kept walking until we saw a woman with a pet parrot resting on her shoulder, and we stopped and asked to take her picture. The lady was very flattered. While she was posing, her neighbor lady came out to greet Fran and gave her a big hug. "I heard you talk at the church in Villa Mella," she said. A lady on the other side of the road waved her hand at us as well. "Please come over for coffee," she said.

While the ladies were talking to Fran, I wandered around to the back of the home, where I heard sounds of men working. There, I found a man burning a round, cup-like cavity in one end of a cutoff tree trunk, about four feet high and 12 inches around. With pride, he explained to me that he was making a pillon, a device the Dominicans used to pound and grind coffee or hull rice. He demonstrated by showing me another part of the tree, a limb that he had rounded off to make a mallet.

A couple of other men were whiling away the day watching him, and one of them spoke to me.

"Are you the Americanos staying in Fernando's house?" he asked. I nodded. "I hope you like it here. I live in a house close by. You must come over and have some rum one night."

I thanked him for his invitation and smiled. He reminded me of Felix, our neighbor in our first home in Ponce, and his nightly invitation to join him for some wine. I thought to my-self, people here are similar to those in Puerto Rico and yes, even in America.

I wished the men a good day and rejoined Fran, and we continued on. By now some children had noticed us, and started to tag along, coaxing us to follow them off the highway where we found more homes.

There was even a baseball game going on among some young boys in a small clearing in an open field. They were very serious about it, even though they were barefooted and they only had one well-worn ball and a tree limb for a bat. We stopped and watched for awhile, reflecting how different this was from the Upper Sandusky Little League where the boys had fancy suits and all sorts of equipment.

Thoughts of home reminded me to take pictures to show to my team back there. At first, the boys didn't see me, so I could get some good action shots, but then, one boy took the bat and stood in front of me, posing in a homerun swing.

"Take my picture!" he said. "I am a New York Yankee." Soon all the boys were starting to run in front of the camera with a special pose.

"Americanos," one boy asked, "you play baseball?"

"Yes, lots of it," I answered.

"Do you have a baseball?" he asked, tossing me the ball they were playing with. I inspected it carefully, then tossed it back.

"You do need a new one, but I'm afraid I do not have one with me." When I saw how disappointed they were, I added, "maybe I can find you one." At this, they all cheered and then went back to their game.

"Well that's one thing I have to do before we leave," I said, as Fran and I started back.

We took our time returning home after a long, leisurely walk during which we met many more Dominicans, all equally friendly. We reflected on it all as we relaxed on the porch afterwards.

"I really enjoyed today," I said. "I really felt as if the people around here love us."

Fran agreed. "They do seem to have accepted us." We smiled at each other. It was a nice feeling.

The next morning, we were both still in a good mood. After breakfast, we both went outside to enjoy a morning visit with the ladies at our well. At noon, I suddenly remembered that I had told Louie I would come to the farm today. They were getting a new tractor, and thought they might need help.

"If you can," Fran said, "come home early. I'll have a home-cooked Dominican meal waiting for you."

Nothing much happened with the tractor, so I was home on time for the promised meal. But Fran greeted me only with a laugh.

"Guess what? We don't have anything to eat tonight!" she said. She had made breadfruit like Marie had taught her, but then the ladies and their children from Fernando's farm came over for a visit. She offered them some of what she was making and they ate it all.

"When it was gone, they just smiled and went back to their farm," she said.

"Well, we wanted to have friends . . ." I said, but I was still hungry. "Guess I'll go to the tienda."

84

Before I could get across the yard however, Fernando and Marie pulled into our driveway in their pickup truck and invited Fran and me to come with them to their farm. Without hesitating, I accepted and turned back to the house to get Fran. Though we were both hungry now, we decided to "go with the flow" of it — we were getting used to the Dominican way. Besides, Fernando had been good to us and if we went to bed hungry, we wouldn't be alone in this country.

The air was very still at this time in the afternoon and the dust from Fernando's truck hung in the air over the driveway as we followed him back to the farm. Even the donkey was quiet as we passed him — which suited me fine. That was the kind of relationship I wanted with him.

Ahead, we could see that Fernando and Marie, plus the two ladies and their children who had eaten Fran's meal for me, were all gathered in front of the rural home.

Everything was very informal and we weren't quite sure what was expected of us. We decided we would just observe and see what happened. If this was a typical Dominican evening, though nothing was planned, something would occur.

Tonight turned out to be no exception. As soon as we joined the group, one of Fernando's laborers came out of the barn with a long pole. He went out to a large avocado tree close by and started to knock down some fruit. When Fernando saw him, he ran over to him shouting, "Wait, wait! The fruit will burst if it hits the ground! Let me catch them!"

It took very little time to observe that the pudgy Fernando was no candidate for the New York Yankees or even the Cleveland Indians. As the fruit continued to hit the ground, despite Fernando's best efforts at catching them, I decided to offer my assistance.

"Fernando, would you like me to try?" I yelled. "I've played a lot of baseball."

Fernando bowed from the waist and motioned with his hand for me to take his position. He was breathing hard and happy to let me try. The laborer with the pole smiled at me. "Ready?" he called.

"Ready!" I replied. The long pole tapped the stem of an avocado and it came flying down. I laughed and made a one-handed catch. Everyone cheered. With each succeeding catch, there were more cheers. Soon, the excitement brought the workers from the barn and a whole crowd was assembled. Now, I had to prove that it was skill and not luck. The laborer with the pole started to knock the fruit down faster and had me darting in all directions trying to catch the avocados. By now, everyone had come over and circled around the tree and was cheering and clapping after each catch. After we had a burlap bag full, another laborer grabbed a different sack and motioned for the men to follow. We headed off to an orange tree, and soon everyone was singing and joking as we picked the fruit.

When we returned with their prizes, the women were making some coffee over an open fire. We joined them and the laborers began peeling the oranges one by one with the large machetes they used for cutting grass in the field by day. By now, the sun was starting to sink in the west, casting a red glow over the horizon. The air cooled and we all started to quiet down to enjoy the beauty of the evening. Fernando, Marie, Fran and I were seated outside of the home, overlooking the field where the cattle were grazing among palm trees. Around us, the women and children, all barefoot, were standing or sitting in the grass. The men were dressed just as they had been in the fields all day, all with no shirts, and some with no shoes. We were all laughing and joking as we sucked the juice from the oranges, ate the avocados, and drank coffee. It was dark before all the events of the evening were finished and we all began to walk toward our homes.

Fran and I had walked slowly down our lane, talking happily together. Everything had worked out all right. It was a Dominican picnic — nothing planned, but with enough food for all, even the laborers and us. I wondered where in the U.S. you could have a family outing and entertain your workers and guests so easily and cheaply.

As we walked, we put our arms around each other and stopped to listen to the children who were still laughing and singing. At that moment, standing there in the dark with the sounds of the Dominican night all around us, we felt magically transformed. We had started out our night as foreigners, observing everything as if it were happening on stage. By the end of the evening, we were part of the action and accepted by the Dominicans. For the first time, it not only felt like home — it was home.

Fran spoke quietly as we neared our home. "Maybe we can still make it as PCVs."

"Maybe," I said.

As we reached our driveway, we discovered that our evening was not quite over. Standing in our driveway was Kiki. She had been waiting for us to return. As soon as her sharp eyes spotted us, she ran over to meet us, yelling in English, "Hello, you friends." In her excitement, she stumbled the last step and caught herself by throwing her arms around both of us. We all three started laughing.

"I've been waiting for you," she said. "I want to sing a song for you." We told her we would love to hear her sing and she gave a joyous laugh, then joined her hands on either side with ours.

"I sing happy songs tonight because tonight I am happy," she said. Then, she began to sing, putting much expression and action in her words raising her arms, skipping on one foot and swaying from side to side. We did our best to follow along with her as we made our way to the porch, our arms willingly rising and falling with hers, our bodies moving with her sways.

We reached our porch and Fran started to speak, but Kiki cut her short. "Sit down and I will finish my song. It say 'I am happy because you make me happy. You make me happy because you came to live here.' " We sat quietly, caught up in the beauty of her voice, then watched as she began to dance after her song was over. The evening ended only when her younger sister, Francesca, came over and commanded, "Kiki, mama say it time for you to come home." Then, both girls ran off, waving good night as they disappeared through the hole that was their path through our hibiscus hedge.

When she was gone, it was as if some magic had faded. Fran turned to me and in the dim light from our porch and the moonlight, I could see there were tears in her eyes. "Lew, I think we had better reconsider our decision," she said, wiping the tears from her cheek.

I put my arm around her. "Definitely! We must have another high level talk with ourselves tomorrow about this most important decision."

In the morning, Fran was up first. I entered the kitchen and found her humming to herself while making breakfast, so I sang loudly, in a voice not quite as beautiful as Kiki's, "I'm happy because you made me happy, because you live here."

Fran gave me a quick smile. "You won't be so happy when you see your breakfast!" she said. As usual, it was coffee and fresh fruit — which as much as we liked it, only made us long for a doughnut or two. We polished off the fruit, then pushed back the dishes for our "high-level" conference at the formal dining table Fernando had built for us on our first day.

"Okay, Lew, you are Chairman of the Board," said Fran. "What do you think?"

"Something interesting happened last night," I began. "There we were with people who could not read or write —"

"But they could sing," interrupted Fran.

"Yes, they could sing," I agreed. "But there they were, without any formal education, training and expertise, surviving better in this country than we are. Obviously, what they were doing works."

Fran looked at me. "But exactly how did they do it?"

I shrugged my shoulders. "Just by being friends with us and letting their feelings show, I guess." For emphasis, I shrugged my shoulders, again in an exaggerated Dominican style.

"Well, that must be part of our answer then," said Fran. "Do you suppose the solution to all our troubles is to just be ourselves and be open to making new friends?"

"That's what worked for us the other morning during our walk in the neighborhood. When we just acted like friends visiting among our neighbors, they responded."

"But isn't there anything that we can do to really help them?" asked Fran.

Something clicked with me. "What was it the padre told you the first night he was here?"

"You mean the part about how if I did nothing but keep house," said Fran, catching on, "the ladies would learn from me by watching what I did and trying to do as I do?"

"Right," I said. "Why don't you try that? I can probably do the same on the farm — I can just work with the laborers until I see a better way to do something. When I do, I'll just start to do it."

We smiled at each other, feeling like we had a clear course of action for the first time. Thanks to our walk, Fernando's picnic, and Kiki's song, things were starting to fall in place. We went to seek a friend, but could not find one there. Then we went to be a friend and friends were everywhere. The only thing we had to do was try harder — try harder to be a friend.

Part 2

Searching For A Route

Chapter 10
Sunday Singers, Night-Time Drummers

"Lew, let's go to church this morning."

Fran's voice drifted into the bedroom where I lay resting on one of our cots, enjoying the cool breeze from a portable fan. She was rattling pans in the kitchen as she spoke, but after awhile the rattling stopped. When I looked up she was standing over me.

"Did you hear me?" she asked.

"Yes, I heard you, but I was thinking."

"Well, when you think quietly — I can hardly hear you."

I yawned elaborately, but she continued. "Padre Miguel has been insisting we come to church and several of the neighbor ladies have invited us."

"There's not much choice about where to go," I said, still lying down.

By now Fran was a little exasperated with me. "It makes me no difference if we go to a Lutheran church in Ohio, or to a Catholic Church in Villa Mella! The important thing is that we go."

She was right, of course, and soon we were in our Sunday best and in a publico on our way to Villa Mella. We had no idea what time church started, but by Dominican standards, our "late" was sure to be their "early." Sure enough, when we arrived at the little church, there were only a few people sitting inside. Not knowing the local customs, we decided to take a seat in the back pew, rather than up front.

The first custom I noted was that we were overdressed. I thankfully removed my necktie and gave it to Fran, who put it in her purse.

"It's no wonder," I replied, fidgeting in my seat. "These pews are not very comfortable." I shifted my weight and almost upset the whole bench — not only were they hard as a rock, they were not attached to the floor.

"Sit still!" Fran cautioned me.

Understandably, we were both still trying to act like we did in our church back home. But as the morning wore on, it was plain the Dominicans didn't believe in quiet prayer.

Next we noticed a little boy who had climbed a ladder through a hole in the roof and started ringing the church bell non-stop. He had been ringing it for about five minutes straight, but people were still straggling in. Without clocks or watches, they needed the bell to call them to mass, and it was evident that Padre Miguel wanted the whole town to have the opportunity to come.

We noticed more differences. Here everyone seemed to sit in the front, rather than the back. And they were all talking — loudly — probably so they could be heard above the church bells, which were still clanging away.

The state of dress was also different. The ladies wore blouses and skirts and most had white rags tied around their heads. Many blouses had no zippers in the back and hung open, which was comfortable and cool for the women, and appealing for the men. It was a shame there weren't that many male Dominicans around — I was outnumbered by at least five to one.

Just when we were wondering if Mass would ever start, a few of the girls started singing, even though the bells were still ringing. Soon, everyone joined in, all singing á capella, for the padre's church had no organ or piano. But that didn't stop the Dominicans — they all just sang along on one song until someone started a song with a different tempo, and then they'd all join in on that one.

At last the church bells stopped, and the rest of the service went on without a hitch until it came time for the collection. The deacon came around with a collection box attached to a pole long enough to reach across the entire pew from the center aisle. He came to us last, and I threw in an American dollar, causing the deacon's eyes to light up. He quickly pulled the box away. Here was another thing to learn, I thought. Next time, leave your dollars with your necktie and bring a few coins!

We were the first to exit after mass was over, and were greeted outside the door, not by Padre Miguel, but by several peddlers. Each had a three-wheel push cart loaded with a 50-pound block if ice. For a few cents, they would shave off enough ice flakes to fill a cup, and pour syrup of different flavors over them. After a hot church service, they knew where to find customers on a Sunday morning.

We lingered awhile to meet the people as they exited — they were all extremely friendly. The ladies all touched me on the shoulder and smiled, then ran to Fran with open arms for a hearty Dominican greeting. Just when we were about to go, a small boy ran up and summoned us to Padre Miguel's office.

He was delighted to see us. "If you do not understand any part of our service, only ask me," he said. "I want you to feel at home."

We headed back, refreshed spiritually from the service and physically from the ice treat, and wondering if a Dominican couple attending our church back home would be welcomed as warmly.

Soon after we learned what Dominicans did on Sunday morning, we discovered what they did "after dark" as well. As soon as night fell, most activities would cease and our neighbors would go to bed. The chatter and noise of the children would vanish and in its place, we would hear the occasional braying of a burro, or a rooster crowing and receiving a faint answer in the distance. There was always the crackle of insects in the yard, and sometimes an occasional car would pass and the noise faded away down the road.

But the biggest mystery of all to us were the drums. We did not hear them every night, but when we did, one night they would be close and clear; the next, so very far away and faint that they seemed like a faint echo. They would always beat a definite rhythm, and often, especially when they were near, we could hear male voices chanting a simple melody over and over again, in time with the drums. It was beautiful but why was it happening and what did it mean?

Finally, one night we had the chance to find out. We had barely settled into the chairs on our porch when we heard the drums. By their sound, they were not too far away. It was strange — our neighbors had invited us to share other things with them, but not one of them had ever mentioned the drums to us.

We were discussing whether or not we should ask our neighbors about the drums tomorrow, when we noticed someone coming our way on the road, on foot. The moon was so bright it was casting a shadow. As the figure drew nearer, we could tell it was Dulci, a neighbor girl who lived with her mother about a five-minute walk from us.

"Hola, Dulci," Fran called to her. Dulci raced over and gave each of us a big Dominican hug and smile that lit up her round face and large brown eyes. Dulci was about 19 and very attractive, with an outgoing, positive personality to match.

"Where are you going by yourself?" Fran asked her.

"I am going to a banco," she said, gleefully raising her voice and her right hand in the air.

"Is that the sound of the drums we hear?" I inquired.

"Yes — it's not far from here. Only a short walk."

"And what's a banco?" Fran asked.

"You do not know?" she asked, surprised. "Why don't you come along with me, and I'll show you and tell you all about it."

Dulci waited for us to get our shoes and close up the house. "It's no hurry," she said. "We have all night."

Maybe there was no hurry, but Fran especially was bursting with curiosity and did not want to waste a second. In less than two minutes, the three of us were walking toward the road. Dulci in the middle, her arms extended to walk hand-in-hand with us. As soon as we reached the road we ran into more neighbors — Kiki, Francesca, Delila and Margo — all regulars at our well. All seven of us walked in a group for awhile, then Kiki forged ahead on a small pathway off the side of the road.

"This is it!" she said. The path wound in and out among the trees and bushes, and our walk down it single file created a spooky Halloween feeling, especially when an occasional palm branch dancing in the moonlight, reached out to tap us in the face. Fran reached back for my hand and about the same time stumbled and gave a loud grunt and groan.

Kiki, who had the only flashlight, shone it at the ground near Fran's feet at a big tree root she had stumbled over. "There will be more," she said. "I'll try to warn you."

"I hope you girls are not leading us poor Americans on a wild goose chase," I said.

"What is a 'goose chase'?" Kiki asked.

"Never mind," I answered.

The pathway ended very suddenly into a large open area, where there were several homes scattered about in an unorganized fashion. At one of the homes, there were many kerosene lights and lamps. It was hard to tell, but it looked like a crowd of 50-60 people had gathered there, under a shelter made of four poles stuck in the ground and a roof of palm fronds. Four men were frantically beating on drums and chanting a simple melody without words. The drums were made of hollowed-out tree trunks. They stood about four feet high and had goat skin stretched tightly over their tops. Some were larger with a deep bass sound and others smaller and higher pitched. The men were barefoot and one had no shirt (but he did have a half-empty bottle of rum in his hip pocket). We did not need to listen long to realize they were excellent musicians.

Any thought we might have had of blending into the crowd was forgotten, as even in the dim light it was easy to spot us. Soon everyone knew the Americans were present. As always, the people were very friendly toward us — greeting us by laying their hands on our shoulders or touching our arms. Soon, a gentleman came with two chairs, insisting that we sit in a special place.

We took them gratefully and sat down to let our eyes become adjusted to the dark. As soon as they did, we realized that we were not among strangers. The women from our well, those who walked by our home each day, those we met at mass, and the laborers from the farm, were all here. Here was a whole new part of the community that we had not been a part of — until now.

After a while, we began to feel as if we were on display in our chairs, especially when some of the children began to gather round and start talking to us. Some of the more timid ones stood back, simply looking and giggling.

"If we are going to live with these people as one of them, we must get off our chairs and mingle around on our feet," I said.

"Right," said Fran. "Right now all we look like are a couple of curious Americans watching them like these kids are watching us."

We rose and began to take in more of the action — everyone was certainly in a festive mood. Some ladies were serving coffee from a tray that contained about a dozen small tin cups. The people would take a cup, drink the coffee and put the cup back on the tray. When the cups were all empty, the ladies would return to the kitchen and refill the same cups over and over again. They spotted us and came over with a fresh tray of just-filled cups. "Here is some coffee for you," one said smiling.

Fran just smiled back at her, looking at the coffee. One of her hands slipped to her side where she could tap me on the leg. I knew what she meant "What shall I do?" Smiling I reached for a cup, looking at Fran.

"I guess if we are one of them, we take a cup of coffee like everyone else," I said to her, in English, while smiling at our hostess.

We both took a tin cup and smiled some more saying, "Muchas gracias." The ladies smiled back, "De nada" (you're welcome) but did not leave. They were waiting for the empty cups, so now, we had to drink all of it. As we felt the damp sticky cups, we knew they had not been washed between servings. Again Fran tapped my leg.

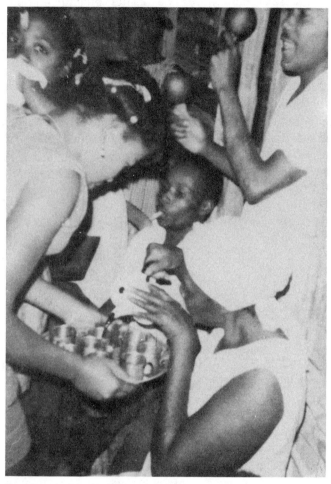

Serving coffee to the guests.

I looked at the cup — it did not have much coffee in it
and the tin was not too hot. Smiling again, I said to Fran under my breath, "keep your bottom lip inside the cup and drink
it fast. Ready?" We both downed our drinks and replaced the
cups on the tray, wondering if we had just acquired the one

PC disease we'd both managed to avoid since we arrived here — Montezuma's Revenge. We could only hope that as older and tougher PCVs we would somehow survive.

At one point, Dulci returned — it was the first time we'd seen her since we arrived — and slipped in between us. "Do you understand what's going on?" she asked.

"Not really," I said. Between the drums, the chanting and the coffee, I would have thought it was a celebration, but there was also an interesting dance going on in one area — only one couple was dancing, very slowly, and barely touching each other. Fran and I were at a loss for anything in our experience to compare it to.

Dulci explained that a banco is a religious service honoring the dead. Bancos were always held on the first anniversary of a person's death. Only one male and one female were allowed to dance, and they must be closely related to the deceased.

"How long will they dance?" Fran wanted to know.

"To the end of the banco, which goes on from sunset to sunrise."

"These same two people?" Fran asked in disbelief.

"They will dance until someone taps them on the shoulder — see?" Dulci pointed at the man who was approaching the dancing couple. As we watched, he moved up behind the male dancer and began to keep the same steps. Once he had the patterns down, he entered and the other dancer stepped out. The woman never changed her step or rhythm the whole time.

"And what about the woman dancer? Will someone relieve her?" Fran was concerned. Judging by what we'd seen of Dominican double-standards, it wouldn't have surprised us if she had to dance all night. In this case, we were wrong. A short time later, another woman replaced her, stepping in the same way as the man did.

Behind the dancers was an altar, decorated with crepe paper and a metal cross. There was a small dish, where some people had placed a few coins. The altar was there, Dulci explained, so that people could pray for the soul of their loved one.

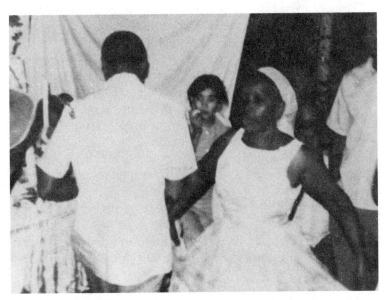

Dancers at the banco.

Drummers beating rhythm all night long.

"With all the drums, dancing and merrymaking going on?" I asked.

"That is part of a custom that goes back to our ancestry in Africa," Dulci said. "The altar, cross and candles are part of the Spanish religion, but we have added them to our bancos."

We stood for a long time, watching the dancers sway, listening to the drums pounding, and marveling at the mix of the cultures in this ceremony going on deep in the Dominican night. The ladies came around with the coffee again, but this time we turned it down, as did Dulci, which made us feel better.

By now, it was close to midnight. Dulci noticed that we were getting tired and offered to lead us home. As we passed by the drummers on our way out, I could see blood on the hands of one of the men from his pounding, but he continued to pound away like he had just started.

It was quiet and peaceful as we slowly walked the winding path toward home, the sound of the drums drifting farther and farther away with each step.

Though we were tired when we returned, we could not resist sitting in our chairs on our porch for just a little while, listening to the drums in the distance once more. They were no longer a mystery to us. We had learned another part of this Dominican life that was so old to them, but so new to us. At last, we headed off to bed, but not before we set our alarm so that we could wake before sunrise to hear the end of the banco. Sure enough, at the very break of day, the drums sounded once more, and then they were silent.

We attended many bancos after this and were always made to feel welcome. It appeared in this, as in other ways, Fran and I shared an experience unique from all other PCVs. When we related our banco experiences to our younger friends in the Peace Corps, we found none of them had ever attended bancos, or even heard of them. They had never heard the drums at night. Perhaps they only played at night near Villa Mella, where people refused to let go of their roots from Africa.

Chapter 11
School Days

Our new plan of helping through our actions proved to be a good one, especially when we demonstrated to the Dominicans our willingness to understand their ways in return.

It became a game of sorts as we exchanged ideas. The natives loved to instruct me on the proper way to swing a machete, peel an orange, open a coconut or show me how to plant native seedlings. At the farm I would then show them how to plant in a straight line for easier cultivation. They showed me how to crank a hand-fertilizer spreader. I showed them how not to overlap the applications for more economical use of fertilizers. Simple things, but progress.

Fran was also achieving some success with the women, as well as getting a little help with her housework. Take Delia, for example. She was about 12 years old and built like a bean pole — tall, thin and straight. Delia's family lived on the land leading back to Fernando's farm. Their home was within calling distance of our kitchen window, so she often came to watch Fran work. One day she was watching Fran mop the floor and finally she asked if she could help. Delighted, Fran handed her the mop, only to discover Delia didn't have the slightest idea how to start. So Fran took the mop back and showed her. Enthusiastically, Delia grabbed the mop back, dipped the mop in the bucket, pulled it out and slopped water not only over the whole floor but three feet up the walls as well. Experiences like these were good for all, for after a few tries, Delia became good at it, and Fran ended up with clean floors as well as walls. They also reminded us of something a PCV friend had told us. "If it were not for good things resulting from bad things, there would never be any good things in the D.R."

There was an enterprising family who lived across the road from us in one of the few concrete houses in the area. The parents made their living stuffing sausage in their backyard, and the oldest of their four teenage daughters was a teacher. They also had a younger son who shined shoes and did odd jobs.

One day, Mama and Papa were discussing the surrounding community and people with us. "There is a dance in Villa Mella," Papa said. "You should go."

When Fran replied "no" — the hot weather caused her feet to swell and hurt — Mama looked at me and said in a very persuasive voice, "then, Lew, you must go and you must have a girlfriend. You can have the choice of my four daughters."

Before I could think of an answer, Fran was on her feet. "Thank you," she said, smiling politely at Mama, "but if Lew goes, I think I will go too!"

This was a good example of many of the cultural differences we had to learn about. For the Dominicans, it was totally acceptable for a married man to enjoy the company of an unmarried lady at dances and parties. Part of the reason for this was strictly cultural — the Dominican men were much more "macho" than the males of our culture. There were also more than enough women around to make this system work. Because of poor sanitation and health conditions, many children died young in the D.R., especially male children, who aren't as healthy at birth. Add to this the island's history of wars and bloodshed, and you end up with nearly two females for every male. Since there was no way that every woman could have her own man, they had to share. This was very acceptable to most women — but not to Fran!

As the weeks passed, the women's morning visits at the well became longer, and they became freer and more relaxed in their talks with us.

One day, Fran was surprised to see them comparing the degrees of their skin color by holding their arms next to one another. Wanting to get in on the act, Fran placed her arm next to theirs, but the minute she did, one lady immediately pulled her arm back saying, "that's no contest with you in there."

Margo quickly replied, "Don't worry Fran, after you live here for two years, you will be as dark as the rest of us."

"That's all right," Fran said, saying what she thought was appropriate, "the color is not important."

Lizzabeth, the first lady, disagreed with that. She picked up her can and placed it on her head, saying, "Yes, it is important. The degree of darkness does make a difference!" With that she left, taking all the ladies but Margo with her.

Fran looked at Margo, confused. "I hope no one was angry," she said.

"No one will be angry with you," Margo replied. "We argue many times about our skin color, but we never get angry." Fran still looked puzzled, so Margo offered to explain it to her.

Over coffee, she told Fran that the original people of the island were Indians. Then the Spanish came and took control, bringing with them their African slaves. As a result, the country today has some lighter-skinned people who are descendants of the Spanish, some black people who are descended from the slaves, and only a few of Indian background. Most natives were a mixture of all three but the shade of one's skin indicated much about one's ancestry, and unfortunately, much about one's place in society as well. Most of the important jobs and land were held by those of Spanish descent, and those with mixed blood but lighter skins had an easier time of finding a job. That was why around Villa Mella, where most of the people had darker colored skin, work was hard to find.

Sometimes, it was through things we didn't even think we could learn from that we learned the most. One time Fran accidentally tossed an empty soup can from an "American" dinner into the trash. She had a few wrapping papers, too, so she lit the fire to burn everything, forgetting the can was there. Within minutes, a couple of boys who had been watching her from the fence ran over and one of them reached his hand right into the fire and pulled out the tin can. He hurried out of sight before she could stop him, waving his "prize." The other boys told Fran that tin cans were valuable — the boy could take it to his mother and they could eat or drink from it. From then on, we set any empty cans outside our door each night for the boys to take to their mothers.

Our neighborhood boys also taught us something about Dominican finances as one evening, they came to the front porch on a business venture.

"Do you want to buy some guavas?" they asked, holding up five of the tropical fruits. "For you, 10 cents for them all."

From our training, I knew the Dominicans always set their price higher, because they expect you to bargain with them. These boys were probably no exception. I shook my index finger at them sideways and said, "No, too much money."

"Then you can have them for five cents," they said, smiling.

I studied the guavas a little more. "Still too much money," I said.

At this point, one boy, apparently new to the game, gave in. "Okay, then you can have them for two cents." I did not expect the price to drop so quickly, but I reached into my pocket and gave them some change. The boys handed me the guavas and laughed. I returned to the house, shaking my head. "I hope that was a fair price for guavas," I told Fran.

Just then we heard a noise from the yard. Fran leaned out the window to investigate, and there were the boys. They had run only as far as our own guava tree and were now throwing sticks and stones at it to knock down more fruit.

"Well, now I know where they got the guavas," I said.

Fran laughed. "I'm happy you did not let the boys outsmart you on that deal." We waited a few minutes, and sure enough, they were soon back on our porch, this time with five more guavas for the bargain price of two cents.

This time I was ready for them. "Since these guavas are from my tree," I said, "I give you only one cent for these, and that is it. No more guavas."

The boys looked at each other, not knowing what to do. If they accepted my offer they would only have three cents total to go among four of them. My heart gave in to my business sense. "Let me have another look at these guavas," I said, and held them up to the light. "Yes, I thought so — these are not very good. Get me two more good ones and I will give you one cent more." They quickly rounded up two more, and our deal was complete.

Later Fran and I had mixed feelings about the incident. On one hand, we felt silly buying fruit from our own trees. On the other, we were pleased that the boys had worked rather than begged for the money.

The next morning, I made a special effort to flag down Fernando, as he drove to his farm, in the hopes that he could shed some light on this issue for us.

Fernando told us that to understand the boys and the guavas, we had to first understand the history of the Dominican Republic. In the past, all kinds of tropical fruit grew in abundance in the wild, and in sufficient enough quantity to feed the then much smaller population. Then, the only agriculture necessary was to gather the fruit when the people were hungry. With a year-round warm weather climate to mature different fruits throughout the entire year, and plenty of fruit for all to pick and eat, the people came to believe that the fruit of the land belonged to everyone.

This custom persists today, even when the trees are fewer and the population is greater. Some Dominicans, like Fernando, were now trying to produce feed for their personal use, which meant they had to take measures to protect their products.

"That is the reason for my guard dogs," Fernando said.

We thanked him for taking the time to explain this to us because it was so different from the way we had been raised. As an American farmer, I had the advantage of learning from my parents, who in turn, had learned from their parents, and so on, all the way back to the mother country in Europe. In this country, people had simply not learned skills that we take for granted, not because they had been waiting around for us to teach them, but because there was no need to know these things until recently.

"I am glad you understand, amigo," Fernando said.

The guava episode proved to have the added benefit of enriching our diets as well. We had already discovered that we could buy bananas for one cent each at the tienda at the end of our yard, and coconut juice had replaced orange juice as our morning beverage. As a result of buying the fruit off our own trees, however, word soon spread that the Americans would pay cash for things to eat. Enterprising children began to roam the country-side to find something they could sell to us. A small girl began to bring a fresh egg every morning for five cents, still warm from being laid. Several peanut peddlers stopped almost daily, each carrying a tin can full of nuts, with a string attached to the top of the can, and another can below with hot coals in it. They sold us hot peanuts for one cent per rum bottle cap full. If I smiled and kept my hand out, they would always give me an extra rum cap more for free. I proved to be such a good customer that they were disappointed if I failed to keep my hand out for extra nuts.

Several weeks of this sort of day-to-day learning passed before Fran and I had a chance to reflect on how far we had come under our new "plan," as we relaxed on our front porch one night, with the cool of the evening surrounding us.

We were both feeling that we had made the right decision to stay in the Peace Corps, right here in Villa Mella. We were now getting along well with all of our neighbors, and had come to appreciate each of them for their own unique personality. Fran was doing well with the women and children, and the laborers on the farm were actually looking forward to seeing me each day. My only concern was the management, who were still pretty much ignoring me.

I shared my concerns with Fran, as we listened to the sounds of the night drifting toward us in the dark. My biggest fear remained that I was not sure if we'd be able to accomplish any of the big things that I dreamed about.

Fran reached over, then took my hand. "Lew, I understand very well and know how you feel. But remember, the Peace Corps does not demand that you make outstanding contributions, only that you do your best."

I knew she was right, of course, but I still wondered, "would my best be good enough?"

Victoriano and Dolores Lopart

Our in-country education was aided greatly when Padre Miguel introduced us to a Spanish couple, Victoriano and Dolores Lopart. They operated a successful dairy farm near Villa Mella.

> *Make new friends, but keep the old:*
> *Those are silver, these are gold.*
> *New-made friendships, like new wine,*
> *Age will mellow and refine.*
> *Friendships that have stood the test*
> *Time and change — are surely best;*
> *Brow many wrinkle, hair grow gray:*
> *Friendships never know decay.*
> *For 'mid old friends, tried and true,*
> *Once more we reach and youth renew*
> *But old friends, alas! may die:*
> *New friends must their place supply*

108

Cherish friendships in your breast
New is good, but old is best:
Make new friends, but keep the old:
Those are silver, these are gold.

— *Joseph Parry*

As time went on, Victoriano and Dolores became very close friends and teachers of ours, both in agriculture and Spanish. And they taught us in the best possible way, through friendship.

Despite our day to day learning of cultures, we still felt a need to improve our Spanish on a formal basis. Fernando came to our rescue, securing Juanita, one of our neighbors, to give us lessons twice a week. Juanita was a local teacher, so we not only learned better Spanish, but received an education about Dominican schools as well.

On one of the first nights she came over, we noticed a change in her voice.

"Do you have a cold?" Fran asked, concerned.

"No, no" she said. "It's from school." The place where she taught consisted of only one room for 30 children. It was divided down the middle with a screen so that two groups could be taught at the same time — that meant the teachers had to talk very loudly to be heard over one another.

Today the other teacher had been out, so she had to teach both groups, leaving her voice hoarse.

"I don't understand how the children can learn very much under those conditions, Juanita," Fran commented. "Nor is it fair to you."

Juanita nodded, but said, "If I do not do this, someone else will be the teacher, and I need the job. I must also give part of my salary to the person who hired me, too."

Fran was alarmed. "You should report this to your government!"

"I don't think it would do any good," Juanita said. She knew that education was not a very high priority in a country with the financial difficulties of the Dominican Republic. Until the economy was straightened out, attention was unlikely to be placed any where else but there.

109

I had been listening up to this point, but now shook my head, also. "What you are telling us does not sound very good for education."

But Juanita was as practical as she was wise. "It's not as bad as it sounds. The schools in Villa Mella and the larger villages are in much better shape than our little school here in the country."

Fran was intrigued. "Could I visit the school in Villa Mella?"

Juanita was delighted with her interest, and made plans for us to go the very next day, even though it would mean she would need to take a day off teaching her own classroom. "I'm sure the children won't mind a day off," she said, "and besides, I need time for my voice to get better."

While this was something I was sure American children would love as well, I couldn't recall the Upper Sandusky Schools closing because the teacher had lost her voice.

The next morning the three of us arrived in Villa Mella before school started. The headmaster, Andre Royes Fortunato Victoria, knew Juanita and proved to be very cooperative. He also proved to have a genuine interest in young people.

"Come, let me show you our school," he said. First he showed us the school's four classrooms, each with large blackboards and desks that could seat three children each. Juanita told us that in her rural school, the children carried chairs from home to sit on and had nothing but their laps to write on.

Next, we stopped outside a room that was different from all the rest. "What is that?" Juanita asked.

"The rest room," Andre replied.

Juanita smiled, "that's another thing we don't have in our school."

"What do the children do — wait?" Fran asked.

"You know children too well for that!" Juanita said, laughing. "But it is a good thing we have the outdoors so handy!"

By now, it was time for school to start, so Andre took us outside, where we could see all the children standing, more or less, neatly in lines. All were in uniforms and had their hands placed over their hearts, as they stood facing the Dominican flag, that flew from the top of the school. Together, they sang their national anthem, then hurried inside.

Later, Juanita explained to us that all schools required uniforms, so that the poor children did not feel inferior to those from richer homes. "If we did not have a dress-code, many would come to school in very shabby clothes. It gives respect to our schools," she said.

"But what if the parent cannot afford the uniform?" Fran asked.

"That happens in places like our area. In that case, they do not go to school until they have the proper uniform."

Now from the American way, that made no sense. But from the Dominican thinking, we had to agree it was a good thing for then no child would then be embarrassed or ashamed.

Chapter 12
The Day The Cows Came Home

After we were settled in, some daily routines developed. Though, since this was the Dominican Republic, we could never be certain of exactly what each day would bring. Which was exactly what happened the day the cows came home.

The day began in its normal fashion, with me slowly lacing up my heavy work shoes to head to work on the farm, and Fran planning what work needed to be done around our home. That morning, as she flung open the wooden kitchen window doors to take a deep breath of fresh morning air, Fran caught a glimpse of Delia, one of our young neighbor girls stirring around outside her home. Fran gave her a loud, "Yoo hoo, Delia, Venga," and the girl immediately raced over to our window on a dead run.

"Que Pasa?" she shouted, breathing fast.

"Can you help me today?" Fran asked.

"O.K." said Delia, always eager to help, "but first I must carry a can of water from the creek for Mama." She headed off on a run again, stopping only to turn around and yell, "I'll be back soon!"

"And what do you plan today?" I asked Fran, knowing full well what she had in store. She had on her best housekeeping clothes and looked ready to clean our home from one end to the other.

"Oh, just wash some clothes, mop the floor, and housework," she answered. Then eyeing me with a knowing look, she added, "You want to help?"

That made me quickly finish dressing. "Sorry honey, I am ready to go to the farm."

Fran smiled understandably. "Hurry along, you never know what kind of surprises will await you today."

I found the first surprise waiting for me when I arrived. It was a visit from Dr. Luna, the farm director, who had never made a personal call on me since I started working for the Foundacion.

"I have good news," he said. "The Heifer Project is sending us 21 Holsteins by air today. We want you to go along to the airport to pick up the cattle."

This was so unexpected, the only thing I could say was "great." The Heifer Project was a charitable effort that arranged for the donation of livestock to farmers in under developed countries, and a project I had hoped to be involved with during my PC stint. These were the first heifers to arrive since I started with the farm, and I was anxious to begin working with them.

Dr. Luna explained that plans called for bringing the heifers to the farm first, so they could become accustomed to the hotter weather and the different types of pasture and feed on the island. He wanted me to observe the group very closely both at the farm and after they reached their new owners.

Then the director added the best part of the surprise yet, saying, "We also want you to give us any ideas or suggestions you may have about how to improve procedures."

Now this was great news, leaving it hard for me to control my emotions. This meant that the Foundacion management had discussed my skills and was now placing confidence in me. All my struggles had paid off! I literally leaped to me feet to grab Dr. Luna's hand, pledging to do my best for him.

"Great," he said, pleased with my enthusiasm. "Louie will drive by your house to pick you up with the farm truck." Louie was the farm foreman, and though not always reliable, the best man they had to put in charge.

"How soon?" I asked eagerly.

"As soon as he organizes the work on the farm," Dr. Luna answered. "It should not be too long."

I headed for home with more spring in my step than usual, greeting each of the friends and neighbors I passed along the way with a cherry, "Hola!" My heart was pumping faster and the adrenalin was starting to flow. At last, I was going to be a useful volunteer to the Foundacion that had brought me here!

When I reached home, I ran through the yard and up the steps. Eager to tell Fran the good news, I forgot totally she and Delia were to mop the floor today. With my first step in the house, my feet flew out from under me and I slid all the way across the room on the wet floor on my back. When I came to a stop, Delia was standing over me, with all the whites of her eyes showing and the mop still in her hand. "Que paso? Que paso?" she asked, laughing.

Fran approached with her hands on her lips, her face half concerned and half angry. "Lew, we are mopping and the floor is wet!" she exclaimed.

I looked up at her and rolled my eyes slowly, then calmly replied, "Yes, I figured that."

I got up slowly — fortunately, no damage was done — and told Fran the news about the heifers. She was excited, but wasted no time in kicking me outside so she and Delia could finish their work. "Let your clothes dry off!" she said.

I spent the next few hours waiting on the front porch for Louie to arrive with the truck. Noon came and went. Noon turned into one o'clock and still no Louie.

Finally, Fran came out and joined me. "Are you sure of the plans?" she asked.

"Yes. Dr. Luna said that Louie would stop to pick me up."

"What time?" Fran asked. I looked at her. Now, she had lived here long enough to know better than to ask that question.

"I know," she said, in reply to my look, "I guess you'll wait here all day, and tomorrow Louie will stop by and laugh and tell you he drove by, or it got too late, or he forgot, or the truck was full, or who knows — maybe you will learn a new excuse!"

"No," I said. "Louie will stop. I just need more patience." Now, it was Fran's turn to give me the same look I'd given her.

"On second thought," I said, "I've had patience enough. I'll walk back to the farm and see what goes."

"Good idea!" she said, "And good luck! I'll see you whenever!"

I set off down the road once more, yelling back to her, "I'll see you whenever," and waved goodbye. "Oh, and keep the floor dry!" I added, as a parting shot. She laughed and waved me on.

I arrived just in time, the farm was a real beehive of activity, as everyone was excited to go get the cattle. Three trucks stood ready to head out. Louie had the pickup truck motor going, with Sexto, a laborer, standing in the back of the truck bed, waiting to ride along. When Louie saw me, he smiled and said, "Good to see you, Mr. Lew — we were waiting for you!"

I climbed into the truck and said a silent prayer of thanks. Then, I remembered Sexto. "There's room in here for Sexto to sit in front with us," I said.

No, no, no," answered Louie, "Sexto is a laborer. Here they never ride in front. They always ride behind or walk."

I hoped Sexto was holding on tight when we pulled out, for as usual, Louie started out with the peddle to the floor. Stones were flying everywhere as we took off. "Are we late, Louie?" I asked, hanging on.

Oh, no, just right. It's 2 p.m. and it takes an hour to drive to the airport. The airplane with the cattle is due in at 4 p.m. That will give us about an hour to get the trucks and everything organized."

I bounced along in the truck amazed that what Louie had just said sounded like American planning! Things were changing — was it possible I could make an impact on these people after all? Even on Louie?

We soon passed my house, and I reached over and tooted the horn. Fran was watching from the porch and waved back. I caught a quick glimpse of her face and read her lips to be saying, "See you whenever!"

Louie was in a very jolly mood today, tooting his horn and waving his hand out the window at every passerby. He hardly slowed up to drive through the town of Villa Mella, but as we passed the town square, three men came running toward

115

the truck, he stopped, and two of the men hurriedly jumped on the back of the truck with Sexto. Just as we started to move again, the third man leaped on with a hearty laugh.

"Are they going to help us today?" I asked.

"No, no, they just want a free ride to the capital."

"Do you know where to leave them off?"

"No, but that's not important. They'll just jump off somewhere when I slow up, or stop for a street. I just drive as if they were not on." I nodded, and hoped that our free-riders knew what they were in for!

The only way to the airport was to drive all the way through the capital, taking Avenida Maximo Gomez to the Caribbean Sea and then turning on Avenida George Washington and on through the city. Near the center of town, there was a statue of Christopher Columbus. As we passed it, Louie laughed loudly, pointing to the statue, and said, "Columbus was loco! (crazy)."

I was puzzled. "Why do you say that? I've read that Columbus loved this island best of all the places he visited."

Louie laughed. "He saw the United States and still wanted to sail here." He made a circle around the side of his head with his index finger for emphasis. "Like I said, loco!"

When we arrived at the airport, the three large trucks were parked outside a large gate along the runway. They all found a comfortable, relaxed positions and settled down for a little siesta.

After a short wait, I said, "Don't you think we should check to see if the plane and the cattle are here?"

"No," said Louie, "the plane is not here yet."

"How do you know?"

"The plane always parks here where we can see it."

"Maybe it parked in a different place this time."

"I don't think so. We just sit here."

I was getting a little impatient. "Mind if I go inside to check?"

"If you wish," he said, sighing but going along with me. But as I started to open the door, Louie grabbed my arm to stop me, then fished into his pants pocket and pulled out a crumpled piece of paper.

"I have a pass to let us in the gate. I'd better go with you."

Once inside the gate, Louie was lost as to where to go and what to do. I used my knowledge of airports to find the main terminal and offices.

It took a lot of asking and hunting, but we finally found the office that knew a little about our flight.

It turned out to be very little. When I asked the attendants how soon the plane would arrive, I was answered with a shrug of the shoulders. "Don't know," one of the men said.

"Can you find out?" I asked.

The man who had answered me again shrugged his shoulders, but then motioned for a girl to check on the flight of the plane. She soon returned with the same shrug and a similar answer. "The plane is a long ways from here. We don't know for sure what time it will arrive."

Now it was Louie's turn to shrug his shoulders at me. I thanked the attendants and followed Louie back to the truck.

The minute we arrived, he climbed into his seat, and like the rest leaned back and tipped his hat over his eyes. "See, Mr. Lew," he said, "I told you the only thing to do is sit here and wait. You must learn to relax, because what is going to happen is going to happen anyway."

I looked around at the rest of the Dominicans, who had never stirred from their comfortable stretched out positions. Soon, they were all asleep but me. Obviously, they were not bothered a bit about the wait.

But I was sitting there in the hot sun with absolutely nothing to do. Finally I got out and took a short walk. Luckily, there was a bicycle peddler selling oranges. He was peeling very thin layers of the orange skin off, and then cutting a small hole in the top. This was a favorite way Dominicans eat oranges, sucking out the juice from the top and then throwing the rest away, usually on the ground or in the street. After a couple of oranges, I felt better and accepted the fact that the drivers had the right idea after all. I found a shady spot to stretch out and relax — the plane would arrive when it got here.

It was almost dusk when finally, a large plane with its lights on came lumbering up and parked near the gate where we were waiting. Now Louie jumped to his feet, moving faster than I knew he could. "Hurry, Mr. Lew," he yelled to me, "We go to the plane — they will need us!"

Louie pulled out his pass, and the two of us hurried through the gate toward the plane. Already the exit door was open, and an American was standing in the door.

He had a briefcase under one arm and his white skin was very noticeable. "Does anyone here speak English?" he yelled at the top of his lungs.

No one responded, so he kept on repeating his plea. If anyone could speak English besides me, they were certainly keeping it a secret, so I ran up to him, grabbed his hand and said, "Hi, Yankee. Welcome to Santo Domingo!"

The man sighed a big sigh of relief, and introduced himself as Marion Lehman, of Indiana. He was of medium build, round face, thinning hair and was sweating profusely from the warm Dominican air. He reminded me of Fran and me, that first moment when we arrived.

I quickly explained that I was a volunteer helping with Heifer Project here in the D.R. "Wonderful!" he said. "You're the person I was told would meet me here and help me clear these cattle through customs."

Now this was news to me! One minute I was along for the ride, the next I was the man in charge. I decided to just go along with the situation, remembering what Louie had told me — what will happen, will happen.

"Okay, Marion," I said, "follow me!" My trip into the airport with Louie earlier now proved to be of some value, for I was able to guide us swiftly back to the office we'd checked with before. The same personnel were still there, but were now eager to go home. They recognized me and asked for the health papers on the cattle. Marion handed me his briefcase and we soon found the right papers. Without saying a word, let alone checking to see if they were correct, the attendant stamped every one of them. It was only a matter of minutes until one man handed back a duplicate of all papers and said, "Thank you, you may unload the cows now and good luck!"

I handed the paprs back to Marion, who stuffed them into his briefcase and looked at me with an admiring smile. "Lew, this is great! I have never seen such efficiency anywhere. It sure pays to have someone like you along!"

"Thank you," I said, returning his smile. This wasn't going to be so bad, I thought, relaxing until I noticed that Marion was looking frantic again. "We must hurry, Lew," he said. "We had to detour for a storm on the way down here. The cattle have been on that plane three hours longer than planned — they're probably in alot of stress due to lack of adequate food and water for that big of a trip."

When we arrived back at the plane, everything, surprisingly, was going like clock-work. The loading ramp was backed up to the plane, and the first truck was parked at the end of it, ready to receive the cows, which could be seen inside the doorway.

Marion pulled his permit out — it was one of the papers that the attendants had stamped — and showed it to the ramp attendant. The attendant took it, looked at it, and handed it back to Marion. Now came the next surprise — this was not so nice.

"That will be $25 for the use of the ramp," he said to me.

"I don't have $25 for the use of the ramp," I looked at Marion frowning.

"No way," he said. The attendant was getting impatient, but not budging, "No $25, no ramp!"

I spotted Louie near the truck and yelled at him. "Do you have $25 for the ramp fee?"

Louie shook his head. "No, the cows are not ours until I get them on our trucks. I can't pay anything until then."

Now the pilot of the plane was getting impatient. "What's the delay?" he yelled down to us.

I yelled back at him, "You must pay $25 for the use of the ramp before the cattle can be unloaded." It was worth a try.

The pilot didn't think that was a very good idea. In fact, he was very upset. "Hell no," he said, "I will not pay $25! I got the cows here, now they belong to you."

Being in charge was suddenly no longer fun. If the cows belonged to the pilot when they were on the plane, and to Louie when they were in the truck, and to no one on the ramp, then who was going to pay the ramp fee?

I went back to the attendant and asked him who paid the fee the last time the ramp was used for the cattle.

He shrugged his shoulders, "Don't know."

For the next few minutes, we all just stood around getting aggravated. Everyone wanted the cattle off the plane, but no one wanted to pay the $25.

The pilot yelled down again, "If you do not unload these cows soon, I'll shut the door and head back to Miami with them."

Marion's earlier admiring smile at my handling of the situation now changed into a frown, and he was muttering something about "never having had this problem before." Though I was thinking fast, no solution was materializing.

Ironically, it was Louie who came to the rescue. "How are things going?" he asked, walking over to me.

"Not good," I said. "I need help. No one wants to pay the fee."

He hesitated a moment, then said, "Let me talk to the attendant."

The two went aside and soon the attendant returned, waving his hand in the air. "It's okay, you can bring the cows down now." No one asked Louie how he managed it — we were all just anxious to get the cattle off the plane.

Free at last, the cows came jumping and bellowing down the ramp like wild buffalo. Even someone who had never worked with animals could understand what it must have been like for the poor cows — they had just had their first plane ride, which was three hours longer than expected. Floodlights were glaring in their eyes, and the air around them was 20 degrees hotter than they were used to. They were hungry and

Lew doubts if the cows will make it home in these trucks.

tired and people were now yelling strange sounds. The more scared the cattle became, the wilder they became, and then the louder the people yelled. I was glad I wouldn't have to clean up the ramp or the inside of the plane after this trip!

It did not take long to load up the three trucks. Louie and I watched as they rolled through the gate. I shook my head in disbelief. The truck sides were only four feet high and the cattle were loaded on sideways with their heads hanging over the top of the sidebaords. "They'll never get to the farm that way," I said, envisioning the cows breaking through the short sidewalls of the truck the minute something on the road scared them.

But Louie laughed, "They'll be all right," he said, "see those men?" He pointed at a laborer standing outside the sideboards on the back of the truck.

"They'll ride there all the way to the farm and make sure nothing happens."

"Just in case," I said, "let's follow them." Louie shrugged his shoulders, but followed along.

We were both quiet on the way back, being just as tired as the cows were. At last I broke the silence, for there was one thing I had to know — just how did Louie get us out of paying for the ramp fee?

"Louie, what did you say to the ramp attendant at the airport?" I asked.

Louie smiled, "I told him no one had the $25 tonight and we would decide who is to pay it 'Manana.' "

It was, of course, the perfect answer. "Manana is one of the most used Spanish words — it means tomorrow or sometime later. The word was a good solution for the pilot of the plane, for manana, he will be back in the United States. It was a good solution for the Foundacion, for manana, we would have the cows without paying the money. And just maybe, it was even a good solution for the ramp attendant, for something told me, he was never entitled to the money in the first place.

When we arrived at the farm, amazingly enough, the cows had made the journey fine. Perhaps they were just too tired to try anything. After they were unloaded, I said good night and wearily began my walk home — there was a lot of work ahead for me — but I would think about that "Manana."

Chapter 13
The First Pitch

We were surprised to discover that baseball — the great American pastime — was a major Dominican interest. The Dominican Republic has more major league baseball players per capita, than any other country in the world. Though sometimes their equipment is not very good, every boy's dream is to grow up to be a major-leaguer. They practice and practice, and their enthusiasm is unbelievable.

I felt right at home in this aspect of Domincan culture. Softball had always been one of my favorite sports, and it was only last year that I decided to hang up my spikes and call it quits.

But Fernando, our landlord, changed everything. He was forever solving problems and creating opportunities for us, sometimes knowingly and sometimes not. So it was that one Sunday, he accidentally gave me back the game of baseball.

That morning, he stopped early to tell us that he was going to bring his family and older sons to our home for a big fiesta that afternoon.

The yard is large and has shade trees," he said. "And we can use your house for the food."

Well, it was his home after all. "Should we leave for the afternoon?" I asked.

"No, no, no! I want you to stay for the celebration with my family!"

It turned out to be a first-class Dominican party. As Fran and I watched from our porch, things began to take shape. First a laborer came with six burlap bags full of coconuts and dumped them in the shade of our lime tree. Then Fernando returned with his family, and four bottles of rum and a sack of limes. Fernando placed them next to the coconuts.

Fran went into the yard to greet Marie. "Who'll drink all the rum?" she asked.

"Fernando's four sons will be here with their families," Marie replied. We had never met them, so Fran asked if they were Marie's children as well.

"No, just Fernando's," Marie said, smiling in a way that Fran asked no more questions. "Some workers may come too — this is Fernando's party!"

About that time, the laborer who brought the coconuts pulled out his machete and began chopping the ends off them. He poured a little coconut juice out and a little rum in, then squeezed in some of the lime juice. He knew how to get a party moving!

A little later on, the four brothers pulled into the lane in their own cars, each loaded with their families. All four boys were husky, handsome and athletically built. They must have inherited that from their mother, for they were in direct contrast to Fernando's round, short figure. But in personality, there was no doubt that they were Fernando's sons, for they all were as friendly as their father, and immediately made themselves right at home.

Within a short period of time, the party was going strong. Empty coconuts began to be tossed everywhere on the ground. We were all beginning to get hungry, when in walked another worker with a large bag of hard crusted bread rolls over one shoulder followed by two others carrying a whole roasted pig. As they laid the hot, golden brown pig on the table, Marie explained to Fran, "Two men roasted the pig all night long, by slowly turning it by hand over hot coals," smacking her lips, she added, "it will be delicious!"

Then a woman entered with a very large pot of hot cooked rice. Everyone knew what to do next. The men dropped all their coconuts and followed the parade into our house. There the men tore into the pig, while the women and children waited. Fernando grabbed my arm and pulled me to join them. I hoped there would be enough for Fran and the girls, but there was plenty to go around.

After all had eaten their fill, there seemed to be nothing planned, so I brought out the horseshoes that I had brought from home. The men watched curiously as I pounded the two stakes into the ground. I tossed the horseshoes to demonstrate, then handed them over to the men, but they only tried it a couple of times.

"Too dangerous," said Tonio, Fernando's oldest son, "We may hit one of the children."

I looked at the horseshoes lying all over the ground (among the coconuts) and had to agree. Unless the Dominicans improved their throwing, it would be awhile before this game was safe for anyone to be around.

I must have looked disappointed, for Tonio looked at me curiously and said, "Don't worry, amigo, we have something better."

He yelled and whistled for his brothers, and they all ran over to the car and brought ball gloves and a couple of new softballs to play with. Soon, all were happily playing pitch and catch.

I watched them, while slowly picking up my horseshoes. Fran came up to my side and put her hand on my arm, "Que paina (too bad) you brought your horseshoes and left your ball glove in Ohio," she said.

I nodded, a familiar feeling of disappointment coming over me, "Yes, mark up another lesson to be learned!"

I sat alongside for awhile, watching them play, my adrenalin flowing, but the men ignored me. Finally, I could stand it no longer. Trying not to look too eager, I strolled up beside one of Fernando's sons and asked if I could join in, even though I had no glove.

"No problem," he said. "My brother manages a baseball team in the capital, and keeps all his equipment in the trunk of his car." He tossed his glove to me and ran after another one.

I entered into the group, but it was clear that they were not going to immediately accept me on an equal level. The men laughed, and I could tell they were throwing the ball very softly to me. This irritated me even more than not playing. With the hot relaxing sun, I was ready to pitch a few.

"Okay, amigo," I yelled to Tonio, "you catch, I pitch!" I dug a small hole with the heel of my shoe. He humored me, squatting into a catcher's position. "Okay, amigo, let her come," he said.

My first pitch was right on target. It felt good, and I threw a second one faster. Again I was right on target.

"Bueno amigo!" said Tonio, pleasantly surprised. "You pitch softball?"

Fran had been watching and spoke up, "Does he pitch softball? I want you to know he is one of the most experienced pitchers in America! He has been pitching softball for over 30 years!"

Now Tonio became excited. "Watch everybody. The American pitches softball!" I continued to pitch several more. First a drop, then a rise that glanced off the top of Tonio's glove, then a change of speed for variety. Tonio went "bananas" and all the men soon gathered around me.

"We need a pitcher," they said. "Can you play this Saturday in the capital? Can you play every Saturday?"

Now I was about to go "bananas." All kinds of thoughts went through my mind. This was very well to pitch a few in my yard, but every week? I am 50 years old — can my legs still take it? And what about this heat? Could this help me to be more accepted and help us do our jobs better? Can I resist the offer? In the end, of course, I gave in and agreed to try it for a couple of weeks.

Saturday could not come soon enough for me — but when the big day finally came, I was the first person to arrive at the ball diamond. I sat down to wait and soon the players began to gather. I didn't know them and they ignored me, not knowing I was a new member of the team. I was relieved when Tonio arrived and was delighted to see me, until he told me the game was a doubleheader and he wanted me to pitch both games.

"Wait, Tonio," I said, "I'm out of condition. My arm is not very strong because I've not pitched for several months."

"Then you throw until you get tired," he said and headed toward the rest of the players.

126

It came time for the game to start. I walked slowly out to the pitcher's mound, grinning to myself, thinking — if that Wyandot County softball nut, Gene Logsdon and all my buddies I played with back home could only see me now. "Here I was in my work clothes with no hat, plodding out to play softball with my heavy work shoes and a borrowed, badly-used glove. I had never expected this to be a part of my Peace Corps experience!

As I started my warm-up pitches, trouble started. The opposing team was protesting my status. I could hear them arguing — "if this American played they won't!" I finished my warm-up, but the first batter refused to step into the batters box. The umpire left the argument to the managers and players.

The debate went on for awhile, and I figured my day in the sun was over. I began to walk slowly toward the sidelines, sure that I would be disqualified. But then I heard some of the most beautiful words I would ever hear as a Peace Corps volunteer. They came from Tonio, who was fighting dearly for me to play, "he is not a foreigner, he works for the Peace Corps. He lives here and is one of us."

That seemed to satisfy the opposition, in addition to pleasing me very much. Soon Tonio motioned me back to the mound.

I pitched three strong innings before I felt tired, and in came the reliever. For the rest of the game, I sat with my team, but stood up to cheer both sides. At the end of the second game, players from both teams approached me.

"Nice to have you playing with us!" some said. "See you next week!" others added.

Playing softball today in the Peace Corps brought me closer to feeling a part of the Domincan Republic than any other experience in our time on the island. And in the end it would prove to bring me more than that, for it was to be through the most American of pasttimes that I would finally understand what it was to be a true Dominican.

Lew pitched his way into the hearts of many Dominicans through his new ball team.

Chapter 14
Finding Our Way

It was a beautiful Sunday afternoon, and we were resting peacefully on our front porch. Suddenly, several boys came running up our driveway followed by a Jeep. The boys were pointing to our home and shouting, "They live here! They live here!"

We could see an American couple inside an embassy Jeep. Fran jumped to her feet and started walking toward the car with open arms, "Venga aqui! Mi casa es su case (our home is your home)!"

The couple thanked us with a smile as they got out of the Jeep and introduced themselves as Mr. and Mrs. Wells. I immediately remembered that we'd met before. Mr. Wells worked for the Aid for International Development (A.I.D.) and we had encountered them when we first entered the country.

"You were very helpful to us when we first arrived," I said. "What can we do for you now?"

"For starters," said Mr. Wells, "may I leave my dog out of the car for some exercise? You have a nice large yard here."

"Of course," I said, for Fran and I both loved dogs.

Mr. Wells opened the car door, and out jumped a big, beautiful black German Shepherd. Though we could tell she was not fierce, the children, who had led the couple to us were not so sure. We all laughed at how fast they ran off as we then wandered over to our big mango tree to relax in the shade. The dog followed.

"How old is she?" I asked, playing with her.

"About two years," Mr. Wells said, watching me and the dog carefully.

In addition to being large, she had a very slick coat. "I can tell she's had very good care." I said.

"That's because we love her so much," Mrs. Wells said. "And she's American like us!" The dog's mother had been bred on the American Embassy grounds, making her pups eligible for registration in the American Shepherd Society.

I had been playing with the dog the whole time and now gave her a big hug. "I can tell you and the dog get along very well," said Mrs. Wells, still watching me.

"I grew up with animals," I said. "I love them all, but especially dogs."

Mr. Wells nodded approvingly, "Good," he said, because we have a big favor to ask of you. We're going to be retiring next month and have many things to do before we can leave. Would you mind keeping the dog here for a couple of weeks for us?"

Fran and I were elated with the idea. Within a few minutes, arrangements were all made and the Wells were driving off, leaving us with a leash, a water dish and a new friend.

"Good luck," they cried, "See you in two weeks!"

Fran leaned over and scratched the dog's ears. "You know, we forgot to ask her name.

"You're right! — well I guess it's going to be just 'here girl' for now. I looked down at the dog and continued. "She looks very intelligent — she should be very trainable."

I set about teaching her a few tricks and by the end of the day, had her shaking hands and sitting down, on command. I continued to work with her for the next two weeks, both late into the evening and every morning before I went off to work. Not only was I pleased with what she learned, but I found myself really enjoying the time I spent with her. It was great "therapy" after the day to day frustrations of working on the farm.

For Fran, the dog proved to be a great comfort as well, helping her to feel safer. Our neighbors were more cautious when the German Shepherd was around, for in the Dominican Republic, they were always used as watch dogs. The dog seemed to sense that being a bodyguard was a part of her role, for while she never harmed any of the Dominicans, she stayed close to Fran, and always remained a little less friendly with them than with us.

At last, the two weeks were up. We took the dog and sat back under the same mango tree to wait for the Wells' return, at the time they'd told us to expect them.

Fran looked at the dog and then at me, "I know this is selfish," she said, "but I wish we could keep her."

"I know," I said, rubbing my hand down the dog's back. "I had been thinking the same thing."

Soon the Jeep pulled into the lane. The dog recognized it at once. She perked up her ears and gave a soft bark, then ran toward the car with her tail wagging. It was a happy reunion.

We walked over after the dog and we shook hands all around. "How'd it go?" asked Mr. Wells.

"Great!" I said. "Let me show you some tricks she learned." I put the dog through her paces; she amazed all with her eagerness to perform. Mr. Wells was visibly impressed.

"I'm so glad you got along so well — it makes what I have to ask you now even easier. He paused for a minute, then said, "Would you like to have a dog?"

Fran and I looked at each other, but then I shook my head. The dog was a very valuable animal, far beyond the means of volunteers. "I'm afraid we couldn't afford her," I said.

Mr. Wells quickly explained that we'd misinterpreted him, he meant to give her to us outright. "I have been looking for some time for the right home for her. People from other agencies speak very well about you, and I want her to be with good people."

"Please," added Mrs. Wells, "You'll be doing us a favor if you keep her."

There was only one answer to that question, of course. "Thank you!" we said excitedly.

We walked the Wells back to their Jeep and said our goodbyes, wishing them good luck in their retirement. Then the three of us went back and sat under the tree again. Both of us gave the dog a few extra pats. For two 50-year-olds, we were happy as five-year-olds with our new pet!

Fran took my hand in one of hers and patted the dog with the other. She said, smiling, "We're now three volunteers!"

It suddenly occurred to me that everything had happened so fast that we'd forgotten to ask the dog's name.

"I guess it's up to us to come up with a new name for her," I said. "What should we call her?"

Fran thought for a minute, a far-away look in her eyes, then said, "Let's call her Lisa." That was our oldest granddaughter's name and we loved her dearly. "It'll remind us of our family each time we call her!"

The dog ran and played, but we sat there a long time feeling grateful for the Wells' bringing Lisa into our lives. It helped us to recapture a little of what we missed so much — home.

While Lisa helped bring much joy to our daily routines, there were still many things we missed about our lives back home. Most were things we took for granted back in the states — like easy ways to communicate. Here, there were no telephones for quick and daily contacts, no daily paper to learn about community activities. The Dominicans had only the grapevine to depend on, which we had learned firsthand was not always dependable or accurate.

Most of all, we missed our automobile. Without a car, we were very limited in the number of Dominicans we could contact, and I was still behaving like a typical American in that I had a love affair with my car and thought I could not exist without it. I had suggested to the PC that they allow us to import our own car and even offered to donate it to the center when we left the country. The PC understood my problem, but explained it would hinder our acceptance as Dominicans if we appeared to be rich gringos, riding around in our personal car.

Still, the lack of ability to reach out to more people was frustrating to us. We continued to feel that the lack of a car was a major roadblock in our ability to do the job the Peace Corps needed us to do, but we resigned ourselves to realizing they'd probably never see it our way.

This time, however, the Peace Corps had a big surprise for us. The next day when I arrived at the farm, Louie hurried to meet me.

He was very excited. "You have a message from the main office laying on the desk!" he said. He followed me over, watching very curiously as I picked up the very official-looking sealed envelope with my name on it.

It was from the director of the Foundacion and was very brief. It consisted of only one line which read, "Please see me in my office this afternoon."

Louie gave me a look that mirrored what I was feeling — this could be very, very good news, or very, very bad news. There was no way to tell, but I remembered the last "official" message I had received led to being "chastised" for my evaluation of the farm's operation. "What did I do now?" I wondered to myself.

I decided to go home right away, get Fran and get to the capital. There was no use putting this off. When Fran read the message, she was concerned too, and we rode nervously into town. Seeing the two soldiers who guarded the bank on the ground floor of the Foundacion building didn't help any, even though they knew we were volunteers and smiled at us as we entered.

We had to wait until the director was ready for us. Another PC volunteer came along and increased my anxiety by telling us how unusual it was for him to see volunteers personally.

Fortunately, the director turned out to be very friendly. He first asked us simple questions about ourselves, but finally got to the point.

"Is there anything we the Foundacion can do for you?"

I hesitated — this was either an opportunity knocking, or a test to see if we respected him. I decided to take a risk and make my pitch for a car one more time.

"We miss our car very much," I said. "We feel very limited in our work because we can only operate within walking distance among our neighbors. If we had better transportation, we could reach out farther and contact more people."

The director seemed to be waiting for just that request. Smiling, he reached in his desk drawer and pulled out a set of keys. "Maybe these will help you then," he said, laying them in front of me.

We were both speechless, but I wasn't going to let this chance slip by. Before I could reach for the keys, the director had his hands back on them. We went back and forth for the next five or 10 minutes — I kept reaching for the keys and the director putting another condition on the offer. When we finally shook hands and walked out with the keys, I felt like I'd just bought a used car.

The keys belonged to an old Jeep the Embassy was going to get rid of. The PC had persuaded them to give it to the Foundacion, on the condition they allow us and other Foundacian PC volunteers to use it. A volunteer showed us how to drive it properly, and how to set the four-wheel drive.

We said, "Yes, yes," to everything as we took our driving lesson, and then very cautiously drove our new car home, not relaxing until it was parked safely outside our home. Then, we looked at each other and laughed — all along, we had wanted wheels and where was the first place we drove once we got them? Straight home!

In the days to come however, we would overcome our cautiousness. If the Foundacion and the PC had worked together to get us wheels, we were certainly going to use them. Their cooperation showed us that we now had the backing to do our jobs, and we weren't going to let them down!

As we had claimed, the car made it possible for us to reach more Dominicans. It also gave us access to a broad range of resources available to us as PC volunteers.

One of these resources was the film library at the U.S. Embassy. I thought about using some of the agricultural films in my work with the farm laborers, but Fran had bigger ideas — she wanted to show the movies in Villa Mella.

At first, it sounded like a crazy idea. After all, there was no building large enough to show movies indoors. But then Fran came up with the idea of setting up the projector outside at night, figuring we could use the back wall of the church for a screen.

We decided to test the idea by the showing a film in our own neighborhood. In true Dominican style, we'd figure out a way to do it when we got there.

Our new transporation allowed us to contact many new groups like these from the village of Villa Mella.

Fran with her new 'Mothers Club' in Villa Mella.

"You know this is not exactly what I had planned to do tonight," I said to Fran, as I lugged the heavy projector to our car.

Fran opened the door for me. "Stop grumbling — doesn't the thought of lights, camera, action, excite you?"

When we arrived home, I noticed that Juanita's home had a solid concrete block sidewall with some open yard space next to it. I thought it would make a decent outdoor theater for our experiment, but now Fran was hesitant.

"What will the neighbors say?" she asked. "Most of them go to bed as soon as it gets dark."

I thought for a moment, but still felt positive. "We'll just have a party then. I'll turn up the volume as loud as possible. No one will be able to sleep, and they will all come out to see what the commotion is about. It'll be our first neighborhood pajama party."

"You had better change that to just a party," Fran replied. "I have yet to see the girls washing a pair of pajamas."

Still unconvinced, Fran watched as I began to struggle to get the projector out of the car again.

"I think I'll go into the house," she said. "I have a bad headache!"

I pushed the film into her hands. "Let's go, this was your idea, remember?"

We walked across to Juanita's home, but found no one outside. Fran looked around as we stood there holding the projector and the film. "You were right," she said. "This really is going to be a surprise party."

"Be positive," I answered. "All we need is a table to put the projector on."

"And how about electricity?" Fran asked. "Do you plan to stick it in your ear?"

Just then Juanita's younger sister appeared. Fran tried to explain what we were up to, but the girl didn't understand. She ran to get her parents to see if they could help us. Mama was behind the house, and Papa was drinking rum with his friends.

Fran gave me an uneasy look, "Papa may not like this surprise."

"I hope Mama shows up before Papa," I said, with equal uneasiness.

Fortunately, Juanita and her mother came to our rescue first. Not only did they like the idea of a movie, they found some boxes for the projector to set on and a short extension cord that was long enough to reach into the house. When Papa arrived, everything was ready to go — including him, since he had enough rum by now that anything would have been just fine with him. By this time it was also dark, and Juanita's entire family had gathered, too, as well as a few curious neighbors.

"Ladies and gentlemen," I announced, flipping the switch, "enjoy the movies." Papa gave a long and hearty laugh.

As the movie progressed, more curious neighbors gathered in the dark, some standing, some sitting on the ground. A late-night publico driver stopped in the middle of the road to watch. The only thing missing was the popcorn, but Mama and the girls came up with a tin of hot coffee for everyone, using the same familiar cups we'd seen at the bancos. This ended the evening on a pleasant note.

Later that night, as we prepared for bed, Fran said, "I guess you were right, Lew. We didn't need a plan. All we need is a place to show the movie. The people will automatically show up." She paused, then added, "Maybe we could show movies once a week in Villa Mella. Do you think Padre Miguel would mind if we painted a movie screen on his church wall?"

"Not as long as you don't show films during his church service," I said, "The movie might draw a better crowd."

Fran was right, of course, that it was our job to reach out to the Dominicans in whatever way worked. Now that we had learned much about their ways, it was our turn to make the effort to find our own way to make a difference.

137

Chapter 15
Jingle Bells

It was December 24th, and the first time ever that we would not be with our family during the holidays. While part of us was fascinated to see that the spirit of Christmas was just as strong here under the palm trees and sunshine, as it was back home under evergreens and snow, part of us was the most homesick we'd been since arriving here.

We'd done our best, of course, to get our Dominican home into the holiday mood. One wall was almost completely covered with Christmas cards from friends back home. We'd also splurged and bought ourselves a few early Christmas presents, like a new refrigerator. Never mind that the latch was broken, we had to keep it shut with a large elastic band from our suitcases — it worked! I'd also found a table and four wooden chairs for $20 which made a nice compliment to the ones Fernando built for us when we first moved in. And we now even had a real bed, having traded in our cots for a mattress and a sheet of plywood, supported by stacks of books, and decorated with a canopy of mosquito netting.

We knew, of course, that even though we thought our new furnishings were a little sorry, they were luxurious, compared to what most of our neighbors had. If we were to live like them, we could not afford too many more "home improvements."

Our neighbors, however, were not to be totally outdone by us for the holiday. Many of them had painted the outside of their homes bright colors as was the Dominican custom. Juanita told us that this was possible at Christmas because all government employees, school teachers and salaried personnel received double wages in December. The 50 percent who were unemployed, however, received double their usual salary too — but twice nothing was still nothing!

I remember looking around our home that Christmas Eve, watching Fran hang up the last of the cards. It was hard not to feel lonely despite our best efforts.

It began to rain, and we joked that if the temperature dropped 50 degrees, we could have a white Christmas. It didn't seem to bother the children, who were running around outside in the rain singing, "Jingle Bells." For some reason, it was a popular Dominican Christmas song, though I doubted if any of them had ever been "dashing through the snow."

I walked to the porch to get a glimpse of the kids, and caught sight instead, of a man walking in the direction of our yard. He came up to our door and said that he had walked all the way here from the police station in Villa Mella to tell us we had a Christmas package at the post office in Santo Domingo. He then handed me a scrap of paper that looked like a receipt, though the scratches and scribbles on it were all Greek to me.

Fran came running up, her eyes lit with excitement. "Let's go!" she said.

We both immediately began to scurry around to secure the house, forgetting all about the poor man who had brought the good news to us. We ran to the road to flag down a publico, but they were busy today. The first one passed us by — it was so overloaded, the back bumper was banging the road on every pothole. It was still raining, so we stood on a neighbor's porch, trying to stay as dry as possible. Luckily another publico with some empty seats soon came along. We boarded, and it had just picked up speed when Fran pointed out the window.

"Look," she said, "There is the man who delivered our notice." The fellow was presumably on his way back to Villa Mella, looking wetter than ever.

I reached over and shook the driver by his shoulder. "Stop, stop!" I yelled, "Pick up that man walking in the rain!"

The other passengers didn't like the idea. "No, no," they said. "He is all wet."

But we were insistent. "The man is my friend, I will pay his fare," I said. That was the magic word — publico drivers were always ready to stop for an extra fare, especially on the day before Christmas when passengers had to pay double.

The man came running up, with his clothes dripping wet, and a big smile. He crawled in beside me. Now I was also wet, but somehow it was a good feeling.

The capital was also crowded and busy today. Water splashed from puddles everywhere. At our first stop, there was not a shelter and we had to walk three blocks to where we could get another publico to take us to our destination.

I took Fran's hand, and like true Americans, we began walking very fast. But suddenly, Fran stopped us.

"Wait, Lew. What's the hurry? We're already wet!"

"You're right. Let's take our time and enjoy the cool, refreshing rain."

We walked slowly, hand in hand, in the rain. Quite naturally, we began to sing "Jingle Bells." After a couple of verses, Fran changed the tune to "I'm Dreaming of a White Christmas." It was not our best rendition ever, but it was one of the best combinations of singing and laughter.

I reflected in passing that this was not exactly typical American behavior. Here we were, December 24th, soaking wet, and no family. We should be very irritable and upset — instead, we were singing and laughing.

Fran stopped singing and joked, "Do you think our brain is starting to leak?"

Still laughing, I asked, "Do you think we will ever be the same again?"

"Would that be so bad?" she asked in return.

Neither of us had any answers, so we continued finally arriving at El Conde Street, where we could catch the publico to the post office. Several other people were already waiting here, and none too happily, for the rain was still coming down hard. We glanced at each other and I started to hum, "Jingle Bells" very softly. The lady next to me smiled and joined in. Encouraged, I hummed louder. A gentlemen picked up the melody and our song began to grow louder and louder, until everyone was laughing and singing along.

Christmas Eve had to be the busiest day of the year in the post office. Everywhere, people were crowded around the postal windows and it looked like a matter of push and shove until you reached the postal worker. Fran waited while I finally made it to the front of one line, and waving my wet piece of paper around until the worker finally took it. He glanced at it and immediately handed it back saying, "Wrong place."

Hanging on to the paper I returned to Fran a little discouraged telling her, "Wrong place."

"What do you mean, 'wrong place'?"

"That's all he said."

"You mean this is the wrong building?"

I shrugged my shoulders, "He only said, wrong place."

A little disgusted, Fran grabbed the paper to join the pushy crowd at a different window. I waited until she returned with the same answer, "Wrong place."

I laughed and said, "Yes, I knew that. We must go to the far end of the building."

Giving the paper back to me she asked, "And how did you get so smart?"

Smiling I told her, "I asked a lady with a package."

Angrily, she put hands on her hips, "Then why did you let me shuffle through that line?"

I answered, "I just wanted you to experience the aspect of Dominican culture."

After that comment I wasn't sure Fran would follow me to the correct place, but she did, because we were both anxious to get our package.

I handed the receipt to a worker who led us to a large, disorganized warehouse with a great many packages in it. There were not one, but two packages for us. Both had been opened and everything unwrapped and examined closely.

One package was from our children. It had been crudely rewrapped, but it had passed inspection so that we could take it home and that was all that mattered.

The other package, however, proved to be a problem. It was a shoebox, full of rosaries from our neighbor, Ida Thiel.

141

The customs agent did not hand this one to us. Instead, he took it and authoritatively said, "There is a tax on this box."

"How much?" I asked.

The customs agent thought for a minute, and then said, not quite so authoritatively, "Maybe about — $50.'

"No way!" I said. I was beginning to get the hang of this aspect of Dominican business.

"Okay, maybe $40 would be about right."

I was still very unhappy with the tax and tried to explain. "I am a Peace Corps volunteer, and I will give these rosaries to your people. They are free to me. I pay no tax."

The agent was not convinced, "Maybe you give them free, maybe you sell them. They are worth lots of money."

I pulled one out of the box, "Look," I said, "This one is not even new. It is used."

"Yes, but that does not matter. It is still nice and worth lots of money." I sighed and muttered something about the "Christmas spirit." The man seemed to respond to that, "Well, maybe $35 tax is enough."

I decided it was time to stop arguing and start bartering. I took the rosary, and held it up. "You're right. This one is nice. it could be worth $35. I give it to you to pay for the entire amount of the tax."

The agent smiled, "Merry Christmas," he said, stuffing the rosary into his pocket.

Shaking our heads, we gathered up our packages and headed for Villa Mella ready to call it a day. All we wanted to do was go home, dry off and open our gifts, but when we arrived, Julio, Juanita's brother, was waiting for us on our porch.

"You are invited to come over for Christmas dinner with my family," he said. We were to come "pronto" and bring a bottle of rum "for Papa."

By now, we were getting used to these sort of impromptu invitations, so we accepted the offer. The only thing we had to figure out was when we should go to Julio's home. "Pronto," means now. "Muy pronto" means at once, and "poco pronto" means now, but don't hurry. Julio had only said pronto, so we guessed that meant we should leave soon.

When we looked out our door, we could see the whole family sitting on their porch, waiting for us. We waved, indicating we'd be over in "un momento."

Fran packed up a few of the doughnuts she had made for us for our Christmas dinner, and then we walked across the yard to the tienda to buy Julio's Papa a bottle of rum — the tienda sometimes ran out of eggs, rice or bread, but it always had rum.

When we arrived bearing gifts, the rain had stopped, making it a beautiful evening. Mama had fixed a special dinner for Christmas — chicken, a vegetable salad, another salad made from green bananas stuffed with beef, hard bread rolls and a tall glass of water for each of us with a chunk of ice in it. Although this was a special meal, the eating custom was the same. Mama served us first at the table, and the rest of the family took their plates and ate standing up, in the same room or out on the porch. After dinner, they served us the usual strong black Dominican coffee with sugar — lots of it.

Papa could hardly wait for the coffee to be finished so he could proudly serve us a glass of wine.

"This is especially for Christmas and especially for you," he said. No sooner did we drink the wine, when he opened up the rum we'd brought. "This is a special bottle of rum, especially for me" he said, and proceeded to pour himself the first glass.

The children also had a hard time waiting for dinner to be over — but for other reasons. Their family Christmas gift was a new television set and Mama had made them wait until after dinner to try it out.

At first, she was able to force them to keep the volume low, but then Papa had a couple of glasses of rum, and decided it was time for his favorite pasttime, listening to the radio, which was in the same room as the TV.

A little game soon started. First Papa turned his radio louder than the television. Then Julio slyly leaned over and turned the volume of the television a little louder. Papa did not notice him but gave a mean look and turned up his radio a little louder. Julio again reached slowly for the volume controls.

Fran and I watched as the girls slipped out of the room, and then we both jumped to our feet. I loudly said, for everyone to hear, "It's time for us to leave, thanks so much for a lovely evening and Felice Navidad (Merry Christmas)!"

When we left for home, Julio's eyes were glued to the television, Papa's ears were glued to the radio, and the girls were nowhere in sight. Mama was nodding goodbye with a concerned smile.

We could still hear the radio as we reached our house, and climbing up on our porch, we laughed about the "battle of the bands!"

Soon Papa's radio snapped off, and we kicked off our shoes and relaxed, enjoying more than ever, the peace and quiet of the evening.

At last I spoke softly, returning again to my thoughts about when we were walking in the rain in the capital.

I related to Fran how surprised I was that we were both in such good spirits, given the rain in the capital, the run around at the post office, and Papa and Julio's battle.

"Here we are," I said, "sitting alone in the dark, far from home and family. If this was our first week in-country, we wouldn't be nearly so happy about all this."

Fran laughed knowingly. "You're right. We'd either be calling it quits or crying on each other's shoulders right now. Instead, we sang in the rain and saw humor in everything." She paused, then added, "And you know what? Right now, there is no where else I'd rather be than relaxing right here with you."

"Why are so many things so different?" I wondered. "Have our experiences here changed us to the point that we are two completely different people, never to be the same again?"

"Perhaps," said Fran. "Or perhaps this is just the real miracle of Christmas — what happens when you try to do something for someone else."

At that moment, we both knew that Fran's last statement was true — both for what we were trying to do for the

Dominicans, and for what they'd done for us in the simple sharing of their homes and lives.

I reached over and took Fran's hand, "Merry Christmas, Fran, and to all our friends near and far!" After a short pause, and with a smile, I added, "and a special Merry Christmas wish for Julio, he might need it."

We rose early Christmas Day, in time to see a beautiful sunrise. We were excited with much to do, for we had invited two volunteers, Jerry Winges and Charlene Hsu, to spend the day with us.

Jerry and Charlene had met in the Peace Corps and fallen in love, and after meeting them a few times we had all become very close friends. Like many of the other younger volunteers, they always referred to us as "Mom and Dad!"

Fran began cooking dinner early, while I went outside to find a few things to decorate the house. I felt like a native scavenging the countryside, coming back laden with palm branches, wild flowers, large leaves from the breadfruit tree, some oranges and five large coconuts from the tree by our house. I then ran to the tienda and found 12 nice bananas and placed everything on our new table against the wall, with all our Christmas cards on it. It made a massive Christmas arrangement.

I proudly called to Fran, "Come, look at your newest decorations for Christmas!"

"That's beautiful!" Fran exclaimed coming out long enough to drag me back into the kitchen to help with dinner. She was fixing ham, peas, potatoes, rolls, butter, coffee and fresh-sliced pineapple. As always, I got the job of peeling the pineapple.

We finished early and sat down to wait and enjoy our decorations, but the sitting and waiting was far from easy. Fran kept looking at the clock. "About now, all our family should be together in our home." We wondered what they would be thinking and doing.

Finally, I could take it no longer. "Let's call home," I said.

"Now?" Fran asked. "But company is coming."

Lew and Fran enjoy the Christmas decorations along with their dog, Lisa.

"We can write a note," I said. We could use the phone at the police station in Villa Mella. With any luck, we'd be back in only an hour or two, and we knew Jerry and Charlene would understand. But before we could set our new plan to work, we heard two loud voices yelling in English, "Merry Christmas — Merry Christmas!" and we knew that for today, Jerry and Charlene would be our family.

We ran out to greet the two young volunteers, who had just arrived by publico and were running toward the house. We joined them in the middle of the yard, and there were hugs and kisses all around, while our dog, Lisa, tagged along, wagging her tail in approval. Arms around each other's waists, we all walked slowly toward the house.

Once inside, Charlene took one look around the room and was clearly moved by all we'd done to bring Christmas to the D.R.

"Merry Christmas," she said again, in a very soft, sincere voice.

146

Fran smiled and started to say the same, but she never finished, for as soon as she saw tears in Charlene's eyes, her voice caught on a lump in her throat. Misty-eyed, we all stood smiling bravely, but soon there were a few tears trickling down all our faces. Like us, Jerry and Charlene were experiencing their first time away from home and friends on Christmas Day, too, and in this case, it made no difference if we were young or old — we all missed home.

Finally, Fran wiped her cheek and laughed, "Come now, Christmas is a time to be happy."

After dinner, we exchanged simple gifts and Fran opened the box from our family that we had picked up in the capital. It contained a blue cotton dress made by our daughter, Gloria.

"Let me try this on," she said. "It's the first new dress I've had since entering the Peace Corps!"

Meanwhile Jerry was busy helping me open a box of canned foods. "Look, you even got a can of chicken noodle soup!" he exclaimed.

We both started laughing, "I think you will need to stay a couple of extra days to help us eat everything!" I said.

Fran, who had disappeared into the bedroom, now emerged with her new dress on, modeling it for us. We all nodded approvingly, and Charlene pointed out the nice large pockets on it. But Fran was more impressed with the fit. "I've lost some weight — see how loose it is!"

"One of the fringe benefits of the Peace Corps," said Charlene.

We were interrupted by a small boy walking into the house, holding a written note in his outstretched hand. I read it aloud to Fran and our guests.

"Hi, neighbors, please come to our home for Christmas refreshments. We live in the stone house with the stone fence in front. Merry Christmas!" The house was only a short walk away.

The walk and refreshments sounded good to all of us, so I wrote on the note, "Thank you, we will be there, pronto," and handed it to the boy, who smiled and ran off.

147

We had no idea whose home we were invited to, but it turned out to be a quite prosperous family of three brothers who all worked in the capital. We all had an interesting time mingling with them.

Jerry spoke with one brother who was very active in one of the smaller developing political parties and who hoped one day to be President of the D.R. I introduced myself to a gentlemen who was formally the Dominican Ambassador to the Netherlands. I surprised him by using a Dutch greeting I had learned from friends in the IFYE (International Foreign Youth Exchange Program), and we were soon reminiscing about Holland and its people. Charlene met a former vice president of the Dominican Republic, who was fascinated by her Chinese background, though not sympathetic to her feelings toward the communist government that forced her family to flee to America. Fran, in turn, spent her time talking with a Canadian nurse, who was a distribution director for CARE. Later Fran would become much more involved with the program, and this proved to be an important contact.

After some time had passed, I worked my way over toward one of the host brothers. Later in our service, he would pay me one of my greatest Peace Corps compliments. Right now, however, I simply wanted to thank him for the visit and his hospitality.

Over our protests, he called for the same boy who had delivered our invitation, and he escorted us home by flashlight.

We were very tired by the time we returned, but Lisa, our dog, was not yet ready to call it a night. She came charging out of the door as soon as I unlocked it, so I roughhoused with her a little while Fran and our young friends relaxed. Then, we all gathered out on the porch, sitting close, the moon shining softly through the palm trees. "Peace on Earth, good will toward men" seemed very real to us all, and we started to comment on how appropriate it was to end Christmas Day with a typical, unexpected surprise invitation for a Dominican party.

"Do you suppose it was the spirit of Christmas that prompted them to ask us to join them?" Charlene asked.

"After all, we are strangers, and they had to know our political and social views might not agree with theirs."

"Not so different," said Fran, thoughtfully, "The Canadian social worker and I felt much the same about the schools and the children here."

"The former ambassador to the Netherlands and I had a mutual appreciation for the Dutch people," I added.

"And my views weren't so very different from the older brother's. We had a great discussion on politics," Jerry said, "And I certainly agree with the admiration he expressed for you two, living here among them."

"That's true," Charlene chimed in, nodding. "But I can't help feeling that it took the magic of Christmas for them to invite us into their home to spend an evening of love and friendship with us."

Touched by her words, I reached out and soon all four of us joined hands.

"May every Christmas be as meaningful and as merry as this one," I said. And even Lisa, sensing something important was going on, joined in, she sat up and placing her paw in my lap, gave a soft bark.

This was too much for Fran! She stood up, in a voice holding back tears, and said, "I promised I wouldn't cry, and so far I've kept my promise. But if I don't go into this house right now —"

I finished the statement for her, "Good night friends and Merry Christmas!"

The next day brought more Christmas festivities, when we attended an evening party for all Peace Corps volunteers, held at the home of Mark Levine, assistant PC director. A big crowd of volunteers showed up, all anxious to visit the capital and see friends old and new. For us, there were meetings with many of those we met in our first days of service.

I ran into Jerry, our Christmas Day guest, and the two of us soon found the buffet table. Shortly afterward all the lights went out, a frequent event in the capital. The party continued undampened, by candlelight, which added a magical touch to the evening. Many volunteers sat on the floor in a circle with a candle in the center, chatting as the light flickered on their faces.

Others wandered outside under the palm trees, in the moonlight. Then the Peace Corps dentist, Rosa, began to play a Spanish guitar, and soon we were all singing Christmas carols both in English and Spanish, in addition to the PC favorite, "Let there be Peace on Earth and Let it Begin with Me."

Finally around midnight, as we began to disperse, one volunteer yelled above the crowd for all of us, "Thank you, Mark Levine, and thank you city of Santo Domingo. What a wonderful idea it was to turn off all the electricity in the whole city, it gave our party a great atmosphere!"

Arm in arm, Fran and I walked down the street, the sound of music and laughter trailing on behind us. We reflected again, on how lucky we were to be here in the Peace Corps with these fine young people. They had taught us still another valuable lesson — how to take any situation and turn it into something beautiful.

Chapter 16
Gifts Of The Heart

Like everyone else, the Dominicans had a different way of celebrating the New Year. It started when Fran noticed the ladies lining up at our "well" for more water than usual. Curious, she went to ask them what was going on. Was there to be a party? No doubt the Dominicans, big festival lovers, had a gala New Year's Eve planned.

But Fran's curiosity was rewarded with disappointment. It seems the custom here is to be clean for the New Year, she told me.

"What is to be clean," I asked, "The people or their homes?"

"Both," she answered. Her voice dragging. "Everything."

I started to laugh, "I think you are disappointed because there is not going to be a big fiesta this evening."

She gave a little smile, "Well — this is New Year's Eve." The smile soon turned into an idea, and before I knew it, she was handing me a dust cloth, broom and mop.

"We're here to live like Dominicans, aren't we? Let's get busy."

It turned out to be a good idea, as together we cleaned every little corner in the house. I'm sure it was never that clean when the house was new, and I knew it would never be that clean again.

Our efforts had a drawback, however. By evening we were so tired that we were ready to go to bed and forget all about fiestas, New Year's Eve or not. It was the first time ever that I could remember that we didn't stay up to see the New Year in, but that seemed normal here. If everything were the same here this night as it were back home, it wouldn't have been a Peace Corps experience. Leave it up to the Dominicans, I thought, to be productive on the one day most Americans reserve for fun!

151

Our neighbors didn't totally forget about the New Year, as it turned out. At midnight, one of them, bless his heart, came and stood outside our bedroom window, and at the stroke of midnight, blasted a shotgun into the air. It was followed a few seconds later by another blast near the road. We both jumped in bed, Fran screamed, and Lisa came running in, with a half-growl, half-bark, ready to protect us.

After we calmed down, we could hear our neighbors yelling back and forth to each other, "Buenos Ano Nuevo! Buenos Ano Nuevo!" And we laughed at how silly we had been.

"Might as well return their New Year's wish," I said climbing out of bed and heading for the door. Fran stayed in bed, shaking her head.

I stepped outside and yelled my wishes at the top of my voice in return. A sudden silence fell over the whole neighborhood. I didn't know if this was what they were waiting for, or if I scared them as badly as they scared me, so I crawled back in bed next to Fran.

"Happy New Year, honey," I said.

Early the next morning, when we awoke, there seemed to be a different atmosphere among the people. It was a new day and a new year, and a feeling of hope could be felt among all we met.

Everyone had on their best clothes as they went from home to home to express their New Year's wishes.

The best part of it was being included in their visits. It was a great feeling to experience the warmth of our neighbors as they stopped at our front porch with open arms, broad smiles, and joyous rings in their voices to give us a New Year's greeting.

I asked several of them if they heard me at midnight when I flung open the door to wish them "Buenos Ano Nuevo." Most answered by nodding their heads, laughing, and saying a long, loud "Si-i-i-i!"

Soon Fran and I joined in the tradition and began visiting our neighbors too. They were proud to have us come into their homes, because, like ours, there was not a spot of dust to be found in any corner.

Since New Year's was a holiday here, just like in the states, we had the rest of the day free. After the visiting was complete, we drove into the capitol for a special day of our own. Once there, we picked up another volunteer, Jeff Davidson, with whom I shared a common desire — to play a little golf. Now, here was something we couldn't do in Ohio on New Year's Day!

Jeff was very excited, but a little apprehensive, as we headed for the capitol's only golf course. It was a private club, not normally open to us.

"What if they don't allow us to play?" he asked.

Jeff didn't know, of course, that I had something up my sleeve to insure we'd get in. "Don't worry," I said, "volunteers can always find a way."

We arrived to find a gate blocking our way into the entrance. A guard came strolling out, gave our beat up vehicle the once over, and asked, "What do you want?"

"We'd like to play a little golf," I said.

"Sorry, this is for members only."

Jeff looked at me as if to say, "I told you so," but then I pulled out my ace-in-the-hole. A while back I had helped a certain Señor Lopez, select some of his top dairy cows and heifers for a special breeding program. Señor Lopez had been very grateful for my help, but since I wouldn't accept payment for my services, he had given me a special note, which I now pulled out and handed to the guard.

"My friend, Señor Lopez, said it would be okay for us to golf."

The guard read the paper, and wished us a good day, and opened the gate.

As we drove through, Jeff naturally wanted to know what was on the paper. "Did I tell you about Señor Lopez," I said, "my friend who owns golf clubs as well as cows?"

The piece of paper got us everything we wanted. They did not have golf carts to ride, however, there were young men waiting in line to caddy, and it was a rule that you had to use, as this supplied more jobs for the people. It turned out to be

153

a very good rule for us, for the caddies made sure they found all of our balls, even though we hit them all over the course.

After the game, we entered the club house and were handed towels for hot showers. It felt great, giving our bodies the same wonderful feeling of being cleaned and refreshed to start the New Year. Then we joined Fran, who had been relaxing in the cool shade of a large Frambosa tree while we golfed. We all paused to enjoy one last look at the golf course, whose gorgeous green fairways rolled gently down to the blue Caribbean Sea in one direction and to the volcanic hills in the other. How very different this was than the view from our home in Villa Mella. This was the good life all right, but how many of the people could enjoy it?

When we returned home, the neighborhood children completed our day with their own special celebration. Still in a joyous holiday mood, they came in groups to see us, entertaining us until we were laughing and crying with joy ourselves. When they left, we were no longer disappointed that there had been no grand fiestas to attend. We couldn't have purchased a ticket to any other place in the world and experienced a more enjoyable way to start the New Year, or have felt more renewed and ready to face the opportunities that lay ahead.

There still remained one more special day for the holiday season. This was "Three Kings Day." In the Dominican Republic, this is the day children receive their gifts in remembrance of the gifts of the Magi to the Christ Child. So naturally, Dominican children were more excited on January 6th than on December 25th.

But if the children were excited, Fran and I were not, for the holiday created difficulties for us. We realized this right after New Years, when most of the small ones, unknowingly to their parents, began to sneak over to our home and ask us, "Tiene una regalo por la Navidad?" (Do you have a gift for me for Christmas?") They asked so sincerely that it broke our hearts to say no to them, but we really had no choice — if we gave a gift to one, we'd have to give a gift to all, and that was impossible. We hadn't even met all the children who lived

154

around us, and there were others who lived far back in the jungle whom we hadn't even seen yet.

Our job as Peace Corps volunteers, was to show the people better ways to live, not to give them diversions. But the small children did not understand this. This troubled Fran, especially since they almost always came to her with their requests, knowing she had a soft spot in her heart for them.

Fortunately, all the children seemed to receive something from their families on gift-giving day. We remarked how clever their parents had been in making do with whatever things were available to them, as one by one, the children came to our home to proudly show us their gifts. There were sling-shots made from tree branches and inner tube strips, carved wooden whistles, push toys made with sticks and can lids, and some even had plastic dolls (which the girls usually refused to take from the box). In all, they seemed happy with what they had, and so we thought the crisis passed. But that evening, after the final child had left, we realized it still wasn't settled. As we sat looking at our wall of Christmas cards, which now had to come down, we were both a little saddened by the idea that the season had passed without us being able to give any gifts to the children of our neighbors, who had accepted us as family.

"I wish there were some way we could pass on the love and friendship of our friends back home to the people here," I said, gesturing at the cards. That gave Fran the idea and an answer to our problem on gift-giving.

"Let's give the cards to our neighbors!" she said. "It would be different than giving gifts, and I know they would like them." I nodded for I had heard several of the girls comment on them when they came to visit.

We decided to try it. The next morning, Fran went to our closest neighbors, and invited them to come to our house, one at a time, where each could choose one card from our wall. She explained that each card represented a wish for joy and happiness from someone we knew and loved and that we wanted to pass this wish to them.

The giving away of our cards worked out very well. Some ladies studied them carefully before choosing one, while others just grabbed the one closest to them, but all were pleased with their selection. By the time word had spread that Fran was giving the cards away, neighbors began to line up outside the door. Fran would let only one woman in at a time, so that each could make a personal selection and fortunately we had enough cards for them all!

By evening our walls were bare again, and despite the joy we had in giving them to others, we felt a little lonely and depressed. But like rainstorms in the D.R., sad times didn't last long — something always seemed to come along to brighten things up. This time it was Kiki, and her sister Francesca and Florinda and her sister Margo. They chose tonight to come running to our door, offering to sing for us again.

"You sit down," Kiki said, "we sing, we dance, we tell jokes. We make you happy."

The girls began their show, and the music — and giggling — soon attracted a crowd. Within a short ime, a crowd of youths, between the ages of 10 to 16 were assembled, all trying to get into the act, each trying to outdo the other. We laughed and clapped after each song and antic, which of course encouraged them to try even harder.

Finally, Kiki asserted herself as their leader. "Quitite, quitite (quiet, quiet). Everyone sit down and listen. I now sing very sad song for you."

She concentrated so hard on the words of her song, that she seemed to be in a trance. Tears came rolling down her cheeks as she sang. Then all of a sudden, she dried her tears with the loose end of her dress. Clapping her hands, she again lead everyone in happy singing and dancing.

Kiki's singing climaxed the holiday season, by vividly demonstrating to us the sadness and joy that are mingled together, and so much a part of the culture of this struggling country.

Chapter 17
Long Underwear

When the holiday season came to an end, it was back to business as usual at the farm. In other words, nothing changed much — until we got word that another load of heifers was arriving.

The last time a plane load of cattle was unloaded I was concerned because of all the problems we had encountered. This time I was concerned because things were moving along too smoothly. The plane landed right on time, the health papers for the cattle were in order, and there was no hassle about a ramp fee, even though it was the same attendant who had helped us last time and he hadn't yet received the $25 we were to pay him, "manana."

Even when the trucks were all loaded, and a guard positioned on the back of each of them, I still couldn't believe it, so I turned to Louie and asked, "Que paso — no problems?"

Louie shrugged his shoulders, "No say, maybe it's still the holidays?"

The same pilot who delivered the last load of cattle and I talked for a bit, until he climbed back in the plane. Then he yelled, "Take good care of the two nice gentlemen from New York."

Without thinking, I replied, "Will do." Then I turned to Louie and said, "What two gentlemen from New York?"

Louie shrugged his shoulders, but this time said, "No say, maybe we DO have a problem!" The pilot was now in his seat, but I ran toward the plane anyway, waving my arms frantically, "What two men?" I yelled.

The pilot stuck his head out of the window, "The two men that rode over with me," he said. "They plan to stay here for a couple of days. Someone from the Heifer Project was supposed to meet them here."

"Oh no," I said, expecting the worst, "what did they look like?"

The pilot tried to calm me down. "They should be no problem to find. They had on winter clothes and were carrying suitcases, and had cameras around their necks!"

Louie and I made a thorough check of the airport, but no one was waiting at the customs counter, or anywhere near the customs gate. At last I found a guard who remembered seeing two American men with winter coats on leave about 30 minutes ago in a publico.

I turned to Louie. "Now, we have a problem!"

Louie was more concerned about returning to the farm to care for the cattle than about finding some strangers. "Don't worry, amigo, they are two full-grown men. They will take care of themselves."

I was not so confident. "Two men lost in a foreign country can become like two boys. We had better try to find them." I paused and then asked Louie, "If you were a publico driver, where would you take two lost Americans?"

Louie drove us to the most likely place — the most expensive hotel in Santo Domingo. I immediately spotted two men who matched the pilot's description. Louie had definitely guessed right, and the men looked definitely lost.

I walked up and introduced myself. They were so glad to see me, they invited Fran and me to dinner.

The next morning, I took the two New Yorkers to Boni, a village new to me, but where there were several farms that had received Heifer Project animals. We had to do quite a bit of walking to find them, while the sun relentlessly beat down on us all day. Near the end of the day, one of the New Yorkers pleaded with me to stop.

"Please, I need to rest," he said.

I apologized and said, "I'm sorry, you must be very tired."

Shaking his head, he said, "and also very hot!" He then sat on a rock, and pulled up his pantleg to reveal that he was still wearing long underwear. "I should have left these in New York!"

A few Dominicans nearby got a laugh out of seeing the Yankees sweating in long underwear in their hot sun, but I realized that where these two came from, long underwear would be very appropriate right now. How many times on American streets had I observed foreigners dressed much differently than we were, and Americans who stopped to stare and laugh, too. Americans can also look out of place away from home, especially wearing long underwear in the Caribbean!

Chapter 18
The Little Ambassador

The use of the Embassy Jeep made it possible for us to make many more trips to farms in the surrounding area. When our roads took us to the Capitol, we always stopped at the PC Center to pick up mail and catch up on the latest news from other volunteers. Our best news on this stop was a letter from Gloria.

We were ecstatic when we read the news that she, along with her husband, Dave, and their daughter, Lisa, was planning to visit us.

Fran immediately answered her letter. "You can be assured," Fran wrote, "all of you will be just as safe here among our neighbors as you would be at home among yours. These people have shown much love and concern for us and they will do the same for you. Please continue with your plans to come — it will be an adventure in living you will never forget!"

The anticipation of their coming visit made the time fly by. On the morning of their arrival, I was awakened before dawn by Fran aggressively shaking my body, yelling, "Wake up, Lew!"

Startled, I asked, "What's wrong?"

"Today our family is coming to visit us!"

Of course I knew that, but to tease her a little I rolled over, yawned and said, "That's nice, hope they enjoy it."

Fran threw her hands in the air in disgust. "I don't believe this. Your very own daughter and granddaughter are coming, and you are not the least bit excited." She fell back in bed with a big thud, pulled the sheet over her head, mumbling, "I am going to be very calm about this. I hope someone wakes me up when they arrive!"

Since I really was (nearly) as excited as Fran, I reached over, shaking her vigorously, and said, "Hurry, we better get started.

160

We could have a flat tire, hit a traffic jam, run into a road block or who knows what." Fran never stirred, as I continued, "You know how important it is for us to be there ahead of time." She then leaped out of bed, "That's what I've been trying to tell you!"

The plane arrived, right on schedule. We pushed our way to the gate nearest the customs counter, even though Gloria and her family wouldn't be able to join us until they cleared customs. We wanted them to see us as soon as possible — we knew how much it meant to see a familiar face in a strange country! Fran waved frantically at Gloria, until she spotted us and gave us a big smile.

After going through customs, they came running out of the gate toward us, our granddaughter, Lisa, leading the way. To our surprise, she greeted us yelling, "Buenos Dias! Buenos Dias!"

Gloria and David followed, a little more slowly, for they were toting two heavy suitcases filled with items we'd requested from the U.S. After some huffing and puffing, we got the bags and ourselves loaded into our Jeep. At first we chatted continuously as we drove along, with everyone wanting to talk first, and a million questions to be answered and asked. Then there was silence, as our three visitors became engrossed with the new and different sights of the capital and countryside.

I watched in the mirror as they responded to life in the D.R. — the boys, who, as usual, ran up to our car at every light, in an effort to make a few cents from washing our windows, the burst of horn tooting all around us for a small fender-bender accident, and finally the ever-present soldiers, who had so surprised Fran and me on our first trip. With each encounter, I could see more and more questions in their eyes, both about the country and about us for choosing to live here.

After we crossed the river bridge that led to Villa Mella, and curved around the first bend, we drove past the military base. Armed soldiers were again in the road, stopping all cars. When they stuck their heads inside the Jeep, I observed Lisa

161

huddling close to her mother, but Gloria looked just as afraid. The soldiers just smiled at us, as they now knew us, and waved us on.

"Are you **sure** it's safe for us here?" asked Gloria one more time.

"Oh, yes, honey," said Fran, "no problem!" But Gloria looked doubtful.

When we arrived home in Villa Mella, a group of small children were waiting in the yard. Fran had told the neighbors in advance, that her six-year-old granddaughter was coming for a visit and the children were anxious to meet her. As we pulled up, some of the children smiled, some laughed and others just looked. Now it was Lisa who looked doubtful, until the car stopped, and she jumped out yelling "Buenos Dias!" with the confidence that only a six-year-old has. This broke the ice and she soon was running around in our yard with the native children laughing and following after. There was no question about her adjusting to our new home and country.

Once Lisa was taken care of, Fran took Gloria for a walk to visit the neighbors. Gloria's concern faded as she saw how honored the neighbors were to have Fran introduce her to them. She was warmly greeted at every house with "Entre, mi casa es su casa." After Fran translated, Gloria's concern disappeared entirely. Later, she told us that she felt like she received a friendlier welcome on her first day here than she did at home among lifetime friends! Soon Gloria was learning how to wash clothes, Dominican style, and stirring rice over an open fire, smiling despite the tears that came to her eyes from the smoke. As for Lisa, that was, **no problem**. There were always plenty of children around for her to visit with and they often ran ahead of Fran and Gloria, delighted to show their world to a new friend.

Meanwhile, I had a nice day on the farm with David, that ended in an even nicer surprise. Toward the end of the morning, the farm director pulled me aside and asked me if I would mind making a special trip tomorrow to visit a couple of farms near Puerta Plata, which just happened to be near a beautiful

Gloria tried her hand at Dominican cooking.

Lisa found it easy to find new friends.

area with nice sandy beaches. Originally the trip was scheduled for next week, but when the director learned of our family's visit, he was thoughtful enough to move it up so that we could show them a little more of the island.

To get to Puerta Plata from Santo Domingo, it was necessary to cross the large mountain range that extends across the center of the island. This was not all bad, as it gave us a chance to show off the beautiful palm covered hillsides and enjoy the cooler air of the higher altitude, a nice relief from the heat. Since we had no time schedule to keep, we stopped several times for photos and relaxing or shopping at roadside stands.

In Puerta Plata, we met volunteer Mike Arnow, who had been working hard to increase tourism in this area of the island — a needed source of revenue — and so he was able to direct us to some of the most beautiful beaches we'd seen yet.

We then drove on down to Mao, where we stayed at a new hotel built for tourists. Since few tourists as yet knew about it, we received royal treatment.

That evening we were pleasantly surprised by a visit from Jerry and Charlene, who had tracked us down. They arrived bearing gifts of Dominican fruits for the visitors to try, and as we sat there on the bed trying all the new tastes, Fran and I were moved by this mingling of our real American and adopted Dominican families.

Our royal treatment continued well into the next morning, when we were greeted with deluxe service for breakfast. First, two waiters came to help seat the ladies. They smiled as they dusted the chairs with cloth napkins and turned over the cups and plates for us to use. They gave each of us a menu, then stood by, very erect, waiting for our orders.

Gloria's order, one egg, sunny side up, proved to be a challenge to them. The waiter hesitated, but then returned with coffee and water and bread. After about 15 minutes the cook himself came out of the kitchen carrying a covered dish, which he took straight to Gloria. He took off the lid, and revealed three eggs, each prepared a different way.

"Which way do you like your egg?" he asked.

I translated, and Gloria pointed to it for him. The cook smiled and returned to the kitchen, leaving Gloria puzzled and still hungry. The waiter soon returned with breakfast for everyone, smiled and said proudly to Gloria, "Sunny side up!" We had done one thing to help Mike's tourism program — given the Dominicans a lesson on cooking eggs!

The next morning Jerry met us again to show us a Peace Corps project he was working on, a nice small home from blocks made from the native soil and water and left to dry in the sun. I asked Jerry if he thought someday there would be many homes like this. He only shrugged his shoulders. As a Peace Corps volunteer, I understood. We do our best, but the rest is up to them.

When we returned home, the children were again waiting in the yard, looking for Lisa. We watched as she joined them, marveling at how well they got along, despite the fact that Lisa had only added one more Dominican word to her vocabulary, "Si." If they were able to play peacefully, with so little in common, why couldn't adults, with equally different backgrounds, work and live together too?

Faster than we thought possible, Gloria's visit came to an end and soon it was time for our family to return home. Only a few days had passed, but lives had been changed forever.

As they entered the car, Gloria paused for a last look at the house and surroundings, then remarked, "Mom and Dad, I admire you both for what you are doing."

"Buenos dias" yelled Lisa.

The trip to the airport was pretty routine, as far as Dominican standards went, and our family got off without much delay. We were both pretty quiet on the way home now that the visit was over, but then Fran brightened things up by informing me that there was a surprise waiting for us when we returned home.

"What did you do now, Fran?"

"It's not what I did, it's what our daughter did. Bless her heart, she meant well, but I think she may have left me a problem."

165

The minute we walked in the door, Gloria's surprise/Fran's problem was pretty clear. There, all over the floor, were Gloria's clothes.

"What's this all about?" I asked.

"That's the surprise." Fran said and explained that before Gloria left, she stepped back into the house, opened her suitcase and dumped out all of her clothes, saying, "Here mom, give these to the neighbors. They need them more than I do!"

So this is what Fran was thinking about all the way home. "What did you decide to do with them?" I asked.

"I decided it's no problem. First we go to bed. Mañana we pick up the clothes and then you'll think of something."

I looked at the clothes and shrugged. "Hasta mañana," I said.

The next morning, I still had no idea, but Fran had already made some tentatitve plans for Gloria's parting gifts. Gloria was right — the neighbors **did** need them more than her — but it was important that they not know that they were charity from Gloria. It was important that no family receive more than one item, so the whole plan took all day to figure out.

By the next morning, however, it was worked out. Fran set about distributing them, by tucking one piece of clothing at a time under her arm as she went about making house calls on the neighbors. The ladies would always ask, or say something about Gloria, giving Fran the opportunity to say, "Gloria packed in a hurry and she left this behind," and then pull the piece of clothing out from under her arm. "I'm sure she would be happy to know you could use this." Regardless of what the article was, the neighbors could of course use it, and this way they felt they were doing Gloria a favor instead of accepting her help.

By the end of the week, Fran had distributed all of Gloria's clothes, except for one of the best dresses, which she wanted to make sure went to Alicia, a very shy girl around 12 years of age who was now very, very friendly with us. Alicia always offered to help clean the floors and pick up sticks in the yard, but never asked for any favors in return. She and her mother

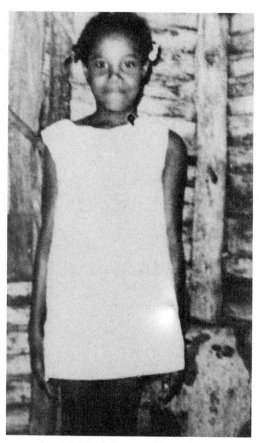

Alicia models her new dress.

were very honored by Fran's visit, as it was one of the few homes in the area Fran had not visited previously.

Alicia and her mother were very happy to help Gloria out by accepting the dress, but would not accept it unless Fran accepted a cookie in return, home baked by Alicia's mother in an earthen oven in her backyard. It was about three feet high, built of mud, with very thick walls and only one small door for an opening on one side. Alicia's mother went on to explain how she would build a fire inside, until the mud walls

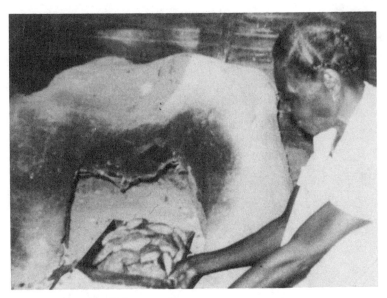

Baking cookies in an earth oven.

were hot, then rake out the coals, put in the cookies, and block the opening shut. The heat from the walls would bake the cookies.

Fran tasted the cookies, smacking her lips. "Um, very good! Do you like to eat mother's cookies, Alicia?"

Alicia's mother quickly moved her finger back and forth in front of her saying, "No! Alicia nor I ever eat any of the cookies. We must save them to sell — they are our only income."

Now, Fran felt a little guilty, taking something so important to Alicia and her family, but she was moved as well, for Gloria's generosity had led to more generosity. While dresses and cookies might not be part of our formal Peace Corps projects, it was a start toward understanding. Then again, perhaps dresses and cookies were one of the many things the Peace Corps was about after all!

Only a few days later, Fran noticed Alicia walking slowly across the front yard, looking at the ground. Fran opened the door, for she sensed there was a problem.

Crying, Alicia said, "My mama is sick in bed for two days, and we have nothing to eat." Still sobbing, she said, "Please help her!"

Assuring Alicia with her arms around her Fran said, "You go home and I'll be over soon."

Alicia reached up, hugged and kissed Fran, and then ran home. Fran went into the house, not feeling quite as confident as she had in front of Alicia. She wasn't at all sure what to do.

"I'm not a nurse, I'm not a doctor, I'm just a wife and mother. But since I'm a PC volunteer, they expect me to be an expert on everything," she thought to herself. But Fran knew she was the only person who could help Alicia and her mother — for even had there been a doctor out here, they could never afford one.

Fran did what any good mother and neighbor would do. She warmed up a can of soup Gloria had brought us, grabbed a bottle of aspirin, and headed for the door, hoping that perhaps it was only undernourishment that was causing Alicia's mother's illness.

Alicia was waiting for Fran. The windows were closed, and the only light entering came through the cracks in the walls. Alicia's mother was lying in bed with a damp rag on her forehead. She weakly said, "I have a headache."

Fran held up her head a little. "I have something here that should make you feel better." Alicia's mother took a few spoonfuls of hot soup, which seemed to revive her enough to insist that Fran give the rest to Alicia.

But Alicia said, "I'm not sick, Mama, you need to get well!" So the mother took a little more.

Before Fran left, she gave Alicia's mother two aspirin, and then gave two more to Alicia to give to her mother in the morning. The next day, Fran again went to visit and was happy to see Alicia greet her at the door smiling.

"Mama is feeling much better," she cried. On entering, Fran found Alicia's mother sitting up and smiling. She held out her hand to Fran saying, "God has blessed me with a beautiful neighbor. Thank you!"

And Alicia said, "Tomorrow, maybe we bake cookies!"

That night, Fran met me on my walk home from the farm and shared the good news about Alicia's mother. We again were amazed with how much the people did, even when they were undernourished and overworked. We were able to help Alicia's mother with soup and aspirin, but how many others needed the same or more?

Chapter 19
No-Plan Planning

Although we now had a Jeep, we still found ourselves without transportation many times. Since the vehicle was registered to the Foundacion, they could have it whenever they needed it, leaving Fran and me with only two bicycles for transportation.

The morning of Palm Sunday, we decided to ride our bikes into Villa Mella for church.

"What's taking you so long?" I yelled to Fran, who seemed to be taking longer than usual.

"Quiet out there," she said. "You sound just like an American, hurry-hurry-hurry!"

"You're right — take your time. The boys at the church will probably just keep on ringing the bells until they see you gliding in on your bicycle."

At that Fran came out announcing she was ready to go, but then I remembered that I'd forgotten to lay clean papers on the floor for Lisa, so now it was Fran's turn to wait for me.

After about five minutes, she yelled, "How long does it take to lay papers?"

"I'm coming, Mrs. America," I yelled back.

"What took you so long in the house, Mr. Macho?" she asked when I finally emerged.

"I was talking to Lisa. When she saw the papers, she put her tail between her legs and gave me that sad dog look of hers. She wouldn't allow me to leave until I promised her I would hurry back to play with her this afternoon."

"Now, you're just like a typical Dominican man. You have two ladies to keep you happy."

"Are you jealous?"

"No, I can be like a typical Dominican woman, too. I don't mind sharing you with another lady — as long as she is a dog!"

I laughed and jumped on my bike, challenging Fran to a race to the bend in the road at the top of the hill.

"I'll do it under two conditions," she said. "First, that you give me a kiss for being such an understanding wife." That was easy enough, so I obliged. "And second, give me a head start." With that she took off, leaving me behind.

Getting to the bend at the top of the hill was the toughest part of bike riding into Villa Mella, as once past this point, the rest of the way was pretty gentle. We ended up in a tie, and then leisurely rode the rest of the way in.

Along the way we spotted several ladies on the road, all wearing white dresses and bandanas and carrying freshly cut palm branches. One of them was a friend, Paula, who explained to us that they were headed to church for a special service that day.

When we arrived, other ladies dressed in white had already gathered. This was all new to us, as these ladies never wore these dresses, even though they were cool and neat and there was a clothing shortage. The service even started on time — for a change, the bells didn't ring forever, either. When they stopped, in came the ladies carrying their palms in a procession, led by Paula.

One by one, they strew their branches in front of the altar, and then across the front of the church, all the while singing, "Hosanna to the Son of David."

After church, we again leisurely rode our bikes home, where I playfully romped with Lisa until she became tired. Then, we all gathered on the ground under the mango tree. This country was a paradox in many ways to us. The women we had seen participating in the service today were the very ones who attended bancos and condoned married men having girlfriends. We were slowly starting to understand the D.R. In the midst of hunger, poverty and bitterness, there were still ways to find joy, laughter and love.

Easter Sunday proved to be a very wild day for us. Not only did Louie give us the farm truck, he invited us to his friend's home for Easter dinner. We attended early Mass, but as we headed toward home we noticed several people entering a building with a sign on the wall that said, "Evangelical Church, Welcome." We'd heard music and singing coming from there the last two Sundays, so today we decided to stop and see what was going on.

We were just in time. The full congregation was singing in a lively rhythm accompaied by a guitar, tambourines and maracas. Afterwards, they had Sunday School lessons for adults and children all in the same room.

We had a hard time hearing, even though the homemade wooden benches we sat on were only three rows back from the teacher. But probably no one could hear — not only were the children and adults arguing with each other, but the church building was only about three feet from the next house, where the people were evidently **not** Evangelical, as they were playing their radio full blast. The church was also situated only five feet from the road, which naturally had cars and trucks passing. But the best distraction of all came when a boy about 10 years old entered along with his younger brother, who wasn't wearing any pants.

Church was not over until almost noon, and we hurried out so that we wouldn't be late for our invitation to dinner with Louie and his wife. When we drove up to his home, however, Louie was chopping grass with his machete. He had no shirt on and was dripping with sweat, but greeted us with a big "Hola Amigos," and invited us in. It wasn't until I reminded him of his inviting us to dinner that he seemed to know why we were there.

With a big laugh he said, "Yes, we go now, as soon as I get a shirt on."

"How about your wife?" I asked. "Isn't she going along?"

"Oh no, she stay home today."

"Where are we going?"

"We go first to my friend's home, then we eat at his friend's home." Fran and I looked at each other. Things were starting to get complicated already and we hadn't even left the driveway.

"This better be good," Fran said, "I'm getting hungry."

When we arrived at his friend's house, Louie jumped out and came back with not one but two men, who jumped in back of the truck and we roared out.

For once, we were glad that Louie was driving because we were on roads that we did not know existed. But in a few minutes it became evident that Louie didn't know they existed either, for he soon stopped the truck and yelled to the men in the back for directions. They pointed straight ahead. A short distance down the road he again asked directions, laughed and took off again, spinning the wheels of the truck. Soon, we approached a lady carrying water on her head. Louie stopped and asked her for directions, and she pointed straight back where we had come from.

"Does anyone know where we are going?" Fran asked, as Louie turned the truck around.

"Oh yes," said Louie, "We just don't know how to get there."

By now it was 2 p.m. The road was full of chuckholes and very dusty, and we were tired and hungry. Louie smiled (but we did not) as he approached yet another lady carrying water, especially when she pointed back the other way again, and indicated a turn to the right. Louie was happy, but we just sighed.

This time we drove on for only a short distance when the two men on the back of the truck began yelling, 'Stop, stop!" and pointed to the left. "That is the road!" they said.

Fran and I looked, but as much as we wanted to see a road, all that was visible was a footpath. But Louie yelled, "Hang on!" and turned on to it, pushing the pedal to the floor. It was all we could do just to stay in our seats inside the truck.

"You better slow up a little, or we may lose your friends behind!" I yelled in between the bumps.

Louie smiled. "They have been on roads like this before, and anyway, if they fall off, they know where we are going."

The two men were still with us and surprisingly still smiling when we arrived at a small Dominican farm. The owner, a very friendly, jovial gentleman, invited us to enter his house and look around. There was a bedroom and a dining room with a table and four chairs. A curtain hung between the rooms to allow the air to circulate during the hot evenings.

The kitchen was located about three steps from the back door. It had a thatched roof, four poles for walls and a dirt floor. Pots and pans hung by wires from the poles and there was a stone fireplace in one corner. A small cupboard hung on one wall and displayed three plates and bowls, while a stand made from grapevines tied together held a small pan filled with kitchen utensils.

From the kitchen, Fran and I wandered outside into a beautiful yard, with banana and citrus trees, and a nice garden of pineapples, eggplant, lettuce and a few plants that we had never seen before.

"This is very nice," said Fran. "Too bad we can't get the people in our neighborhood to do this."

"We'd just have to get them to move to a remote location like this," I said, "where there are no children or close neighbors to destroy or steal the vegetables and fruits."

The garden reminded us of how hungry we were, so we were pleased when Louie and the owner joined us in the yard. But we were not pleased with what Louie said next.

"We have a little problem, Amigos. Early this morning a friend of their's came and asked his wife to help with their Easter dinner. They had an illness in their family and the owner felt obligated to help, especially since they will pay his wife for her work."

"So we must go?" I asked.

Louie just shrugged his shoulders and gave his jolly laugh as everyone climbed back into the truck, including the gentleman who lived here. If we kept this up, I thought, we'd need a bigger truck.

As Louie started up the engine, Fran turned to me and whispered, "What time is it now?"

"After 3 o'clock," I said. "Time sure goes fast when you're having fun."

"But not when you're hungry," Fran answered.

This time, Louie seemed to know where we were going, for we didn't stop to ask any man, woman or child for directions. It was no wonder, for Louie took us to the home of Paula, a woman we all knew well and who sometimes cooked for the farm when there were visitors at the guest house.

Paula invited us into her home, which fortunately had enough chairs for all of us to sit on. She offered coffee, which Fran opted for, and one of the men came up with a bottle of rum, which I decided to be conservative with.

"Don't worry, Amigo," one said, "If this starts to run low, I know where there is another one."

While I joked with the men, Fran's attention wandered out the window, where she spotted more entertainment for the day. Outside, two young girls were chasing a couple of ducks. Finally they caught one, and a few minutes later, Fran could see Paula and the two girls frantically plucking the feathers from it. About an hour later, it showed up as part of our Easter dinner, along with some vegetables in a gravy. The men seemed to prefer duck because, by the time the bowl got around to us, it was mostly vegetables. However they were good, in fact by now, most anything would have been good.

It was almost dark by the time Louie finally delivered us to our home, and then took off in the truck to drop off his friends. All we could see were the three men bouncing around in the back as Louie drove wildly away.

Fran stood looking very seriously at me, "How did you manage to work out this most unusual Easter dinner for us?"

"It was easy," I said. "I used Dominican planning!"

Chapter 20
Grandpa's Visit

Several months after our daughter's visit to the D.R., it was our son, Steve's, turn. Steve was in college and wrote to tell us that he, a friend of his, Dick Summit, and my father were coming to visit us.

We were naturally excited about the news, but this time, instead of worrying about Lisa, our granddaughter, we wondered about Grandpa. My father was 80 years old at the time, and while his favorite saying was "I'm not old, I've just stayed young a very long time," he had also never been outside the United States, or even on a plane.

We picked up three cots from the PC center, cleaned our house and arrived early at the airport the following Wednesday to wait for their flight. We started waving to them as soon as they came down the steps from the plane, but their "better" greeting came from the Dominican Tourism Bureau, which today was giving out free rum to all arrivals.

The rum made up a little for the customs agents. We had a hard time explaining to Grandpa why they had to wallow through his suitcase, especially when he could not get it shut again. But by the time we made it through the gate, everyone was smiling again.

Grandpa took a handkerchief from his pocket, "It sure is hot today!" he said.

Fran took the cloth and wiped the sweat from Grandpa's face. "I hope this won't be too much for you," she said. "This is the way it is here all the time."

I drove back through Santo Domingo with the windows open, which helped to cool Grandpa and all of us down. We passed some small boats that had just come in from fishing in the Caribbean Sea. The bottoms of the boats contained several inches of water, with live fish swimming in them.

"Now where in the world could you buy fresher fish?" I said, but Grandpa said nothing.

Steve and Dick had a good laugh when Fran gave them a tour of our Dominican home. Grandpa just followed and again said nothing. His silence was saying more to us than any words, however.

The first night was a little confusing for our dog, too. Lisa was not sure about the three new invaders in her home. Several times during the night, she got up just to make a bed check of the three cot sleepers. Grandpa, who could not sleep, seemed to appreciate her company. Each time he gave her a few pats, and soon became good friends.

The next day, we headed into the capital for supplies and sightseeing and to borrow a bicycle from the PC center. With three visitors, we thought that maybe the extra wheels would come in handy. While walking to the center, Grandpa lagged behind and ended up doing business with some street peddlers who charged him full price for an amber necklace for his girlfriend. Naturally, Grandpa didn't know he should bargain, so he paid the whole amount.

"Here you must bargain," I told him, explaining that they usually ask twice the amount they expect to receive.

"That's crazy," replied Grandpa.

I put my arm around his shoulder. "That's right, but it can be fun. Next time, let me bargain for you to show you how it's done."

On the way back home, we stopped at a large open-air market at the outskirts of the capital, where merchants sold everything from fruits to clothes and jewelry. This particular market was not exactly picturesque. In fact, the government was trying to close it down because it was so filthy it created a bad image for tourism. But it was a good experience for American visitors to see, and what it lacked in atmosphere, it made up for in price — which was good if you lived on a Peace Corps Volunteer's salary.

Grandpa was delighted when we found a beautiful stalk of bananas, completely intact, as it had grown on the tree.

"That is the way they were hung from the ceiling in our grocery store when I was young," he said. "Can we buy these?"

"Good idea," laughed Steve, "we'll have a whole feast of bananas!"

We were now starting to draw the sellers' attentions, as they sensed the Americans were going to buy something. I pointed to the large bunch of bananas and asked in English "How much?"

The merchant, thinking he found a group of American tourists, pushed them toward me with a big smile. "Very nice, very cheap — only $9." I pushed them back. He had overpriced them, even for bargaining.

"Hey Carumba!" I said in Spanish. "Esta muy carro (Goodness, they are very expensive)."

He smiled, held up five fingers and pushed them back toward me. I turned my back and said, "we will look for others."

Before I could move, he grabbed my arm and said, "how much you pay?"

I held up one finger.

The merchant laughed, "The bottom price is $3."

I shook my head, and turned away again. "Come everyone," I said, "we'll look for other bananas."

The merchant again grabbed my arm and pulled me back. This time, he pushed the bananas into my arms. "One dollar."

I turned to Grandpa. "Give the man a dollar," I said.

In disbelief, Steve said, "Dad, I'm ashamed of you. Instead of helping these people, you steal their bananas." I explained to him that was the going price in the market, but he still looked questionable at my tactics.

Dick offered to carry the bananas, but we were now surrounded by Dominican boys who wanted to carry them for us. I chose a boy not much larger than the stalk, who wore tattered clothes, and waved at the other, to "vamos (go)."

Dick turned around to see the poor boy struggling along behind us with the stalk as we walked to our car. "Are you sure we shouldn't be carrying them?" he asked.

"No," I said, "he is happy to do it, and this way he can earn a few pennies."

At our car, several boys were already waiting. One had his hand on the car door ready to open it for us. Others were cleaning the windows, or washing the tires. Those who could not find anything to do flocked around, asking to help.

When we had to shove our way past them to make a path for the boy with the bananas, Steve was even more concerned. "Does this go on all the time?" he asked.

I nodded saying, "It can get a little irritating. We usually tell them to "vamos" but on the other hand, they have no other work to do and want to make money."

"Then I'll give them something," Steve said, and gave the banana carrier 10 cents. It was a good tip, and the boy immediately ran full speed back to the market, either to look for other Americans or buy food for his family. Steve gave the other boys a penny and a banana each and everyone was happy.

We were soon rolling along, eating bananas, and enjoying the countryside, until we hit an exceptionally large chuckhole. The next thing we new, the jeep started to rattle. When we stopped to check it out, we discovered a broken piece hanging from the rear axle. It didn't look safe, so we decided to leave the car along the roadside and walk the rest of the way home.

The boys took it in stride — Dick offered to carry the bananas, if Steve gave him a nickel, since we'd eaten half of them — but Grandpa was tired.

"Is it far to your house?" he asked. It was less than half a mile, but we did have the bike, so I offered it to him. This made Grandpa happy. He still rode a bike at home, and since it was all downhill to our house, it should have been "no problem."

As he went down the road, however, the bike began to pick up speed. A mother sow and her three little pigs decided to complicate things by crossing the road right in Grandpa's path. He tried the brakes with his feet and was shocked when nothing happened. Grandpa had never ridden a bike with hand

Steve eats his first Dominican banana.

brakes, and there was no way to tell him now. We watched as he went flying between pig number one and pig number two. All we could do was yell, "Watch out!" and all he could do was hang on. Other people walking along the road quickly jumped out of the way as Grandpa went buzzing by them. It was fortunate that he didn't meet any cars or hit any chuckholes after that.

When we arrived home, some of the neighbor children were in the yard, laughing hysterically. "He just went past the house on a bicycle, flying like lightning!" they said.

Just beyond our house was the bottom of the hill, where Grandpa had finally slowed to a stop. We ran to look down the road for him, and soon spotted him, slowly walking back. A boy was following him, pushing the bike.

"That was not very funny," he said, when they reached our yard. "I'll never ride a bike again!"

181

"Cheer up," said Fran, "I have a special treat for everyone — fresh bananas!"

"Who-o-o-pie!" said Grandpa.

The next day, we postponed our sightseeing so I could fix the Jeep. Grandpa decided to relax on the porch, and the boys wanted to explore the neighborhood.

While we were making plans, in drove Fernando. He left his pickup truck in the driveway and came bounding into the house with an invitation for us to join his family for dinner that evening. He also invited Dick and Steve to take a look around his farm while I was out.

"You can even ride two of my horses," he told the boys. Steve liked the plans. "Dad told us you were a great landlord," he said.

Fernando looked at the floor, smiled and then put his hand on Steve's shoulder. "Your father and mother are also 'bueno' tenants."

After he left, Steve said, "It's just like you wrote in your letters. Things are not always planned here but they just seem to happen."

Fernando was waiting for Dick and Steve at his barn. He motioned for them to wait, as the guard dogs were barking and lunging on their ropes. No horses could be seen, but the donkey was putting up a fuss.

"I hope we don't have to ride that!" Steve said.

But when Fernando and his laborers came out with the horses, Dick told Steve, "Maybe we would have been better off with the donkey."

The horses were a sight to behold. They were not much larger than ponies and thin as rails, and each had an old cloth over its back. Fernando proudly pointed at them, and then with a sweeping gesture, indicated that it was okay for the boys to ride anywhere in the open countryside.

Dick and Steve hopped on the horses, all six-feet plus of each of the boys. Fernando gave a loud war whoop, the dogs barked, and the horses took off on a fast walk. With each step, however, they went a little slower. Dick finally shook his head in disbelief. "They will never make it up the next hill!" he said.

Dick Summit, Steve and Grandpa Gottfried and Fran enjoy a Dominican meal with Fernando and Marie.

Steve agreed, "I think we should reverse this, maybe we should carry the horses." The boys decided it would be best if all of them walked, and spent most of the day wandering about the farm. They found some wild fruit to eat and discovered a nice cool stream where they sat to cool their feet in the water. As they splashed their feet, Steve realized that downstream, some ladies could be collecting the same water for their families drinking water. They had much to learn about the D.R.

While the boys were enjoying themselves, Grandpa was having fun on the front porch. One of the neighbor boys had come to visit, with his portable shoeshine kit. Since Grandpa's shoes were in need of a shine, he hired the boy, who did a fine job. Grandpa never told any of us how much he paid, however, the word got around to the neighbor boys. It was not long before they appeared with their shoeshine kits, too. Before the day was over, Grandpa had his shoes shined five times.

All day long, children gathered around Grandpa. They beat rhythms on tin cans, sang, danced and told Grandpa all kinds

Grandpa gets his shoes shined one more time.

of stories in Spanish. Grandpa did not understand a single word, but he enjoyed every minute of it.

Meanwhile, I was tied up with the Jeep, which fortunately was not seriously damaged. All that was needed was a new brace for the axle, which a blacksmith in Villa Mella forged for me while I waited. That allowed me time to make plans for a trip to the countryside for next day, so that I could see a few heifers that had been given out and show my family a little more of the area.

The journey inland proved to be a fitting climax to Steve and Grandpa's trip, especially the last village we stopped at, which was one of the most interesting places we had the opportunity to visit.

We had almost given up trying to find it, so hidden was the little community. We crossed a creek where the water was so high, it came in the doors of the Jeep, and the four-wheel drive barely got us out. Then we traveled across an open field with no trail but a sparsely-used footpath to guide us.

Finally, we could go no farther with the Jeep, and had to walk. Even Grandpa decided to come with us, though we had offered to allow him to wait in the car.

We were all very thirsty, but since the water wasn't safe for our visitors to drink, we forged ahead. I saw a rather well-used footpath winding between the creek and the trees, so we headed toward it single file. After a short distance, we could hear the voices of children playing and then suddenly, a large open area appeared and in front of us was a quaint little village. The settlement had approximately 20 palm-front thatched roof homes, built wherever someone decided to stick four poles in the ground. Everything appeared neat and clean.

No doubt we had been watched very closely from the time we left the Jeep, as four boys were already at our side, directing us to follw them. We were led to a hut where three men were visiting and drinking coffee. They immediately offered us all a cup, though I was the only one who could accept their hospitality. After a couple of sips, I identified myself and the purpose of my visit. The three men were grateful, and eager to show me the cow that was a gift through the Heifer Project.

We followed a zig-zag path among the homes, and there at the village-edge stood the cow. She was a very large Holstein, standing in the shade of a palm tree, contentedly chewing her cud. There was no sign of a rope or halter, and as we watched, children ran ahead to pet her and throw their arms around her neck, she never moved. There was no doubt, she was the queen of the village, her milk shared among the entire population of about 100 each day, with the children and pregnant women always getting priority. It was like a dream, so well was the cow serving her people, so well were they serving her.

As there was little need for me to offer any suggestions, we turned to go. The three men walked with us as we started back toward the Jeep. As we entered the narrow path by the creek, they gave each of us a farewell hug. In the background, it looked as if the whole village had followed. There were women carrying small babies in their arms, and they raised the children's hands to wave goodbye to us along with everyone else as we heard "Adios amigos" echo in the air.

We were silent as we wound our way back to the Jeep. Steve finally broke the silence. "I cannot believe this. We were four strangers wandering into their village and when we left they treated us like national heroes."

Dick laughed. "Yes Lew, tell us, what did we do?"

"It's nothing we did." I replied, "It was who we represented."

Nodding his head, Steve answered for us all. "Yes, I think I understand. The village just seemed to explode with love as a result of the gift of the cow. It would have been wonderful if all people who donated money to the Heifer Project could have seen what we just saw."

Back at the Jeep I had a wonderful feeling of joy in more ways than one. I felt that the other three were starting to understand a little of the inner joy of being a PCV, and was glad for the opportunity to share it with them.

While all of us were happy to get back on a marked road heading toward home, we agreed to stop at the very first tavern or bar we came to. We all needed a coke or a beer after our hot journey inland.

I pulled up at the first little tavern we came across. I explained to Grandpa and the boys that beer would be the best thirst-quencher, but Grandpa shook his head.

"This will take more than a beer," he said.

I went into the bar to order for everyone, while Steve and Dick went to find us a nice shady spot outside. But when I arrived outside, I found Grandpa was missing. In a minute, he emerged from the bar, happy, and carrying a small bottle of whiskey that he had spotted among the rum bottles. He had somehow managed to successfully communicate to the owner that he wanted to purchase it. "Look," he said, "this shall quench my thirst!"

Before anyone of us could say anything, he had the cap off and took a long swig of whatever was inside. Immediately, he started to cough and blow air over his tongue, then started to gasp for air and bend to the ground. He finally ended up flat on his back, fanning himself.

"Are you all right?" we all cried, standing over him.

Grandpa looked up, and then rolled over to find the whiskey bottle lying beside him. He picked it up, rolled his eyes, and then turned the bottle upside down, watching the remainder of whatever was inside it pour out onto the ground.

"I don't know what the stuff was, but it wasn't meant for human consumption!" he cried. I picked up the bottle for a look, but there wasn't any label on it, and we never did find out what it was Grandpa tried to drink.

The next day all three visitors were smiling again as they said farewell to the D.R. Steve gripped my hand tightly. "I learned a lot these last three days and I understand now why you are here." But Grandpa's last words were only, "I'll remember this trip for the rest of my life."

Chapter 21
Strangers At Home

Once we were truly settled into our home in Villa Mella, we had no plans of returning to our Ohio home in Wyandot County during the remainder of our stay. One day, however, a letter arrived that changed all that. Our youngest son, Ron, was getting married!

"Are you sure you read it right?" I asked Fran.

"Of course!" she said, handing it to me. "Here, you read it for yourself!"

She was right, of course, but I scanned it anyway. "I wish we could go to the wedding," I said. It was the first thing that came to my mind.

"What do you mean, you wish we could go to the wedding?" Fran exclaimed. "We **are** going to go to the wedding!"

"Wait," I said, trying to calm her down. "Peace Corps might not give us permission to go."

Fran was adamant. "They can't refuse to allow us to go home. This is an emergency. If they refuse, I'll quit, I'm a volunteer!" Again, she was right, so we made plans to go and see the new Country PC director, Mr. Carossco, the next day.

Like Frank Rey, he was a very understanding man, but he cautioned us about returning. "This may not be as easy as you think," he said. "It's been almost a year now since you two have been back in the States."

Fran was in no mood to hear that the return home might be difficult. "Things at home cannot have changed that much," she said.

Mr. Carossco smiled. "I was not thinking about changes at home. I was thinking of changes in you. You may see things differently than you did before."

Fran's mind was still thinking of the wedding only. "I believe we are both very open minded," she said. "The fact that we're here in the first place proves that, doesn't it?"

Mr. Carossco spoke a little more firmly, explaining that many PC volunteers who terminate their duty early report that the readjustment to the culture in America was harder than adjusting to life here. "I'm not suggesting that you don't go — but only that you keep your trip very short."

Fran interrupted him. "I only want to go home for one hour."

Mr. Carossco gave up. "I understand, Fran, as long as both of you understand that you are going home for the wedding only, not to get involved with your regular way of life there, not at this time. Both of you are now doing fine here in the Dominican Republic and we want to keep it that way."

He rose and reached out to shake our hands. "I hope it is a lovely wedding and that you enjoy your time with your family."

We thanked him, but as we turned to go, Mr. Carossco had one more thing to say. "Just so there is no misunderstanding, this will be considered vacation time."

We understood — the PC paid nothing toward vacations. If we wanted to go home, we had to foot the bill. That was the only part of the conversation we knew we could count on before we walked in!

The time before we were to leave passed swiftly. Each day brought discussions like, "What shall we take home from here?" "What should we bring back to the D.R.?" and, "What do we do with our dog while we are gone?" A Peace Corps volunteer named Max came to our rescue on that one — he was delighted at the chance to stay in our home, and Lisa would have a new friend.

From the moment we started our return trip, we continually compared people, places and things. We also found that Mr. Carossco's predictions came back to haunt us many times during our brief trip home.

At our first stop at Miami airport, we found that English sounded odd to us. Styles of dress seemed to have changed dramatically, especially the women in their revealing attire.

Noticing my apparent interest, Fran said, "Oh, come now, Lew, after all of the non-working zippers and naked children around Villa Mella, you shouldn't even be interested."

Smiling, I replied, "What really interests me is how well fed everyone appears to be." It made me realize how we must appear to the people of Villa Mella, even though we each had lost about 15-20 pounds over the past year.

Smiling, Fran suggested, "Shall we try to gain our weight back this week?"

I just sat silently, with a big smile, dreaming of thick steaks and strawberry sundaes.

Fran interrupted me. "On second thought, remember what Mr. Carossco told us. I think you better stick with your bananas and oranges."

Another surprise to us was the hurried pace everyone seemed to be in. It soon began to get on our nerves. On the other hand, the orderly lines were a welcome change. After getting bruises from pushing and shoving in the so-called Dominican lines, it was a pleasure to stand patiently.

Once we boarded the plane to Ohio, we stopped comparing cultures and began to focus on our family. All three of our children were there to welcome us when we landed, and we both got lumps in our throats when we saw them. Fran stopped and wiped tears from her eyes.

We spent a busy two or three days of "re-meeting" our friends and neighbors before we finally had time to relax alone in our home and reflect on the differences between our old and new lives.

While everyone seemed happy to see us, there was something missing. Here, the men extended their hands at full-length to greet me — in the D.R., we had grown used to warm, friendly embraces, and hands on our shoulders. In America, by contrast it seemed to us that everyone was afraid to get too close for fear of catching a germ.

All the questions were very similar, also — "How do you like it over there?" "Are you glad to be home?" "Will you be going back?" "Can you give a talk or program for us?"

Fortunately, our time on this trip was too short to worry about that. We were having a hard enough time sorting out what we were feeling, let alone give a talk on it.

Ron's wedding took place in the country church about four miles from our farm. My great-grandparents had helped to build it and so it had much meaning for us. The ceremony was simple, but beautiful and afterward the bride's parents had a lovely reception at their home.

We again found ourselves comparing things — how lovely the table setting was, how orderly the people were when they helped themselves to the food, how the furniture and home all looked like new, how the men kept their coats on and complained of the heat. And where were the rum bottles, or the children looking in the windows, waiting for someone to give them some food?

It was all so strange to us at that at one point we both wandered into the back yard, just so we could get a few minutes alone to confide in each other what we were feeling.

"Here we are with our family," said Fran, "and yet I feel uncomfortable."

"It's as if this is a foreign country," I said, nodding my head.

Later on in the day we had a meaningful discussion with Pastor O'Brien, that helped us put things in perspective. He had performed the marriage ceremony earlier, and was a very close friend of our family.

"Have you come to love the Dominican life more?" he asked us, when we explained our feelings to him.

I shook my head. "No, neither one of us can say that, The more we live there and understand the people, the more we do NOT understand."

Pastor O'Brien looked at us in a wise way, much the same as Padre Miguel might have. "Do not worry about it," he said, "today is like being in the middle of a forest. You cannot describe it all because all you can see now are lots of tall trees around you. Later, it will all make sense."

The Pastor's words proved to be true to us, though "later" would be a long time coming. Perhaps it was only years after we had returned from the D.R. that we realized how much, in our attempt to change others, we ourselves, had been changed. For now, we were still in the middle of our journey, with a few more adventures to go!

Part 3

Arrival

Chapter 22
At Home With Strangers

Our way back to the D.R. found us at the airport, once again wondering if we had everything as we had the **first** time we left for the Peace Corps, more than a year ago. But this time, we weren't concerned about things we needed — we had learned that we needed very little to get along there — instead, we worried about the special requests our neighbors had made for things to bring back for them. We had lost the list in all the excitement, but had managed to recall most of the items from memory.

It was time to start boarding our connecting flight in Miami for Santo Domingo. Suddenly I sprang to my feet, "Fran, I forgot, Fernando had asked for a dress hat." I made a mad dash through the airport for it. I heard Fran yell, "You don't have much time." I didn't have time to answer back. I grabbed the first hat I saw, tossed the cashier an extra dollar bill and ran to where Fran stood, waiting with our carry-on bags at the gate. They closed the door right behind us as we boarded, breathlessly I laughed, "That was a close one."

Fran never laughed. In fact, she never did speak to me until we were almost ready to land in Santo Domingo. Then she grumbled, "I hope Fernando will like his hat."

Our first couple of hours back in the D.R. were very tiring and unpleasant. Not only were there again no bands or parades to greet us, but we had to fight our way back home on the publico system during the heat of the day, which meant exchanging publicos four times, all the while carrying extra baggage.

Our neighbor, Antonio, spotted us waiting at our last stop, and wildly waved both arms for us to board his publico. He seemed very proud to be the one to bring the two Americans back to Villa Mella. As he drove through the village, he tooted the horn and waved to all his friends. When he neared our home, he drove very slowly, yelling out the window to our neighbors, "the Americans have returned!"

When he pulled in the driveway, we were immediately surrounded by all our neighborhood children. Before we could work our way past them, out came our neighbors from all directions, some walking, some running, some laughing or shouting. They all came directly to us and each gave us a big hug and a friendly, "Welcome home!"

Everyone stayed until well after dark, as our homecoming was a good excuse to visit with each other as well as us. As for Fran and me, we were so touched by the outpouring of love and concern, that we forgot how tired we were until we were finally alone on our front porch with Lisa beside us. It was very dark, with the only light coming from the moon shining on the palm fronds. But it was enough. It had been a very typical Dominican homecoming — nothing planned, but everything happening. Somehow, knowing we were needed and wanted, made it so much easier to return.

"And that includes you too, Lisa," Fran said, laying her hand on the dog's head.

Early the next morning, Fernando arrived with his entire family before we were even out of bed. They had seen us in Antonio's publico yesterday and were anxious to come over and see what Fran had bought for the children, as Marie had requested something for each of them.

The children's eyes were glistening as if it were Christmas morning, when they entered the house. While Fran hurriedly made some coffee, I explained to Fernando that we had not had time to unpack, but he just said, "That's fine," and the entire family set about making themselves comfortable in our living room. It appeared they were just going to wait. At that, Fran motioned for me to join her in the kitchen.

"I'm not sure where everything is," she whispered.

"That's all right," I said, "this is the D.R. remember? Just pull things out. It will all work out."

"Okay," Fran said, "the next party is about to start!" She went into the bedroom and brought out a package which the children quickly tore apart. Since Tony was the only boy, his shirt was easy to find. The girls soon spotted their new dresses and undressed in front of everyone to try them on. Fernando said nothing during the wild excitement, just standing back smiling, as the girls modeled their new clothes.

"They fit fine!" Marie exclaimed. "You are a perfect shopper."

The girls were now anxious to show off their clothes in Villa Mella, so the whole family rose to go, and the girls gave Fran a big hug. Fernando laid his hand on my shoulder and said, "You make my family very happy. Let me know how much they cost and I pay you tomorrow."

I nodded. "No problem, Amigo," I said, but as the family turned to leave, Fernando whispered something to Marie. She then turned to Fran and said quietly, "Fernando wants to know if you found a hat for him."

I ran back into the bedroom as Fran shouted loudly for everyone to come back. I carried the hat in my outstretched hands, saying "Es por tu, Amigo (This is for you, my friend)!"

Fernando smiled from ear to ear. "Muchas gracious."

Like the children, he tried the hat on immediately, but it turned out that I had not been as good a shopper as Fran. The hat was too large and everyone laughed as it settled down on top of his ears. Fernando didn't laugh, however. Instead, he spotted one of the bags the clothes had come in, which he quickly folded up and placed inside the band of his hat. When he placed it on his head, it fit just fine. "No problem," he said.

From that moment on, Fernando was never seen in public without his hat, and he always made sure everyone knew it was from his American friends. Even Fran had to agree that it was one of the best gifts we ever bought, even if we did almost miss our plane to get it.

Chapter 23
Problems Again

Now that we had returned to the Dominican Republic, both of us felt very optimistic about our remaining time of service in the PC, especially after our neighbor's homecoming party for us. However, as usual, the D.R. had other plans.

First, we discovered that we had no water. Fernando told us that it was "bad, very bad!" as the pump in Villa Mella was broken.

"The last time this happened, it took three months to fix it," he said.

I ended up bringing home water from the farm well every day for Fran and me. Our neighbors were not as fortunate, and had to resort to the creek. Soon the road in front of our house became very crowded as the women and children carried water back and forth. The boys, pressed into service to help, made a little game of it, stringing six plastic jugs on a pole and running down the road passing the girls.

While the farm had water, it had other problems. The price of milk was low, so the manager began to juggle figures to break even. This involved keeping unprofitable animals, because the inventory value made the books look better. The squatters in the stables were a continual problem, of course, for they used the electricity at no cost to them and at plenty of cost to the farm.

On top of this, Fran and I had our own additional problem of no Jeep. It had been taken to the garage for repairs while we were home for the wedding, and since they were looking for parts, it could take as long to fix as the pump in Villa Mella.

As I walked home from the farm that night after finding out that news, I had a strange feeling. It seemed like old times, in fact, just like it did when we started here over a year ago. I hoped our entire Peace Corps experience was not starting all over again!

We needed some good news, and fortunately, we got it the next day when the Foundacion offered us the use of a motorcycle, which belonged to a PCV named Roger who was on vacation for two weeks. We used it every day during that time. Fran and I made an excellent team. I watched for chuckholes, and Fran directed traffic. The motorcycle even allowed us to get out to some homes we hadn't yet visited, as the bike could get down footpaths that the Jeep could not.

We were just really starting to enjoy this new way of commuting when the two weeks were up and Roger pulled up in a publico at our house. Ironically, we were seated on the motorcycle at the time, ready to go on another errand.

We both just sat there, stunned, while Roger apologized for giving us such short notice, and announced that he was here for his bike. We were both silent, realizing that our wheels were once again leaving us, but Roger was insistent.

Fran crawled off the motorcycle, but I was still reluctant to give it up. "What do you hear about our Jeep?" I asked, looking for a bright spot. "Is it repaired?"

Roger only looked at me and shrugged his shoulders. "The Foundacion only told me you had my bike and I was to pick it up."

At this point, I had had it. We had no water, there were problems at the farm I could not solve if we lived here 100 years, and now we had no transportation again. Realizing that the Foundanion was probably not as concerned about our transportation as Roger, I said, "Tell them I will be happy to give back your bike when they return our Jeep."

Now it was Roger's turn to be shocked. "You mean you are not going to give me back my bike?" he asked.

"That's right," I said, "not until we get some kind of transportation."

Now, Roger was an excellent volunteer, who understood my frustration, so he made no effort to stand and argue about it. He just shook his head and said, "I hope you take good care of it," as he walked away to wait for another publico.

I continued to sit on the bike, thinking about what I had done. After a moment, I began to feel ashamed of my actions and I got off the bike. I laid it down, then slowly walked toward the road to join Roger. I held out my hand, saying, "I'm sorry. I was wrong. My transportation problems are not yours. Come back and get your bike."

By now Fran had returned to the house and had some coffee ready. When she saw Roger and me walking back toward the bike, she stretched her arm out of the window and dangled an empty coffee cup from it. After that, we were all friends again, but we still felt a little sorry for ourselves after Roger drove away on the bike. We knew that things would get better, but right now they only seemed worse.

I decided to walk to the farm to see if I could find some good news there, and to my surprise, I almost did — there was the Jeep, in front of the office. I could hardly believe my eyes and I ran over to it jubilantly, my heart beating fast. Rafael Abreau, a Foundanion staff member, was getting out if it, and I greeted him, "Mi guagua, mi guagua!" I cried, "You have brought it here for me?"

Rafael quickly explained to me that this wasn't necessarily the case. Because the repairs had cost so much, the Foundanion had decided to reserve the Jeep for use by staff personnel only rather than PC volunteers. Smiling, he added, "I'm sure we can work something out manana."

Now, I had worked here long enough to know what that meant. To do something "manana" meant you were going to do nothing because "manana" would never come — it would always be "manana."

I don't remember what happened next. I'm sure I must have looked very stupid, for I probably just stood there, staring out into space. I remember Rafael put his hand on my shoulder and told me to have a nice weekend, but I don't remember when he left or how long I stood there. I only knew that I ended up slowly walking home, taking the short cut through the field, my head bowed, seeing only the ground in front of me. Every once in awhile, I would stop and slowly move the dust around with my foot. It helped me to think. And what I thought was, "this is more than a feeling of starting over, things are just the same as when we started." Except that now, I found myself lacking the enthusiasm of new adventure. It seemed like I had been walking for an hour. I wished it could take a year, then I could go back to Ohio.

I must have thought this way until I was almost home. Then I stopped and took a deep breath and shook my head fast.

"This is silly, Lew," I told myself. "You are over-exaggerating a small setback. You cannot let Fran know how you are feeling. You must try to be positive." For the first time, I began to walk erect, quickening my pace until I reached home.

Fran and Lisa were waiting for me under the mango tree. I think Fran, too, must have been trying to think positively, for she greeted me cheerfully saying, "Hi, honey. Any good news from the farm?"

"Yes," I said, holding both arms outstretched. "I have two bottles of fresh well-water instead of one."

"That's wonderful. I have good news for you, too. We are going to have something different to eat tonight."

"I'd like something different, what is it?"

"Fried bananas."

"Fried bananas! What's different about that?"

"I sliced them in larger chunks!"

That made us both laugh, and we ran hand in hand toward the house, Lisa barking along beside us. When we reached the porch, I threw my arms around Fran and gave her a big embrace.

"I have something else important to tell you," I said, "I love you!"

Chapter 24
May The Road Rise Up To Meet You

Rain in the D.R. was a good experience, particularly after a long dry spell, when it brought everyone out to enjoy the welcome showers.

On days like this, even the donkey would celebrate in his own way, with his own heinous sounds. Perhaps he was singing for a day off, or more likely for the refreshing feeling of the warm rain water pounding on his back, carrying away the dirt that was embedded in his hide.

The children enjoyed it most of all as they dashed in and out of raindrops and splashed in the puddles on the road. We watched Amelia, one of our neighbor girls, as she stood at the end of our house, enjoying the warm water that was rolling off our hot roof. She smiled as she lathered her hair, face, arms and legs, and then washed her dress without removing it.

"One of the things I miss most is a hot shower," Fran said.

"Here," I said, handing her a bar of soap from the kitchen table. "Go out with Amelia and enjoy some of the luxury living we have at our fingertips."

"No thanks," she replied. "My dress isn't too dirty today and let's not waste the soap!"

After the rain, all of nature seemed to be revived, as everything had a vigorous, crisp, clean appearance. Our neighbors too seemed to have been transformed, as now there was a happy sound in their voices, and each "Buenos Dias" carried a melodious sound.

Fran and I were affected, too, as our laughing and joking with each other about a shower revealed. This morning truly felt like a sign of better things to come, in nature, in our neighbors and in ourselves.

I got ready to leave for the farm, and Fran decided to walk with me, as she often did. As usual, too, Lisa tagged along very close to our feet, her ears erect and her tail wagging from side to side. When the three of us reached the small footpath that marked my turn-off to the farm, however, something moved Fran to stop me and say that she had been thinking about the Irish doxology.

"How very much its words that we love seem to be with us today," she said.

The doxology was always a special prayer to us. We had repeated it many times to each other through the years, but at that moment, it meant more to us than ever before. We found ourselves holding hands, in the middle of the road, facing each other, and with Lisa sitting down between us, said the words outloud.

> *"May the road rise up to meet you.*
> *May the wind be always at your back.*
> *May the sun shine warm*
> *upon your face and the*
> *rains fall soft upon your*
> *fields, and until we meet*
> *again, may God hold you*
> *in the hollow of His*
> *hands."*

As we parted, I continued on down my path to the farm. The truth of those words seemed to be revealed all around me. the breeze was blowing at my back, the sun was shining warmly on my face, the rain had fallen gently on the fields, and there was no doubt as we struggled through out Peace Corps experience, that God was indeed, holding us in the hollow of His hand.

There was only one part missing — that line about the road rising up to meet us. As I plodded along the path, all I could see were my own two feet trampling down the path; no road was rising to meet me! Or so I thought, until I reached the farm and Louie greeted me with a twinkle in his eye.

"Someone is waiting to see you," he said, motioning toward the office, where I spotted a young Spanish man. He

Lew chats with the new farm manager, Camilo Suero.

was a little under six feet tall, had thick curly black hair, thin features and a pleasant smile. I had never seen him before. He met me as I was halfway to the office, extending his hand in greeting. To my surprise, he not only knew my name, but spoke excellent English.

"My name is Camilo Suero, and I am the new farm manager," he said. He then invited me to join him in his office, where I learned his amazing fluency in English was a result of four years of study at the University of Texas.

"I never could learn to feel comfortable in your fast culture," he said.

Laughing, I replied, "I understand."

From that moment, we forged an immediate friendship, which helped us to talk plainly about the farm. Camilo wanted to know all about the operation of the Heifer Project. He was also interested in Fran's work, and in my personal feelings about the management of the farm.

"I know that in the past, there has been some misunderstanding," he said. "The board of the Foundaion has discussed with me, and informed me that they feel problems were due mostly to a lack of communication. In fact, that's the main reason I got the job. They feel my knowledge of English will be very valuable to you and to them."

We continued to talk, and then toward the end he finally pushed back his chair and asked me if there was anything he could do for me. I immediately asked him for transportation.

In reply, he put his hand on my shoulder, saying, "We will have to work things out together. The pickup will soon be fixed and you can use it when it is available. For longer trips, you can probably still use the old Embassy Jeep. We'll work it out one day at a time."

It wasn't a complete answer, but since it was more cooperation than I had seen in a long time, I felt I was walking on air. Our feelings about today being the beginning of a new time for us in the D.R. were really true — for now, while walking home, even the road was rising up to meet me.

Chapter 25
All's Fair At The Ferria

Because we were born and raised in a rural area, Fran and I loved our county fair, where the best of our farming community's products were featured. While the Dominican Republic did not have any county or state fairs, there was one big national fair. The Ferria Granadera Nacional, it was held every summer in the capital and was the biggest event for the country and its agriculture. This year, it was also the best opportunity I would ever have to implement any changes I had in mind, now that I had worked in and come to understand many things about Dominican agriculture.

I realized that the very best source of help to the poor farmers of this country were the large landowners, who were attending the fair to exhibit their purebred livestock. My business background as a breeder of dairy cattle would enable me to talk with them here on an equal basis, and perhaps have some influence on them. I could only hope.

In preparation for the fair, I worked with the new manager to select the cattle that the farm would show. Sexto, a good dependable laborer, was assigned to help me.

In Ohio, I would put blankets on the show cattle to make their hair soft and shiny, but here the heat would be too great, so we had to brush them everyday.

"Not only will this make their hair look good," I told Sexto, "but it will show the cattle that you are not going to harm them."

I also worked to show Sexto how to lead the cattle. We began by tying them to a post so that they would learn not to pull away when a rope and halter were attached to them.

Sexto was a good assistant, though he laughed when I explained to him that the cattle did not understand English or Spanish, that all communication had to be done with actions, and that if we observed carefully, they would tell us when they were hurt, or afraid or did not understand.

"I never realized that the cows sometimes tried to talk to me," he said.

By fair time we had attained a good understanding between us and the cows. All went fine except for one day when the large black and white Holstein cow became nervous and Sexto forgot my lessons on how to communicate properly. He yanked on the halter and shouted loudly, "Settle down!" This only made the cow more nervous. She pulled the rope from Sexto's hands. In a minute, she was off and running with Sexto giving full chase, followed by the children of the squatters living in the old horse stables.

I watched the side-show, unable to help, until luckily the cow turned in my direction and I was able to guide her into a corner. Exhausted and frothing at the mouth, she was now glad to stand still, allowing me to approach her easily and wrap the halter around the post. This cow had been the farm's best prospect for a grand champion but we would be lucky to save her life and keep her in the milking herd now. I couldn't tell that to Sexto, of course, who was obviously feeling badly about the incident.

"So sorry, Mr. Lew," he said, slowly walking up to me and looking at the ground. "I have failed. You find someone else."

"No, Sexto, we don't quit because of one setback," I said, "We just work harder."

The day of the fair, Fran found me busy writing at our kitchen table before dawn. "What's so important that it couldn't wait until later?" she asked.

"The big fair is today," I said, continuing my work. "I want to make sure I'm prepared."

Fran laughed. "You have been working with the cattle for several weeks. Now, you're getting yourself ready to be on exhibit, too?"

I wasn't amused by her comments. "There will be many influential people there to share my ideas with. Sometimes opportunity knocks only once.'

"Yes, and sometimes here in the D.R., things do not work as planned." She was right on that point, and, sure enough, we encountered many surprises throughout the fair.

Although there was no need to hurry there on the first day, since Sexto was to have full charge of the show cattle, we found ourselves anxious to leave and soon started to gather things together for the day.

"What are you making?" I asked Fran, who was filling up our thermos.

"It's for Sexto," she said, "hot chocolate." Since he would probably be sleeping in the barn next to the cattle, I was sure he'd like that.

I then came out of the bedroom carrying my old work shoes and pants under my arm. Now it was Fran's turn to ask me what was going on.

"I'm going to take them along just in case. I don't want to get caught wearing dirty, stinking clothes at the wrong place." Fran just nodded. I guess she figured her warning on surprises had sunk in.

When we arrived at the fairgrounds, we were both amazed at the large crowd of people who had already assembled. We took a quick walk to get an overall feeling of what it was going to be like — while it was not as large as our Ohio State Fair, it did beat our Wyandot County Fair. By contrast, there were very few commercial stands, the emphasis instead being on educational exhibits and displays. And except for a ferris wheel near the parking lot, the rides and games for the young were obviously missing.

Arriving at the barn, we decided to check on Sexto. He was feeding the cattle with Louie and both men seemed happy to see me.

"We need your help, Amigo," Louie yelled. "It's high time we clean the cattle to get them ready to show."

I was puzzled. "But judging doesn't start until tomorrow," I said.

"Tonight is the big show when we will be on television," Louie explained.

207

"Television? No one told me about this," I said.

"Yes, there is a big parade — the president and all the important people will be there." Louie said. He then explained that every exhibitor of beef and dairy cattle was expected to lead one male and one female into the arena, and then line them up according to breed so that there would be one row of Holsteins, one row of Brown Swiss, one row of Brahma and so on. All exhibitors would then be introduced.

"Okay, Amigo," I said, hearing one of my opportunities knocking. "I'll help you, just as soon as I change."

"I knew it was a good thing to bring those work clothes along," I said to Fran as we walked back to the car to get them.

"Stop bragging," she said. "I already gave you a blue ribbon for preparation."

Working together, Louie, Sexto and I gave the animals a quick beauty treatment, making sure hooves were polished, ears washed, tail hair fluffed and every hair brushed into place. Finally we sprayed them with oil to make them glisten.

"They look great!" I said, stepping back to admire, while Louie and Sexto, pleased and excited, smiled back. "Stay here," they said, "while we change so we can look good, too!"

When they returned, still smiling, they had on new white coveralls, with the Foundacion insignia in large, black letters across their backs. Sexto even had shoes on, a rarity for him. Now Fran gave compliments all around, telling them how sharp they looked.

Louie laughed. "Yes, Sexto even washed the inside of his ears. He wanted to be as clean as the animals!"

By now, it was time to lead the animals into the arena where the participants were to be organized for the parade.

"Let's hurry and get a seat," I told Fran. "We don't want to miss anything."

"What about your shoes?" she asked, pointing to my feet, which were covered with the results of our work with the cattle.

"I don't have time to change. They will be all right," I said. "Let's go!"

We headed for the arena only to find that this close to show time, the seating area in the arena was filled and people were

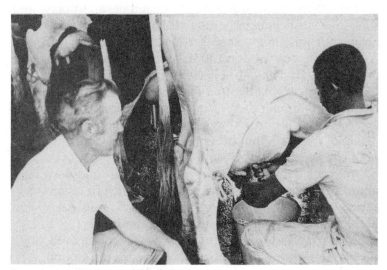

Lew helps Sexto at the fair.

crowded at all the gate entrances. We finally managed to work our way to one of the gates, only to find a guard there telling everyone to leave.

"Please," said Fran, "we are Peace Corps volunteers and have been helping prepare some of the cattle for the show. Is there room anywhere for us?"

The guard smiled politely, and asked us to wait a moment while he checked. He returned soon, smiling and then opening the gate to allow us to enter. An usher came running down the aisle to meet us and motioned for us to follow him. You can imagine how excited we were when he directed us to two seats in the first row, right in the middle of the arena.

I looked at Fran and said triumphantly, "This is great! Right on the 50-yard line."

Fran wasn't so sure. "Something's wrong," she said. We both glanced around and saw lots of empty seats behind us. They all said "RESERVED."

Directly in front of the arena, a band began to play, and soon the seats behind us began to fill up. Fran glanced around again, but this time turned her head quickly forward.

"Oh no, Lew — don't look. Everyone behind us is formally dressed. The ladies have on long gowns."

Somehow we had gotten ourselves, workclothes and all, right in the middle of the dignitaries' section.

"Did you see our American Embassador?" Fran asked.

"No," I said, "but he's probably seen us and is wondering how we got here."

We both decided the best thing to do was to look straight ahead and hope no one would notice the stench from my workshoes, or Fran in her 87 cent yellow plastic raincoat. "You had to say it looked like rain!" she grumbled.

That strategy worked — until the news media arrived. Soon they were flashing pictures of everyone in our section.

"Keep your shoes under the seat," Fran said.

"Don't worry honey," I said, trying to see the humor in our situation. "I may crawl under the seat with them."

Fran was still upset so I went on. "Relax, Fran. Everybody is probably wondering who those two important American hippies are in the number one seats. They will probably never ask anyone though, because they won't want to admit they don't know us!"

That made both of us laugh — until the floodlights were turned on and the President of the country was ushered into a special box seat, directly behind us. We watched, our mouths open, as he majestically strode up to the microphone to open the fair on live television.

After that, the show went on, right on schedule. We soon spotted Louie and Sexto proudly leading their animals past the reviewing stand. Sexto could not help glancing up to catch a glimpse of the President — but instead, he saw Fran and me in the front row. Fran winked at him, and gave a little "hi" wave. Sexto stopped, with his mouth open, almost forgetting to lead his animal forward.

Following the show, the band played while everyone in the reserved section filed past the President for a greeting. That is, everyone except us. We decided to delay the privilege for another time, when we were in appropriate attire to show our respect.

The next morning, Fran fixed some more food and hot chocolate for Sexto, and I came walking through the kitchen, dressed fresh and clean. But again, I carried my work shoes. Fran turned for a second look.

"Just in case," I said.

At the fair that day, I again found my "Just in case" shoes in need. When I arrived, Camilo the new farm manager and Louie were having a conference in the aisle behind the cattle. They motioned for me to join them.

"We're making plans for the judging," Louie said. "We want you to help Sexto get them ready this morning."

Camilo shook his head in agreement. "We can't afford any mistakes today," he said. "The competition is going to be very keen." I thought a little. I wanted Sexto to show the cattle, but knew that might be risky. I decided to suggest a compromise. "Okay, I'll show a couple of the cows, but Sexto must show a few also. I'll be right at the ringside helping him." That seemed to satisfy Camilo, and we worked hard all that morning getting the cattle in shape.

At lunch time, a couple of Americans came strolling by in the barn.

"These cattle are in fine condition," one said in English. I turned around, and to my surprise, found myself face to face with two Holstein breeders and cattle exporters whom I knew from America. It was a happy reunion and ended with the men inviting me to join them for lunch.

Although I was conscious of how dirty I was, the men didn't seem to mind, so we all headed toward a small restaurant on the exposition grounds. As we approached the door of the restaurant, we ran into three prominent Dominican landowners who had imported cattle through the two men I was with. They stopped to exchange greetings and soon the landowners joined us for lunch.

I looked down at my attire. Again, I was caught with smelly shoes and dirty clothes, this time with some of the landowners

I had been waiting to make contact with at the fair. At least they understood farm work, I told myself, as we walked in.

Everything went along fine, until one of the Dominican men jubilantly rose to his feet and said, "Here comes one of my dearest friends!" and went over to greet a very beautiful young lady. He soon brought her over to our table and introduced her to us — she was Miss Dominican Republic, and ended up joining us for lunch, too. Of course, they seated her right next to me.

"I've heard so many good things about the PC," she said. "I'm impressed to meet you and all the American visitors."

Believe me, I was also impressed. I also kept my shoes under the table. I was sure Miss Dominican Republic would understand the phrase "The show must go on!"

Experiences like this set the stage for the entire fair, as strange things just kept happening. First, the official dairy judge turned out to be John McKitrick from Columbus, Ohio, who had judged many shows I'd participated in much closer to home.

Later, as I was leaving, I ran into Walter Olefke, a sales representative of NOBA, one of the top bull farms in America, and located close to our home in Ohio. Walter explained that he was here to try to increase the use of artificial insemination among the large dairy farmers.

I stopped, suddenly aware that here was another of my opportunities knocking when I least expected it. One of the biggest problems of the Heifer Project was the difficulty of bringing live cattle here — not only was it very expensive, but it put a tremendous strain on the cattle as they had to adjust to the climate and feed changes. For some time, I had wanted to change the program to eliminate the shipment of cattle and import bull semen for artificial insemination instead, so that cattle breeding on the large farms could be improved. Then the large, local farmers could donate native cattle to the poor, small farmers. While sometimes the rich were not entirely enthusiastic about helping the poor, in this case the ones I had talked to had agreed they would be willing to give some cattle in exchange for good bull semen from America. I explained it to Walter, and we soon had the making of a deal that would help both the Dominicans and Walt's business as well.

There were also some surprises, pleasant and unpleasant, for other fairgoers. First, an American swine judge was bitten by a boar he had just crowned grand champion of show. Then, a large Brahma bull that was also named champion, broke free from the man who was leading it. Everyone panicked as the bull jumped and bellowed around the arena — and then everyone ran when the bull got loose in the Exhibit Hall. Frightened, the bull somehow found its way to the parking lot. Running at full speed, it finally stepped on its lead strap with his front feet, fell, and rolled over head first, landing with a tremendous thud right on the side of a new Mercedes Benz automobile. The bull gave a loud mournful groan, as he lay beside the car, but not half as mournful as the first man on the scene. Not only was he the owner of the car, but just moments before his bull had come in second to this Brahma that had demolished his car. The poor man was given the honor of shooting the bull that had broken its neck and his car.

The real entertainment, however, took place that night with many kinds of audience participation relays and contests. It was wild-wild-wild and so Fran and I decided to sit back and enjoy the entertainment. We had volunteered for the Peace Corps, not to commit suicide.

In one contest, a scoop shovel was tied by the handle behind a car. One boy had to sit on the shovel and hold on to the handle, while the car pulled him the entire distance of the arena. The first car to make it to the other end with a boy still on the shovel was the winner.

There was an obstacle car race between and around barrels, first forward and then backward. In addition, the driver had to stop the car at one point, jump out and drink a bottle of Coke, while his partner changed into clothes out of a suitcase. About halfway through, they traded drivers and started all over again. Sometimes, the riders would jump out of the window before the car stopped or crawl over the roof while the car was still moving.

There was also a little wild west rodeo, when a group of Brahma cows that had never been milked were turned loose in the arena while contestants tried to fill empty pop bottles with their milk. It ws an action-packed 20 minutes of chasing after uncooperative cows that were running and kicking both hind feet straight up in the air. No one was able to get any milk in any of their bottles.

The final day of the fair was reserved for the Dominican youth. We decided to take along Kiki and some of our neighbor girls, thinking the educational exhibits would be good for them.

When they came to our house that night for a ride, however, I hardly recognized them. Gone were the barefooted girls running around in rags. Before us were four very beautiful young ladies wearing nice dresses and a little bit of make-up.

"I must watch Lew very closely tonight," said Fran, as she smiled. "You all look beautiful!"

We arrived early in the evening at the fairgrounds, with plenty of time to see the model rural home, the agricultural exhibits and so on. However, the girls kept asking, "Is it time to go to the arena?"

"Why the hurry?" Fran asked. "You told us in the car that you had never seen the fair before. Don't you want to see everything?"

"Oh yes," Kiki said, "but on the radio, they said that all the best bands in the D.R. will be here tonight and we want to get a seat!"

We gave in, and headed toward the arena, which, as the girls had anticipated, was already starting to fill up with people far earlier than usual. Excitement was everywhere as the bands performed, each doing their best to please the audience. The Dominican youth acted just like Americans, clapping their hands, and crying and hugging each other. Before it was over, everyone was in the aisles in the arena, or standing on their seats, jumping and screaming to the music. Fran and I seemed to be the only two still sitting down.

214

"I guess these seats were made to dance on," Fran said.

"You're right," I yelled, pointing down, "and guess what? Tonight I don't have my stinky shoes on to keep under the seat."

Soon we too, were standing on the seats, jumping and jiving, trying to mock everyone else. The neighbor girls spotted us, and soon circled around us and began clapping and cheering. They loved to see the older Americans dance and try to act like them.

Fran and I looked at each other in the midst of it all, filled with the energy of the night, and with hope for the D.R. and its people. The Ferria Granadera Nacional had lived up to its expectations and given me new contacts that could help the farmers long after we had gone. With all its surprises, good and bad, the fair seemed to give the Dominicans something else — PRIDE — the source of making all hope for the future a reality.

Chapter 26
Seeds Of Friendship

While I had the advantage of working through an organized program, Fran's only way to help the Dominicans was through her day-to-day contacts with the women. Her opportunities were much more spontaneous, and she had to take advantage of each situation as it occurred, or to create them herself.

One way she did this was by accompanying me to the softball games. This encouraged the other players to bring their wives and girlfriends, giving the ladies the opportunity to talk during the games. Many times they would be laughing in the bleachers while the men were arguing on the ball field.

Another time, she discovered a large supply of garden seeds at Church World Service that had been donated by a major American seed company. With approval, she distributed them to the volunteers throughout the country, who in turn, gave them to the native peoples. In this way, she really was sowing seeds of friendship through the countryside.

Fran also developed a very close friendship with the young children in the neighborhood who would come to visit most any time of the day or night. Sometimes they came in groups of two or three, but many times there were as many as seven or eight at a time. They had all heard Fran say, "My home is your home," and apparently took her literally.

This was all right with Fran, as she loved the company during the day. Neighbors would just walk in when she was home, usually yelling "Hola Francisca." Some of the more shy girls would quietly enter and sit down on a chair and just look around and smile. Many times, while working in and around the house, Fran would look up and find some children just sitting in a chair, watching her.

The children had many questions like, "How big is your home in America?" and "What is snow like?"

We had tacked different maps to the wall, including a map of the world; a favorite game was to ask the Dominican children where the Dominican Republic was on the map. Garcia, a bright boy, pointed at the Soviet Union, since it seemed to be the largest country of all. When Fran pointed out the Dominican Republic, the boy thought she was teasing him.

"The D.R. is a big country," he said.

Fran had only a few difficult times with the neighbors. One morning, bright and early, one of our neighbors, Florinda, came by our kitchen window on her way for a can of water. She stopped and leaned her arms on the window sill.

"What can I do for you?" Fran asked.

"Nothing," she answered.

Fran thought that perhaps she wanted to talk, but as her day was planned she had no time. "Lew and I have a lot to do — can we talk another day?" she asked.

"Okay, adios," Florinda replied, giving a big smile as she walked away.

Fran continued to make breakfast, but soon discovered that she could not find her paring knife. It was her only one, and she suddenly realized that she had laid it on the window sill, where Florinda was leaning. Now, it was gone. It was not the value of the knife that bothered Fran, but how to handle this. It was the first time any of our neighbors had taken anything from us.

I suggested to Fran that she talk to Florinda about it the next time she came for water. A day later, Florinda walked past without stopping, so Fran hurried around the house to "accidentally" meet her.

"Hola Francisca, I have time to talk today." Florinda smiled and put her can of water to the ground.

"I have a problem," Fran went on. "I lost my only knife and I cannot find it."

"Oh, I'm sorry," said Florinda, as she wiped her face on her dress.

"Would you know where it is?" Fran asked. There was a silence, and immediately Fran knew for sure that Florinda had taken it.

217

"Florinda, you are my friend. If you find my knife, put it on my window sill, as it is the only one I have." Florinda smiled, picked up her water can and went toward her home.

The next morning, Fran found her knife lying on the window sill. When Florinda came by for more water, she stopped and said, "Francisca, did you find your knife?"

"Oh yes," said Fran, "thank you very much." From then on, Florinda was a trusted friend.

It was in these daily challenges that Fran learned that the PC wasn't about big things so much as it was about the day-to-day events.

Another little problem developed on one of the many visits that the young people made into our home to entertain us. This time they continued well into the night with loud singing and laughter. We knew the neighbors would be trying to sleep. Fran also knew how to end the party. She slipped into the bedroom, to her secret hiding place, and hurriedly placed a piece of wrapped candy in a dish for everyone. Triumphantly reentering the room, she exclaimed, "For the wonderful party tonight, I have a treat for everyone." She was shocked when the first two girls grabbed all the candy and passed the empty dish on.

Fran ran over and grabbed the dish commanding, "Now, let's put all the candy back into the dish."

She again proceeded to pass the dish, explaining, "If everyone takes only one piece, there will be enough for all."

When it reached the last girl, there were two pieces, she reached for both pieces, then smiling, said, "Look, there is even one left for Francisca."

Fran also used her psychology on me. Later, when we retired, she passed the candy dish to me, this time with two pieces of candy. With a big smile, she said, "And you thought the party was all over!"

Eating our candy, we crawled into bed. She was right, the party was only starting!

Fran's seeds of friendship continued to grow and included special occasions like my birthday. On this day a lovely lady, Senora Rhina, walked nearly five miles along with her two daughters, to bring me a cake that said, "Happy Birthday Lew."

I accused Fran of planning it, but she denied it. Then she really did plan a birthday party that evening, attended by Louie and his wife. After they left, I turned to Fran.

"Okay, you little devil, what other surprise do you have?"

But she only smiled and held up her hands saying, "Honest, the only surprise was Louie. I knew nothing about that cake."

I held her close and said, "I don't know why, but I believe you."

It turned out that there was one more surprise — it came late that night when we both awakened suddenly by the sounds of a strumming guitar and several voices singing a ballad outside our bedroom window. I looked at Fran, but she whispered, "Honest, I didn't do it."

We sat up in bed, enjoying the beautiful music until it stopped, but just as we started to settle back in for the night, there was a strum again on the guitar, and the music started some more. I got up and whispered to Fran, "We'd better go out and see who this is, they might sing all night."

We wandered out in our pajamas, hoping they could not see us in the dark any better than we could see them. When they finished singing, we both softly clapped our hands and called out, "Very beautiful! We thank you! Do we know you?"

They laughed, "No, you do not know us." Then came the strum of the guitar and they started to sing again. I turned to Fran, who could only repeat, "Honest, I know nothing of this."

Thinking out loud, I said, "then this means they are serenading us in hopes of getting a little tip," so I went inside and got a few coins, which I gave to a youth who appeared to be their leader. He bowed in the moonlight as he said, "Gracias, Senor," and then disappeared in the dark.

As we re-entered our house, Fran said, "Now do you believe me?"

I answered, "Si, but it was a beautiful birthday surprise anyway."

219

Chapter 27
Hungry Today

One evening we were sitting on our porch, quietly relaxing, when Jose Ernandez Gonzales de Marco, one of our neighbors, approached in the fading twilight. As he came closer, and we recognized him, we invited him to join us. While Fran brought him a chair, he started to quickly tell us why he had stopped.

"I need your help," he said.

"Okay, we'll try," I said. "What is your problem?"

Jose looked me directly in the eye. "You have been living among us and will understand what I want to say," he began. "I am poor, very hungry and very unhappy."

It was easy to see that he was poor — he was barefoot and his calloused feet had probably never seen a pair of shoes. He wore no shirt, and his ribs could be seen plainly as the sweat rolled down his chest. Although he was still young, his smile already showed some missing teeth.

I nodded my head. "I understand, but why are you unhappy tonight?"

Jose looked at both of us. "I want to live a better life," he said. We were silent, so he continued. "You see, I don't know who my father is. I still live with my mother. She may know who my father is, but she never told me. He may be living near here and perhaps I could have other brothers and sisters here, too."

We kept listening patiently. "We understand all this, but we cannot change the past. What is your problem tonight?"

"Tell me how I can make lots of money."

I did not want to disappoint him, so I said, "Okay, Jose, it will not be easy, but I do have some ideas . . ."

For the next hour or so, we talked, while I outlined a plan I thought could at least get him started. What he needed first,

I explained, was access to a small piece of land for a long period of time. Jose told me he could get squatter's rights to some of his neighbor's property.

While the idea of using something that belonged to someone else was against my principles, Jose looked hopeful, so we continued. I next told him to get some ripe coconuts from the beaches, or the islands, wherever he could find them. I told him how, with some attention, we could get them to sprout and then plant them along with some mangos.

At each step of the way, Jose kept telling me he understood, but how was that going to make him rich?

"It will take time," I said. "But if you protect your seedlings and keep the grass and weeds away, in a few years you will have a beautiful, shaded area where you can raise pigs which you could buy from selling the coconuts. You could then sell the pigs, or butcher and sell your own meat. There are so many things you could do because now you have something to sell." I paused, then looked him in the eye. "Does that sound good to you, Jose?"

He was silent for a moment, then slowly got up from his chair and shook his head. "Mr. Lew, you do not understand. I am not concerned about 10 years from now. I am hungry right now. I will go to bed hungry tonight. God only knows, 10 years from now, I may not even be alive. I'm hungry today!"

We watched as he turned his back to us and slowly walked away, a strange sadness growing inside of us. How could we ask these people to plan for tomorrow, when they had so many problems to solve today?

Chapter 28
The Tourist's Unexpected Tour

More often than not, when we planned to do one thing, we ended up doing something completely different. You had to be pretty flexible and not be disappointed easily to survive in the D.R.

I had been an active member in the Lions Club in Ohio, and, since it was an International organization, I figured there might be a club in Santo Domingo. I kept asking about it each time we visited the capital until finally someone remembered seeing a Lions Club meeting sign in the lobby of the Hotel Embajadore. So one day, we stopped at the hotel and sure enough, there was a sign reading, "Lions Club meets here the first Monday of every month." I inquired at the desk but neither the desk clerk nor the manager was of much help.

"But you have a sign in the lobby that says they meet here on Mondays," I said.

"Oh yes," said the manager, "they did meet here, but that was over a year ago."

"Then why do you keep the sign up?"

"We haven't found anything else to put there," he replied. I had been here long enough to understand the good logic in that statement.

I walked back over to Fran who had been busy watching the people. "Who do you think that nice looking, American lady is?" she asked, pointing out a very beautiful woman to me. "She seems to be wandering around like she has nothing to do. I think we should go over and talk to her."

I gave the lady a quick once over. She almost looked like she was ready for a fashion show. Her shiny black hair was well groomed, and her clothes were of the latest style and in excellent taste. We watched her, as she walked gracefully in her high heeled shoes; all indications were that she was well-educated or was raised in a family with a good social background.

I was hesitant. "Maybe she is not alone here in the D.R.," I said.

But Fran still wanted to go over and talk to her. "She may need help," she insisted. "Remember how we felt here for the first time? And we had each other."

So we went over. The woman, whose name was Audrey Pico, was startled at first, but quickly warmed up to us. She lived in New York and worked for Pan Am Airlines and was here to check on the service of the Hotel Embajador, which Pan Am owned.

"What an interesting job!" Fran said, but Audrey shook her head. This was her third trip down here, but since she knew no one, she always stayed in the hotel.

"Actually," she said, "it's rather boring." Fran and I looked at each other (she gave me an "I told you so" look) and we both invited Miss Pico to spend the day with us at Villa Mella. "I'll guarantee that you will not be bored!" Fran said.

Audrey decided to give it a try, so we quickly made arrangements to pick her up the next morning. Fran told her to wear her most comfortable walking shoes and a plain, simple dress. "Wear no make-up and leave all your jewelry at the hotel," Fran said. We also warned her that her transportation would likely be an old dirty farm pickup truck, but she must have really been bored for she became more enthused as we talked.

"I'll look at it all like a new experience," she said. "I'll be ready!"

The next day, Audrey and Fran spent the day walking to the homes of our many different neighbors. At first, Audrey followed Fran and did nothing but stand and look. But before the day was over, Fran had her holding hands with the children and even got a few of them to sit on her lap whenever they stopped to rest or visit.

At our house, Audrey ended up sitting on the ground, helping our neighbor girls wash clothes. Her own dress, already soiled from a day in Villa Mella, only got more dirty in the

223

process, but she looked up at Fran and said, "You know, Fran, I'm never going to wash this dress. I will keep it dirty forever as a remembrance of this day."

That night, as we drove her back to the capital, Audrey could not stop talking about her experiences, or her gratitude to us for showing her a glimpse of a different side of the D.R. "Is there anything I can do for you to show my appreciation?" she kept asking.

Fran looked at me and then at her and then said something that surprised us both. "There is something you can do for me. I would love a hot bath."

"No problem," Audrey replied. "As your neighbors would say, "mi hot tub es su hot tub" and smiled.

As soon as we entered her hotel room, Fran and I argued about who would go first, while Audrey called the front desk to order us pina coladas. In the end, Fran let me go, saying, "You first, because I might stay in there all night."

I wasted no time. I filled the tub until it felt like a jacuzzi and jumped in. In a few minutes, there was a gentle tap on the door and Fran's voice said, "Your piña colada is here. If you don't come out in five minutes, I'm going to drink it."

"No, you're not. You are going to bring it in here!" I said, then added in a pleading tone, "Please?"

There was a pause, then Fran graciously entered, placing the glass in my outstretched hand. "Oh, for the easy life of a Peace Corps Volunteer," I said to myself, as I settled back to enjoy the tub, siping on my piña colada. But all too soon Fran finished her drink and came charging back into the bathroom.

"Okay, sir," she said, "your easy life is about to come to an end."

"No way," I said, sinking back into the tub.

"Oh yes," she said and reached in and turned on the shower. On her way out, I heard her tell Audrey, "A little cold water has changed many a man's mind!"

While Fran took her turn, Audrey and I had the opportunity to visit a little more. "I suppose you think Fran and I are crazy for living out here in the country and missing so many of the good things in life," I said.

"Oh no," she said, leaning forward in her chair. "Just the opposite. I envy you two very much. You are having a beautiful adventure. I see you as having an experience no money can buy. You are living life to its fullest."

As we drove home that evening, I reached over for Fran's hand, and thanked her for insisting that we introduce ourselves to Audrey Pico. She had made us both feel good, physically and mentally.

"Yes," said Fran, "I guess we both need that once in a while."

"Si," I said.

Chapter 29
Inner Voices

Some of our most enjoyable times in the PC were the short one or two day trips we made into the heart of the Island to visit compensinos (small farmers) who had received Heifer Project animals. Most of these farmers had minimal contact with the outside world, but they proved to be some of the nicest people that I have had the privilege to meet. They were eager for my visit and would follow my suggestions. I do believe that if I had told them to let their family sleep out under the palms so their cow could sleep in the house, they would have done it.

One day, I visited an extremely beautiful family consisting of a father, mother, eight girls and one boy, about 12 years old. As with most families, when I was about to leave, they wanted to give me something to thank me. Usually it was something from their garden, and while I knew it was a sacrifice for them, I usually accepted, because it would have hurt their feelings not to honor their gesture.

This particular family insisted on giving me a coconut from one of their trees. The father directed his son to climb a tree and pick a nice one for their "American friend." I watched as he hesitated, then walked toward the tallest tree. It looked a little dangerous, as the wind was blowing strongly, so I told the father, "It's not necessary. I'll return some other day when the weather is much nicer."

But the father told the boy to continue. He obediently and skillfully shimmied up the tree using his feet and toes as well as his hands and fingers to cling to the trunk of the tree. We were all tense by the time he reached the top, for by now both the boy and the tree were swaying in the wind.

"Hang on tightly with one hand," the father yelled up to him, "and then twist off the large coconut."

The boy wrapped his feet around the tree trunk, took a firm grip with one hand, and began reaching for the coconut. Just then, a gust of wind blew a large, sharp palm branch into the boy's face and his hands slipped. His outstretched arms and head were left dangling in the breeze, as he clung to the tree with only his feet. The father ran quickly beneath the tree in case the boy might fall, while the rest of us stood, frozen in our tracks, until the boy was able to pull himself up and regain his hold. He was successful at his next attempt and everyone was relieved as the coconut came tumbling to the ground, followed by the boy sliding rapidly back down the trunk. His mother gently patted the boy's head while his proud father gave me the coconut in his outstretched hands.

I thanked them and continued on my way, using a narrow footpath to take me to the next neighbor's home. The experience made me think — here I was, far away from home and friends, walking this dusty hot trail, sweaty and thirsty, with nothing to drink but the juice from a coconut, that I had no way to open. I started to feel sorry for myself and the big sacrifice I was making to be here, until I thought of how I'd gotten that coconut. That father had been willing to risk the life of his only son just to thank me. I walked on feeling I wasn't making much of a sacrifice after all.

Suddenly, a compensino approached me from the opposite direction with a machete hanging from his belt. When we met, his right hand reached for the machete and his left hand pointed at my coconut.

"Are you thirsty?" he asked. "I can open it for you." I watched as he skillfully sliced it open — no easy task — and then handed it back to me, smiling.

I took two swallows before I realized the man was now watching me intently. I guessed he had been working in the field all day and was probably thirsty, too, so I handed it back to him and said, "Please you have the rest, I do not want anymore."

He took it gratefully, our eyes meeting in a friendly gaze and then I walked on. Suddenly I remembered the words of

Audrey Pico, "You are having an adventure." My thinking was suddenly changed. I was no longer hot, tired or thirsty — I was enjoying a walk along a beautiful trail, with many friends. How lucky I was!

The Foundacion operated several agencies other than the Heifer Project and after Camilo came on board, I was asked to help out in other areas as well. One time, I was sent on a village-to-village survey to find their most urgent needs, and then draw up a list of recommendations about how the Foundacion could help them.

In most villages I visited, the experience followed a similar pattern. The people would be eager to talk to me, and share good, legitimate requests, like a water supply, marketing cooperatives for their crafts and farm products, sewing machines, small tools, and schools for adults as well as for children. I also discovered that it was hard for them to understand that I was only conducting a survey, and that they were not going to receive all these things just because they asked for them.

On my last stop, however, I received a totally different response. In this village, I was directed to an elderly gentleman whom everyone seemed to love and respect. He was partially bald, with gray hair around the sides and back of his head and a neat, well-trimmed beard to match. He was a big man, well over six feet, and in very good health, and when he spoke, his wrinkles were accented by the bright sunlight.

I asked my questions and he answered immediately, without hesitation. "My people most need a baseball stadium and a first-class ball diamond with good equipment," he said.

His comment took me by surprise, for as I walked through his village, I had seen many children with large stomachs, indicating parasites and starvation, filth in their streets, and poor housing. And he wanted a baseball stadium?

"We have tremendous athletic talent in our young men and boys," he explained, laying down his pipe and speaking in great earnestness. "With the proper facilities and equipment, one day one or more of them could become a superstar on one of your major league baseball teams." He then grasped my arm and moved close to me, speaking in a low voice. "Do you understand? They would become **rich**. They would never forget us, and would return to help us with all these things you see we need." Then he released his grip on my arm and backed away a step, but still held my gaze. "You see, my friend, in this way we could have the chance to solve our own problems. Do you understand?"

I understood. These people did not want handouts, or others to do things for them. What they needed most were the means to help themselves.

"Yes," I said, "I understand. I will report to the Foundacion the things you have told me. Now, do you understand that I may not be able to grant you your request?" This time, he nodded his head and said he understood.

I kept my word and discussed it all with the Foundacion. While they heard me out, their answer, as I feared, was that all the people and agencies contributing money would be a little upset to see their dollars used to build a modern baseball stadium out in the middle of the country. But the words of the elderly gentlemen in that small village kept ringing in my ears. Maybe he was a wiser person than me and all the agencies put together.

Chapter 30
A Court For All

Alone, just the two of us, Fran and I could achieve very little in the D.R. To accomplish even the smallest of projects it took the cooperation of many agencies and many people. But sometimes, we could be the catalyst that brought those people and agencies together — and sometimes, that was all that was needed.

One of the most successful programs we worked on started at a meeting between Padre Miguel and Andre Royes, the school headmaster. Now, just getting the two of them to sit together was quite an accomplishment for Fran and me, so if they could agree to anything, it would be icing on the cake.

To get them to come, Fran had to talk with each fo them separately. They were both leaders in the community, but while the Padre was very dedicated to his church, the schoolmaster never attended Mass or church activities and often inferred that the church was limiting community growth by draining the people of their time and money.

The Padre, on the other hand, hinted to us that the schoolmaster limited religion and community growth by scheduling youth meetings on Sunday mornings and church holidays. But somehow, we thought that no matter when Andre scheduled his meetings he would have attracted the crowd, for the boys were fascinated by his interest in karate, and the girls by his dark, wavy hair.

When they arrived for the meeting, Fran and I were both a little nervous, especially sitting between the two men. But as long as we kept the subject on their common interest of helping the people and improving living conditions, they both were very cooperative.

Fran started the meeting by saying that we should first do some American "brainstorming," and then going on to explain exactly what she meant by that.

"We start out by dreaming big dreams," she said.

"That sounds easy," said Andre Royes, "We're always doing that."

"Good," said Fran, "then you start."

The schoolmaster jumped in eagerly. "I would like to see a modern sports facility for the youth. A new baseball field with grandstands and lights. A new air-conditioned basketball auditorium. A whole sports complex."

Padre Miguel interrupted. "I would like to have an organ in my church, fresh milk for all the children, playground equipment in the park, clothing available at a minimum price for the people, a train or modern bus service to the capital, and telephones in all the homes." He smiled and hesitated a moment, then added, "I can keep on going if you wish."

"I think that might be enough," Fran said. "Let's sort out the things we might be able to do."

For the first time in the meeting, there was a pause in the conversation, but then both men got rolling again. Soon the idea for an outdoor basketball court began to take shape, one that could be built in the large open space between the church and school. "It could be used by the school for basketball and volleyball, and by the church for large activities," said Andre.

Fran and I remained silent while the two men talked. They were making good progress. But then Andre turned to us and said, "but we have one big problem — no money to buy equipment."

The Padre seemed in deep thought, then said, "Maybe I could convince Catholic Relief Service to help a little."

I sensed this was a turning point so I was quick to jump on the band wagon, "We could use our influence with other angecies," I said.

Andre leaned forward in his hair. "And I could organize the youth to help do some work. That way they could help raise money for the basketball court."

At this, Fran nearly jumped out of her chair. This was what we had been working so hard to see happen — the people working together to help themselves. She threw her hands in the air and exclaimed, "This may work!"

The four of us departed with hearty handshakes all around. We weren't sure how the Padre and Andre felt, but Fran and I were bubbling over with enthusiasm. "This could be the start of real progress for Villa Mella!" Fran said.

The next morning Fran was ready to leave for the capital at daybreak, so anxious was she to push the basketball project forward while everyone was in a cooperative mood. I tried to calm her down so that she wouldn't be disappointed if things didn't work out, but she was determined.

"I know that things may not work out, but we have to start now and show an example of following through on our agreements," she said.

I agreed, and canceled my other arrangements for the day to go with her. This was the time I knew I had to give her my full support, just as she had done for me so often in my work on the farm.

The first agency we saw was Church World Service, where we had visited several times before. We rattled off the list of things we needed — baseballs, bats, basketballs, a truck load of lumber — but the director shook his head to each one, until we came to clothing.

"Clothing? I have lots of that!" he said, leading us to a warehouse full of bales of clean, used clothing sent from the United States, most of which had just recently arrived.

"Our problem is distribution," he explained. "The last time we started giving away clothing, people came from all directions. We soon ran out. Those that received were happy, but those that didn't, were angry."

We nodded to all he said. We had had a similar experience one night when we decided to make some popcorn. The sound and scent attracted the neighbor children, and without thinking, I handed one of them a few kernels out of the window. Soon there were more children than we could feed, and we ran out of popcorn. But they just kept on coming. We finally had to close the shutters on the windows, but even then, we could still hear the children tapping, wanting more. In our process of making a few people happy, we made many unhappy because they went to bed hungry.

"If you have any suggestions," the director said, "please let me know." We looked around. The piles and piles of clothes were the ingredients we needed. We just had to come up with a way to make it work.

Suddenly I had an idea. "Let's take the clothes from here and let the youth group sell them in Villa Mella for a few pennies apiece. The money they raise could go toward the basketball court."

Fran nodded. "It makes sense. The agency can distribute the clothes without the worry of making someone angry, the Padre can get used clothing for his people, the youth can make some money, and we can use it to build the court. Everyone would have a hand in it."

The director liked the idea, and said he would recommend it to his superiors. "I'm sure they will agree, so long as you give me a full written report on the details of the sale, and any suggestions you might have for future projects."

The next day we met again with Padre Miguel and the schoolmaster, who both accepted the idea whole-heartedly. Andre even offered the use of the school building for the sale, and the help of 10 or 12 of his best youth to help us.

We set the date for a week from that Saturday, and Fran spent most of the next week alternating between nervousness and excitement. Finally, on the Friday before the sale, we took the Jeep to pick up the clothes, waiting until after dark to return so that no one could see what we were carrying. We didn't want people to know about the sale ahead of time, as this could cause difficulty if some heard before others.

Early the next morning, we left for Villa Mella. We arrived to the welcome sight of several youths waiting for us. They were very quick about helping us carry the bales of clothing into the school building and just as quick to burst them open. Naturally, their first reaction was to dig into the piles to find something for themselves, but Fran soon stopped the fun.

"These are to sell, remember?" she said. But our hearts went out to them, especially little Carmelitta, who moaned, "Qua Paina," (too bad) as she put a very pretty dress back on the pile.

We put the youth to work helping us to divide up the clothes into stacks and to carry them to different rooms, so that we could distribute them easier among the crowd. There were three rooms, and while Fran worked to divide the clothes in one, I worked within another. Unfortunately, this left one room unsupervised, and naturally, a little hanky-panky went on. One girl came strutting toward Fran, wearing a dress twice her size with a blouse on of matching colors, flopping over her shoulder.

"Do I look like one of those rich New York society ladies?" she asked.

"No," said Fran laughing, "you look like a Dominican clown."

Then a boy entered with a lady's dress on, wearing a bra on the outside of it. He placed his hand on his hips and asked in a beautiful falsetto voice, "anyone want a date?"

I gave him a date all right, I sent him off to the police station to get two officers to come over in case we had any problems — but not before Fran made him change his clothes!

After we got the clothes sorted, Fran set about pricing them — most at one cent, though some were five cents and the very best, 10 cents.

In the meantime, I organized things outside. I put a card table near the entrance with a large sheet of paper on it for each lady to sign her name. I planned to give each one a number in the order that she arrived, so that there would be no pushing or fighting to get in. A new lady could go in as each one exited and paid Fran, who was the acting treasurer. To make sure the clothes lasted all day, we limited each person to no more than three pieces of clothing or 15 cents worth of purchases.

At last, things were ready to go — but since no one knew what was to happen, only a few curious people came by to sign up at first. This was great, as it gave us time to see if our system of handling the crowd would work. Fran and I stayed outside to watch the line, the youth stayed in the rooms to watch if anyone needed any help, and the policemen, who were well liked by the villagers, insured that everyone followed the rules.

After a few of the ladies had bought their clothes and told their friends, things began to move at a much faster pace. The children told us later that inside it was a three-ring circus, as ladies grabbed and threw clothes everywhere trying to find the right article. We could have saved a lot of work of sorting and hanging up, for the ladies seemed to like the throwing and hunting best of all.

By the end of the day it was evident that the sale had been a huge success. Everyone who was willing to, or could, spare a few pennies had a chance to shop, leaving only a few well-worn articles left. We gave these to a couple of ladies with no pennies to buy anything, who had been lingering around most of the day. Then, they, like their neighbors, left with happy smiles.

The clothes were gone, leaving Fran and me with tired feet, eyes and minds. But there was joy in our hearts as we gathered with our friends in the shade of the school building afterward, especially when one of the ladies returned to show us her new dress. The youth had stayed all day, even Carmelitta, who had so wanted the one dress that Fran made her put back.

"That's okay," she said, "we were helping you!"

With a smile, Fran closed the lid on the money box, and handed it to Andre, so that Carmelitta and the others could see. "You were not only helping us, you were helping yourselves," she said. "The money you earned today will go toward the recreation center. If we continue to work together, we should have it very soon."

One of the boys thought that was good news, and smacked my palm in the air saying, "Amigo, we shall do!"

We had one final meeting with Padre and Andre, where we learned that the clothing sale had raised enough money to buy stone and an oil base to make a hard, level surface for the recreation area. All that remained was to carry out our promise of contacting the other agencies for additional supplies. When we told them our story of how the youth had raised the money, and how the church and school had worked together, they all contributed something to help.

When we left Villa Mella, the recreation center stood as a lasting reminder of the fact we had made a difference. But ever more importantly, it was a reminder to the youth, that when they worked together, they could accomplish things. And that would be important long after we left, for the next projects would be tougher and up to them alone.

The outside basketball/volleyball court soon became a busy place for all.

Chapter 31
Tres Weddings

There came the time, when out of the blue, Fran was invited to three weddings.

An American wedding invitation came from our son, Steve. He was going to marry his college sweetheart, Jo Ellen Dowling. In the same mail was an invitation for an American-Dominican wedding between Pat, a PCV and former Catholic nun, and a Dominican street vendor. The third wedding invitation came at the last minute and it was as typically Dominican as anything we had ever experienced yet.

Despite the fact we had little time to make arrangements, Fran decided she needed a new original "Dominican" dress for all these social events. She decided to go to a seamstress in town to have one made.

Her visit proved to be most interesting. The seamstress assured Fran she could make it in a week, though she had only a foot-powered sewing machine and hand scissors. She had no patterns so Fran sketched out the dress she had in mind on a piece of paper. The seamstress quickly measured Fran and told her to buy 3¼ yards of material. She never wrote anything down.

After her visit, Fran felt a little uneasy, but decided it best to demonstrate confidence in the woman, so she returned the next day with the material plus a zipper for the back.

The seamstress shook her head. "The material is fine, but the zipper is too long. Here we use only short zippers, and we don't even usually zip them up. It's cooler that way, you know."

Fran knew that well, but told the woman, "I am going to wear the dress in America, where it is not as hot."

The seamstress smiled and asked Fran to come back in three days to try it on. Fran left, more concerned than ever, as this was only two days before we were to leave for Steve's wedding. But when she returned, she was amazed to find that the dress was just as she had imagined and fit almost perfectly, even though the woman had kept all the measurements in her head — only a few small adjustments were needed before Fran could finally pick it up. When she did, she was even more amazed than ever, for the dress was perfect, and only a three inch scrap of material was left over. The only flaw was the zipper, which the woman had sewn only half-way in, leaving part of the zipper dangling free inside the dress.

Once Fran had her dress, we organized everything else for Steve's wedding. This was fortunate, for Fran received invitation number three only a few hours later, all on the day before we were to leave.

Our neighbor Juanita came to the door late that afternoon, asking Fran if she wanted to go to a wedding in a nearby home of the neighborhood. Though Juanita had said it was close, it was more like a half mile walk, but Fran didn't mind, as it was fun to walk with Juanita and her mother and the several other ladies who met them along the way. Finally they arrived at the home, where some other ladies greeted them with the news that the wedding was going to be at the church instead.

Juanita led the rush back to the road to flag down a publico. Fortunately two came along, but with all the ladies pushing and shoving to get in, Fran somehow ended up being left behind. There wasn't much she could do but wait until another one came along. So Fran made up her mind that whatever direction it was going — to Villa Mella or to our home — she was taking it. Fortunately one came along quickly headed toward town, so once more Fran was going to a wedding.

When she arrived at the church, she found about 25 women and three men (including the groom) present, and the Padre pronouncing the blessing. Then the bride and groom stopped to sign some documents at the altar, while everyone else left. Alone once more, Fran waited until the bride and groom walked down the aisle with Padre following. The padre told

Fran he was to have married the couple at the bride's home at 6 p.m., but they had showed up at the church at 5:30 p.m. instead.

"What happens next?" Fran asked.

"There should be a big fiesta at the home," the Padre replied, "that's where everyone has gone." Fran looked out the entrance of the church toward the road, just in time to see the last publico pull out with the bride and groom. She turned to the Padre and threw her hands in the air in frustration. "Most of the time I'm impatient here because things move too slow. Today things are moving too fast!"

"The ladies are not being rude," the Padre said, "you are just being too polite. This is good, because it shows that the ladies are now considering you as one of them. It is also good that you are showing good manners. Cheer up — you are doing a good job!"

About this time another publico pulled up and Fran ran after it, feeling better. "See, Fran, have faith in me," the Padre called after her.

When she arrived at the wedding reception, things were in full swing. About 50-75 adults, plus children, were gathered in and around the house. Juanita saw Fran climb out of the publico and came over to meet her. "Where have you been?" she asked, laughing, and then led Fran into the house to meet the bride and groom.

The newlyweds were both in their teens. The bride wore a white cotton dress and a head piece made of cheese cloth which hung in a straight panel down her back to about a foot above her ankles.

While the ladies served coffee and cake (which soon ran out), Fran spent most of her time milling around in the crowd, observing the action. She noticed a man carrying a fighting cock emerge from a publico and walk around to the back of the house, though no one seemed to pay any attention to him.

When it was starting to get dark and most of the people were leaving, Juanita's mother took Fran's hand and said, "Come, we will say hello to my compadres." She led Fran to

239

the next home, which was only about 10 feet away, where they entered to find two men eating by the light of a tiny oil lamp. Both men stood up to give Mama a big hug, who turned to Fran and said, "I want you to meet the father of the bride."

Even though it was dark, Fran recognized him right away — he was the same man that had gotten out of the publico with the cock under his arm. Apparently he had attended a cockfight in the arena while his daughter was getting married less than one block away. Now he was eating with a friend next door instead of being at his daughter's wedding reception. "Will I ever understand this fascinating culture?" Fran asked herself.

Our trip home was very rushed and even shorter than the last trip in for Ron's wedding. We really never had time to talk about anything until we were once again on the plane headed back to Villa Mella. I looked at Fran and said, "Something has been bothering me. In the middle of Steve's wedding, right when Jo Ellen's father gave her in marriage, I had observed you laughng to yourself. What was so funny?"

Fran told me the story of how the bride's father had gone to a cockfight instead of his daughter's wedding in the D.R., and soon we were both laughing, thinking of the differences — of Fran's Dominican formal, and Jo Ellen's mother's American dress, of the nice wedding, and the reception at the Country Club. Fran began to wipe tears of laughter from her eyes.

"You better brace yourself, Fran, you still have one more wedding to go!" I told her.

Pat's wedding turned out to be an interesting combination of American and Dominican customs. It was held in a small Catholic Church in Santo Domingo. She wore an attractive street-length dress with a shoulder corsage, while Nini, the groom, looked handsome in a business suit. The priest performed a simple marriage ceremony, and then gave his blessing to the newly married couple.

From that point on the wedding became more Dominican, with many noisy people and, of course, children, rum and Coca

Cola, fried meat cakes and wedding cake. We stayed, like most of the guests until the food was gone, but Nini, who had changed clothes much earlier, had disappeared to join his buddies drinking rum.

The three quick weddings helped us to "crystalize" a lot of serious thinking we had been doing about the different culture and living patterns that exist throughout the world. Pat's wedding had been a blend of American and Dominican cultures, true, but both of these cultures are blends of others. The Dominicans have Spanish, Indian and African heritage, while our customs in the U.S. are a blend of even more nationalities. Cultures continue to change, just like the world we live in, where volcanoes, erosion, earthquakes and wars continually change the face of the land.

We now have the privilege of living in a world that is different than anyone has ever lived in before, and that no future generation will ever live in again. Were we, as Audrey Pico felt, really taking advantage of each opportunity to enjoy life to the fullest? Were we taking an active part in changing our world for the better? While we hoped then, as we do now, that the work we did in the D.R. made a difference, we recognized it for what it was — part of the continued exchange of ideas between countries that is as much a part of life as the changing of the seasons.

Chapter 32
A Wild Ride

Once it was recognized that the new farm manager was doing a good job and had the help of an experienced PC farm volunteer, there was a big increase in shipments of Heifer Project animals to the D.R. Each time a load arrived, Fran and I were called upon to meet it, especially when it was accompanied by visitors from the U.S. who donated to the project.

One such visit especially stands out. The visitors this time were Larry and Janet Rosenbohm, who owned and operated a beef cattle and grain farm near Graham, Missouri. We immediately took a liking to each other, although they were much younger than we were and still active in farming and raising their family. They were a delightful couple to entertain, and we visited several farms with Heifer Project animals, as well as Santo Domingo during their stay.

Things were pretty routine until their third and last day with us, when Dwight Walker, from the PC office, asked if I would be willing to take a trip inland with two young PC volunteers who, as the director put it, could be ''very adventurous.'' We persuaded Larry and Janet to extend their stay so that Larry could come along with me, while Janet visited longer with Fran in Villa Mella.

Bright and early the next morning Larry and I rode into the capital to meet the two young volunteers, Ed and Dick. Ed was tall and thin with blond hair and blue eyes, while Dick was shorter with a round face and straight dark hair, already thinning a little in front. Ed was seated behind the wheel of the PC Jeep when we arrived, and Dick jumped out so that Larry and I could climb in the back. Mr. Walker had warned me that this was the first time these two boys were being permitted the use of a PC vehicle other than a motorcycle, but

I figured it was safe enough as long as Larry and I were in the backseat as chaperones.

The wisdom of that could have been questioned from the moment we took off, for Ed had a heavy foot and soon we were speeding off down the road, our hair flying wildly. We joked and laughed and sang Spanish songs very loudly and off-key, with even Larry joining in.

Our first stop was a large farm managed by a Dominican priest which served as a collecting point for Heifer Project goats. Here the goats received special care for a short period of time to help them adjust to the new climate and living conditions. The priest had been expecting us and had coffee ready in a small dining area. After introducing ourselves, the farm manager became interested in Larry and wanted to know why this "American farmer" was along.

To give Larry a legitimate excuse for accompanying us, I told the priest that Mr. Rosenbohm was a well known "goat expert" from Missouri visiting for a few days with Heifer Project and that we had insisted he join us. This excited the priest, who from then on directed much of his speech at Larry. Since neither spoke the other's language, Larry had a good excuse to dodge the technical questions and still be believable as a "goat expert."

After coffee, the priest insisted on taking us out to the field, where the goats were running free in large lots and where several workers were to meet us. On the way over, Larry pulled me aside and said, "Lew, I raise hogs and beef cattle at home. I know nothing about goats!"

I put my arm on his shoulder. "Relax. Over here an American farmer like you is an expert on all agricultural subjects. Besides, none of us knows anything about goats either."

Soon we had all gathered in the middle of a large field, with several hundred goats running free around us. The farm manager and the foreman explained their program to us, and then turned to Larry and asked if he had any questions. "No, it appears you are doing a fine job," he said, but seeing that they wanted more from him, he decided to get into the part.

"Would it be possible for me to examine that goat?" he asked, pointing out one of the herd.

The foreman signaled and directed his men to catch the goat — which was not that easy. For a while it looked like a wild west goat rodeo, with men and goats running in all directions. In the midst of the commotion, I moved over beside Larry and quietly asked him what he was doing.

"I'm stalling for time trying to think what a goat expert would do in this situation," he said. Soon hard-breathing men came over carrying a bleating nanny goat. Larry put on a good show as, in a very professional manner, he checked its teeth and eyes. Then he noticed a small metal tag attached to one of its ears and took a note pad from his pocket and recorded the number very officially. "She has a little age on her," he said, releasing the goat, "but in all, seems satisfactory. Bring me another one.

In all, Larry checked four different goats, then placed the pad in his pocket, saying that he would do some checking on the goats' breeding back home and complimented the priest on his fine work.

As we reached the highway again Ed said, "Lew you never told us Larry was an authority on goats."

"He also never told me!" Larry said, and we all laughed. "Are there any more surprises I should know about?" Larry asked me.

"Probably," I said, "but I don't know what they'll be just yet!"

For the rest of the day things went well, and I became impressed with the knowledge of the young volunteers and the business-like manner in which they conducted themselves.

At the end of the second day, however, the PC director's warning came true. It was late in the afternoon, and Ed looked at his watch and said, "We have a big problem. There's no way we can make it to our next scheduled visit where our lodging is."

Before Larry or I could suggest anything, Dick took a look at the map, "I know this territory well," he said, "If we take a sharp turn here, we can make it. Turn right!" We lurched onto a dirt road winding around and down a steep mountainside, barely wide enough for two burros to pass.

"What if we meet another car?" I asked.

"Don't worry, I doubt if any cars use this trail!" Ed yelled.

"What if we meet a donkey?"

"That will be the donkey's problem!" Ed replied.

We kept winding down the hill with Ed continually blowing his horn — until it started to rain. Soon, Ed needed both hands to try and control the Jeep to keep it from slipping around each curve. I glanced out the window at one point to see our wheel within inches of the road's edge, with no guard rail to protect us from tumbling over it.

I put my hand on Larry's leg. "I think we should start to pray!" I said.

"I've already started!" said Larry, staring straight ahead.

When we reached the bottom of the mountain, Ed stopped the car and gave a big sigh of relief. "I never want to do that again! Take over, Dick, I've had it." Dick was very calm, telling us all that there was a new highway ahead and that we were going to make it.

We drove for a short distance and came to a village with what looked like a motel. It wasn't our scheduled stop, but Dick thought we could work something out. In fact, he seemed happy when Larry and I agreed that we should stop here instead of continuing on.

As we entered, we found out why, for it was obvious this was not an ordinary hotel. A lady greeted us, then seated us around a large table. Another girl came in immediately with coffee for all of us. Before we could drink it, girls were coming from all directions to join us.

Larry looked at me. "I think you just sprung another surprise on me," he said. While I was trying to explain that this was just as big a surprise to me, a girl started to rub her hand through Larry's sparse head of hair, saying "El es mi novio (He is my boyfriend)?"

Larry smiled, then told her, "Sorry, I don't understand a word of Spanish." Because she didn't understand a word

245

of English, she left him to join me. Even though I understood her, I followed Larry's lead and told her the same thing.

The strategy worked perfectly, as soon as we were left alone. The first lady who had welcomed us, then approached us and asked in English if we would like a bed for the night. She led us up a stairway, using a small oil lamp to guide us.

Our room was anything but a luxury suite. There were two bunk beds with well-worn mattresses, no springs no pillows, no covers and a large opening in the wall, looking right out into the outdoors. Our hostess took the lamp with her when she left, leaving the two of us to enjoy the room by the moonlight coming through the hole in the wall.

We finally got settled on the lumpy beds, stumbling against each other as we removed our dirty trousers. But, the mosquitoes had other plans. Attracted by the smell of good American flesh, they must have come in for miles. Simultaneously, we jumped out of our beds, banging our heads together, while feeling around in the dark for our trousers. We collapsed on our beds, laughing so hard we could hardly talk.

"If our wives could see us now!" Larry said.

"Shall we tell them about this?" I asked.

"NEVER!" Larry answered.

Meanwhile, Janet and Fran were having a good time in Villa Mella too. While the sleeping arrangements were a little better, Janet had a hard time sleeping on our beds made of plywood propped on stacks of books. Distracted by the electric fan, she ended up getting caught in the mosquito netting, where she stayed until Fran woke up to help her.

The day before she had had a good run-in with some chickens in a publico. When Janet had started to back out of one that had chickens on the floor, Fran had pushed her back in saying, "Relax, livestock ride first class here!"

Janet saw Dominican baking standards firsthand by watching boys dump hot loaves of unwrapped bread onto the sidewalk to count them. For lunch the girls went to our favorite pizza store. After two hours of drinking coffee and waiting, they were told no one was there to make the pizza. In all, the girls thought they had quite an adventurous tale to tell us!

The next evening, Larry and I returned home, smiling but weary from our travels. Janet's first question was, "How was your trip — did anything unusual happen?"

Larry thought for a minute, then said, "No, not exactly. We saw lots of farms and countryside. It was 'very educational.' How about you?"

"We had all kinds of excitement," Janet said, and then approached Larry to try and coax him into staying longer once again. "You may never have this opportunity again," she said.

Fran came close to me, saying, "PC is not for everyone, but I think Janet would make it. How about Larry?"

I just smiled and said, "Si."

Chapter 33
Bloom Where You Are

We always welcomed our contacts with American visitors during our two years as volunteers. Our guests welcomed having a knowledgeable guide, while they in return brought us new, fresh views and observations that helped us keep our PC experience in perspective.

This was extremely valuable to us, as once we became used to our daily routine, we were sometimes almost callous to some of the very problems we'd come to solve, just as we'd grown used to the heat and climate. The observations of one of our guests, Herman Schoenberger, while visiting the Foundacion farm had one of the biggest impacts on me.

I had just finished showing him the livestock and then pointed out a hibiscus hedge on the farm that had always fascinated me. The workers had severely trimmed the old bushes, cutting them so close to the ground that I figured they would die. But the bush had rebounded into another vigorous, healthy plant with beautiful flowers. Even more amazing were the new bushes that grew from stems that the workers had stripped the leaves off and had poked into the ground. While some had died, many took root in the rich soil, and thanks to the sun and rain, they too, had grown into large bushes with beautiful flowers.

While I was marveling at this, Herman had drifted away to something that interested him even more — a small plant that was struggling to grow on the side of an old concrete wall. The frail, spindly little stem had somehow succeeded in bursting out into a single, little flower with four dainty-yellow petals, proudly swaying in the breeze.

"Now, this is what impresses me," he said, pointing it out to me.

I stopped in my tracks and stared at it with him. I had been working nearly everyday within a few feet of it, and had missed it. The hibiscus were beautiful, yes, but this was truly a Dominican flower. God had caused the seed to be placed on this barren, concrete wall, but somehow it had sprouted. No one had transplanted it into fertile soil. No one saw or cared about its problem to survive. The seed had only one choice, to struggle to bloom where it was planted. After months of life in the D.R. wondering what, why, and how — here was the answer to all our PC experiences, summed up in one tiny flower, "Bloom where you are."

That image stayed with me throughout the rest of our time in the D.R., and long after, but it never hit home more profoundly than it did a few days later, when Kiki posed to us the toughest challenge of our PC careers.

She had come to visit us often during our stay, always brightening our days with her beautiful songs. But one day, Kiki, was so very quiet, just sitting in our chair, when Fran went over and asked her if anything was wrong.

"I have been doing lots of thinking," she said.

"It's good to do that," Fran said, placing her hand on her shoulder. "Do you want to tell me about it?"

Kiki was silent for a moment, than jumped to her feet in a completely different mood. "I sing for you!" she cried, and began making up the song as she went along. But this time there was a message for us, "If you go, don't leave me behind, I your friend. I go with you, I do what you do."

As she sang, Fran and I exchanged glances, listening intently to her words. When she stopped, she looked at both of us and said, "You understand?"

I joined Fran by Kiki's side. "Yes, we understand," I said. We had often wished Kiki could go with us — we had come to love her and were sure that with her talents, she would blossom in the U.S. But until now, we hadn't known Kiki's thoughts on the matter. "There may be many problems involved for you to leave your country, and more problems when you got outside," I hesitated, "Do you understand?"

Kiki nodded her head. "Si, but I would be with you!"

Fran clutched Kiki's hand. "You go home now, Lew and I must talk about a lot of things."

After she left, Fran gave a big sigh. "Well, we got what we asked for," she said. "What do you think?"

I shook my head. "There are too many things against her. She has had only three years of schooling, and her entire life has been spent running around in bare feet, dressed in rags. Can you imagine the adjustments she would need to make?"

Fran thought a minute. "There's more. Many times she told me she was eagerly looking forward to getting married and having a family. Plus, she is very close with her mother and sister, Francesca."

Fran and I were thinking the same thing. Kiki knew only of this culture. Here, she was able to sing and laugh. She was a very beautiful, young and fragile girl and drastic changes could easily shatter all we loved about her. On the other hand, we were (and still are) both strong believers in exchange programs between nations that create better understanding and promote peace. But we couldn't introduce Kiki to the U.S. without changing her life completely, and that wasn't fair.

"So," I said, "how are we going to tell her?"

While we were talking, Fran looked over and spotted some paper and crayons that she often used with the children. "Maybe a picture would help," she said. I watched as she drew a flower pot with a single stem reaching high, with a single blooming flower. I looked at it. It was the Dominican flower on the wall at the farm. It was the story of the D.R. It was Kiki. It was perfect. The flower pot was the D.R., where the seed had been planted. She was the flower. If we were to transplant this flower into a different type of soil where it snowed and froze, it could wither and never bloom. Kiki might understand that.

The next morning, Fran took the paper with her and went over to talk with Kiki and her mother. When she arrived, they were discussing the very same subject. They listened intently while Fran tacked the drawing to the wall and explained it to them.

"You must bloom where you are," she told Kiki.

Kiki was silent. Mama placed her hand on Kiki's shoulder. "Fran is right, you stay here."

Kiki looked Fran in the eye. "I never, never, never want to see you again!"

Fran was slow to answer. "I hope we meet again, but in the meantime, I will always remember you as a beautiful flower. Whenever I smell the fragrance of a blossom, I will think of you." She paused, then added, "You see, you will always be with me."

Kiki hesitated then replied, "Then when I smell a fragrance of a flower, I think of you." She then seemed completely changed. Laughing she said, "I get married, I have lots of kids, and I have big flower garden."

As Fran left the home, Kiki yelled, "Before you leave us, I gather the neighbors, we come to your home and sing and dance for you and Lew. You like?"

Fran waved back. "Si, mucho!"

As the time went by and more and more people learned we were soon going home, more and more of them asked us to take them to America too. Thanks to Kiki, we had an answer. "We understand that life can be difficult here," we told them, "but this means you must work that much harder, dig in with all your might, and bloom where you are."

Chapter 34
A Real Family Outing

One of the brightest stars among the volunteers was Lucy Marks, a beautiful blue-eyed blonde from Wisconsin, who always had a smile and a positive attitude. One day, she came bouncing into the Peace Corps library while Fran and I were checking on a few books. As we talked, and Lucy realized that we would be leaving in only two months, we all became rather serious, realizing how tough it would be to say good-bye to each other and all the volunteers.

"I know what we'll have to do," Lucy said, "we'll have a big farewell party!" She was always good at spur-of-the-moment ideas, and before we knew it, plans were in motion for an old fashioned picnic, complete with games and contests, to be held at the Foundacion farm where I worked. Another PC volunteer, Janet Klepper, came up just then and we quickly drafted her to help on the planning committee.

The plans evolved to include a volleyball match between the PC volunteers and the Villa Mella youth on their new basketball court in the morning, followed by a softball game betwen officers and employees of the Foundacion and the volunteers in the afternoon. Janet got into the swing of things and agreed to get the food from the cooperative where she worked and organize a committee to do the cooking.

Lucy was now all gung-ho and ready to go. "I'm going to write a letter today to every volunteer," she said. "Let's set the date for one month from today to give everyone time to plan their work so they can be here." "Let's all call it The First Annual PCV — Dominican fun day," I added. Fran and I were glad as we liked this idea much better than a farewell party.

The response to the invitations was great. Volunteers started to pour into the capital from every corner of the island the

Dominican ladies teach PC volunteers to pluck and dress chickens.

day before the party. Janet soon had more than enough people to help her prepare the food. It was a very cooperative adventure, as two of the Dominican ladies from the farm worked side by side with the American volunteers. Together they cleaned 12 chickens, starting from scratch by chopping off heads and plucking feathers by hand. But it was fun, as one of the volunteers remarked, "I don't know about the rest of you, but I'm having a ball!"

In true Dominican style, the volleyball game turned into something a little different from the youth group/PCV challenge I had envisioned. When I had contacted the youth group in Villa Mella to make arrangements for the match, I had tried to build a little enthusiasm into the game by saying, "The volunteers love to play volleyball. It would make me happy if you could beat them." They took the challenge seriously, and at game time, six strong, very athletic young men came

253

strolling onto the court dressed in matching, shiny black shorts. They definitely weren't our local youth group! Once we saw them warm up, we realized the Dominicans had imported some outside talent.

The six Dominicans proved to be a very well organized team, setting up the ball to each other, and then spiking it hard at the volunteers. It was a short game, and the Dominicans won it 15-0. Then they won the second game 15-0, even though the women and some of the less athletic boys had dropped off the American team.

For the third game, the Dominicans proved to be good sports. They gave the entire court to the volunteers for a game among themselves, and mingled among the players, giving a few tips and demonstrations on how to play. So, it was not a complete flop — it gave us something to joke about and it was good for the Dominicans to beat us and see us smile in defeat. It also helped their egos to be teaching the volunteers.

Now it was time for the next big event, the softball game at the farm. Unfortunately, we forgot to arrange for transportation out there, but several publicos came to the rescue, saying they would take us for free, if they could be part of the party. Things were growing — for now, in addition to the drivers, the Dominican volleyball team and the youth club were all part of the happenings.

When it came time for the game, we were in for another surprise. After the Foundacion office received my challenge for a softball game, they had held a practice session. Everyone enjoyed it so they organized an official team, buying new gloves, equipment and flashy, matching orange shirts for their team. The Foundacion boys really looked sharp, practicing on the field with their new uniforms, and our boys were getting worried.

"Looks like another set-up to me," one said.

"Yeah, and not in our favor," said another.

"Relax, some of those boys look a little old to be playing softball."

"That just means they have more experience."

"Where is Lew? He gets us into this, then disappears."

"He's probably getting a truck load of half-starved kids to go through the chow line ahead of us."

I was, in fact, helping with the food, but only in trying to get everything set up at the guest house where we were to eat. I could hear the game in the distance and my mind started to wander, so the women pushed me out the door saying, "You are starting to get in the way — go to the ballgame!"

When I arrived, the volunteers were actually doing quite well. They were only behind 4-2 and it was already three innings into the game. At the backstop, I was spotted by Julio Tomois, a Dominican who worked as a chauffeur for the U.S. Embassy and also for the PC and who played in the Saturday softball league with me. He ran toward me excitedly, saying, "Mr. Lew, our boys need us! You pitch, I catch, we win!"

"When did you join the PC?" I yelled to him, smiling.

"Every Saturday you play with the Dominicans, today I play with the Americans. Besides I'm the only one here who can catch your pitches. It be okay?"

I put my arms around him. "It be okay amigo, let's go!"

Julio was a real clown to watch and listen to. As he became progressively more excited, he began to jump up and down behind the batter's box, and yelled over to the Foundacion bench, "After Mr. Lew finish with you guys, Yankee no go home, Dominicans go home!"

When the next batter came up to the plate, he yelled at Julio, "Shut up and put your catcher's mask on before someone hits a foul tip and knocks all your teeth out."

Julio laughed, picked up the mask and threw it toward the Foundacion bench. "No need mask, you guys not touch the ball."

Fortunately, few batters did hit the ball and the volunteers were jubilant for the first time that day, as we ended up winning the game.

Afterwards the players joined the rest of the group in contests led by Fran, including swimming in the pool, which was filled with fresh water just for today.

255

Meanwhile, the women were busy with the meal. Soon, the table in the education hall was loaded with Dominican goodies, like rice with chicken, fresh sliced pineapple, oranges and bread. There was plenty for everyone. Like the whole day, it was an excellent blend of American and Dominican culture.

The committee stayed late into the night to make sure everything was back in its original order, then took a few moments to evaluate the day's activities. All of us were satisfied. The PCVs had needed a day like this to get together for food and fellowship. Fran and I were glad for this last chance to see so many of them. And, best of all, it demonstrated that the Dominicans and Americans could work and have fun together, which was one of the things the PC was all about.

Chapter 35
Renewal

As we started to come to the end of our two-year service, we began to wonder if we would be able to identify with American culture when we returned. After living "outside the forest" for a couple of years, we weren't sure we'd recognize it or if we'd be comfortable when we were back inside of it again.

A final visit from a group of Americans removed all doubts from our minds, when they demonstrated to us that Americans were still a nation of caring people.

The Congregational Church in Orange, Massachusetts, became interested in the Heifer Project after they heard about the D.R. from a visiting minister. So moving was the story he told that the church got their whole community involved in a fund-raising effort for Heifer Project — an auction night — when they raised enough money to buy and ship two heifers, plus two delegates, to observe the D.R.

The two heifers were joined by others in a planeload donated from the New England States and the two delegates were joined by other people from the same area who also wanted to journey to the D.R. to make sure their gifts would be of help. So by the time the group reached our island, they were a true cross-section of America — they included the minister who had been so inspiring, Rev. Morse; Dave, a firefighter; Henry, an engineer; two students, Nancy and Jim; and an educational aide, June Henley.

Naturally, their trip was a little better organized on the American rather than the Dominican end. The arrangements had been made for them to stay at the guest house on the Foundacion farm. While not luxurious by any means, it would have been adequate for a group of all men.

The two ladies were a surprise. Fran solved the problem at the last second when she said, "The women are welcome to stay with us."

Our dog, Lisa, seemed very happy when she saw me get out the cots for June and Nancy to sleep on. She hadn't forgotten the enjoyable visit of Grandpa Gottfried.

The next morning Nancy was bright eyed with excitement while June stretched and yawned. "When does your dog sleep? Every time I awoke during the night she was standing by my side," remarked June.

We hurried breakfast and took off for the farm where we found the men at the bunk house, sitting around a table loaded with dirty dishes, all joyfully singing. They had everything under control and were anxious to accompany me on a trip to a Dominican farm that had received Heifer Project animals.

The compesinos seemed very pleased to have such a large group of Americans visit them. One farmer told me, "I'm very touched to know that Americans are so genuinely concerned about my welfare." While visiting another farm the Americans were treated to fresh coconut juice picked by a small boy who shimmied up the tree to get them for us after John Forrester had tried and failed several times to climb the tree. The farmer took pride in chopping the tops off the coconuts, one for each person.

Watching the Americans, I remembered the enjoyment it had been for me when I tipped a freshly-cut coconut to my lips for the first time. Everyone was smiling and wiping their mouths just as I had done.

Later we found Tottie, a beautiful Dominican girl who had visited in the home of Rev. and Mrs. Morse as an exchange student. Tottie arranged a small party for the New England group and a few of her frineds. The bonds of friendship grew closer as Rev. Morse showed American slides, Tottie played Dominican music and we all danced.

The ride home was the most memorable of all. The truck was overloaded as we stacked in people two and three deep. Equally full was the joy in everyone's heart. As the truck slowly wandered down the lonely country road, everyone burst out in song filling the still of the night with music. How beautiful it must have sounded to the people in scattered houses along the road, as the Americans leisurely passed by singing "Amazing Grace."

It was especially meaningful to those of us who were cramped in the truck, as the closeness made everyone pour their hearts into the song. I could not tell how many people had misty eyes during that journey, but I know there was at least one, especially when someone started leading the singing of "We are Climbing Jacob's Ladder." Different persons added their own words to the song and someone said, "God bless Fran and Lew for all they do." We were very touched and could only say, "God bless you, too!"

When the New England group left the D.R., they left with more than just an understanding of the Dominican people — they left with love for them in their hearts.

We will always be grateful to this group. They helped us rediscover our love for the America we'd left behind. And even more important, they helped us realize the greatest discovery made while serving in the Peace Corps — WHERE THERE IS UNDERSTANDING, THERE IS LOVE. WHERE THERE IS LOVE, THERE IS HAPPINESS AND PEACE. And for this to happen, it didn't matter if you lived in America or in the Dominican Republic.

Chapter 36
Farewell Friends And Lisa

One of our final things to leave behind was Padre Miguel's small church which we'd been attending regularly for almost two years. The last services we attended there turned out to be a fitting farewell, though unusual, it was not planned that way.

That day, the church was full and for the first time, we had to look around to find a seat. Then other new things began to happen. First, the congregation stood to sing in an orderly fashion. Then Antonio Cruz, a small, kind elderly gentlemen decided he did not approve of the lady's dress in front of him. She had failed to make any effort to zip up the zipper, which ran the full length of the back of her dress, so while she was singing, he reached forward and carefully pulled the zipper completely up. We watched as the lady slowly turned around with a puzzled look, but said nothing, just kept on singing.

When everyone sat down, Antonio remained standing, then walked to the middle aisle and shook his head at the disorderly alignment of the pews. Antonio went to the first pew and asked everyone to stand. Then he pushed the bench forward and straightened it out. He went through the whole church this way, until every pew was straight north and south. As he did this, Padre Miguel stood in the pulpit, grinning but saying nothing. The whole procedure took about 15 minutes, but the people cooperated beautifully.

Fran and I were sure that if all this commotion would have happened the first time we attended church there, our reaction would have been much different. We would likely have been joking, wondering if we were really in church. However, instead we both just sat still, observing just like the Padre, with approving grins on our faces too.

In addition to the sudden organizing of the church, Padre Miguel surprised us with a special closing message. Standing in the middle of the aisles, he told the people of us and how as PC volunteers, our mission had been to help them improve their living conditions and the world around us, but that we would soon be leaving to go home to our friends and families, never to return.

"They have set an example of loving one another," the Padre said, "and we need to follow it and love and help one another. We have many problems in our community, but everyone must work together to solve them."

After the Padre finished, we could hear a few voices saying softly, "Si." Tears came to our eyes, and we found ourselves thinking of what Padre Miguel had told Fran when we first arrived, "If you do nothing more than live among these people, you will bring about change." We had been doubtful then, but today, we were believers.

There was a faithful companion that had touched our lives by living with us. It was now time to make a very tough decision — WHAT DO WE DO WITH OUR DOG LISA?

We sat on the porch one evening, Lisa by our side, sitting as she had so many times while we discussed our problems. She knew her turn would come when we were finished.

I placed my hand on her head. "You are a very intelligent dog," I said, "I wish you could take part in our discussion and tell us what to do."

Fran's hand joined mine, "Yes, Lisa, you have been a wonderful dog. You have never harmed a single person, but your bluff has sure protected us."

I looked at Fran. "I've always thought that if someone really would have tried to harm either of us, it would have been more than a bluff."

After a short pause, Fran asked the question again we had both been thinking. "So, what are we going to do?"

I could not bear the thought of leaving her behind, as she had helped both of us when we needed it. "I want to take her back to Ohio with us," I said.

"Oh, good," said Fran. "So do I."

Giving it a little thought, I said, "I hope we are not being selfish. Other people want her, and maybe she would be happier staying here." Neither of us had an answer to that, so I jumped up and Lisa bounced into the yard, barking, and our discussion was completed, at least for that night.

We both had many things to do in the capital the next day, but we made time to check on the possibilities of taking Lisa home with us. We found it would be very complicated, but possible, to take Lisa to Ohio. However, when we made our initial stop that day at the CARE office to talk to the director, another option was offered to us.

"There is something I've been wanting to ask you," he said. "Would you sell your dog when you leave the country?"

My children have been begging for a pet, and Lisa would be very welcome to join our family."

I smiled. "We have been checking on some things today. Drive out to see us tomorrow."

When we arrived back home, we had a lot to think about. We knew it was possible to ship Lisa home, but we also had a beautiful family to leave her with. We had come to admire the CARE director who did so much with so little, and we knew that his family would treat Lisa well. We both went out to sit under the mango tree in the moonlight, with Lisa, who put her head on my lap to wait for us to talk.

After seriously discussing what was practical, the decision was easy. It would be difficult to ship Lisa, and we didn't know for sure how we could handle all the necessary arrangements. Here, she could make another family very happy. We decided that when the CARE director came to see us tomorrow, we'd let his family take her with them. Then, Fran and I jumped to our feet and romped and played for the last time with Lisa.

The next day, the director came on schedule along with his wife and two children. The children flung open the car doors and ran to Lisa — the friendship was immediate.

As we watched them play, the director asked, "Are you going to sell the dog?"

I shook my head. "No, I'll never sell Lisa." He stood with a disappointed look, so I continued. "The dog was given to me with a promise that I give her a good home. I will give her to you if you promise you will do the same."

He laid his hand on my shoulder. "You have my word," he said.

I wanted to say more, but I was starting to get choked up, so I turned my back and walked toward the house. Fran came over and said to him, "I think you had better take your dog and go before Lew changes his mind."

I turned around to join Fran and we watched the family drive away. Lisa stuck her head out the window and gave a few barks, the children clinging to her with all their might.

Lisa had been born on the grounds of the U.S. Embassy which made her an American dog. She had spent one year with Aide for International Development, two years in the Peace Corps, and now, she was starting a new career in CARE. But that was not the end of her service. Soon after we left the D.R., we learned that the CARE director's family had been transferred to Bogota, Columbia, and Lisa had gone with them, as she was now a precious member of their family. There, Lisa, the American dog that had never set foot in the United States, went on to serve her country faithfully and well.

But we did not know that as the car disappeared out of our driveway. Then we could only stand quietly, tears in our eyes, as we softly whispered, "Goodbye, Lisa."

Chapter 37
Strike Him Out, Lewie

Finally, there came the night of my last Dominican softball game. It began with Fran waiting on our front porch for me. It was taking longer than usual, so she yelled in, "Lew, you have been changing clothes for a long time. Are you all right?"

Inside, I was still slowly pulling my baseball shirt down over my head. "It's okay," I yelled out, but Fran came into the bedroom anyway.

She stood by the bed where I was seated. "You have been very quiet. Is there a problem?"

"No. I was just doing lots of thinking. Tonight could be my last ballgame."

"I've heard that many times."

"It's true. I'm over 50 and the warm climate here in the D.R. has kept my muscles loose. Next week we leave the D.R. When we return home again, my body may change in the cool climate."

"Many things will change when we return," Fran said, but she continued to sense that I wanted to reminisce, so she sat on the edge of the bed with me.

"Playing here has made me feel young again," I said, "not to mention giving me a chance to work off all the frustrations from the week."

"We sure had our share of those," Fran said.

Softball had been good to me through the years, but here, it had been a great morale booster and enabled us to touch the lives of middle class people, publico drivers, merchants, college students and office workers we would have never met through our normal PC contacts. There we met only the very poor, the very rich, or government officials.

Fran laid her hand on my shoulder. "It not only helped you, but me too," she said, referring to the wives and girlfriends who had come to watch the games with her after the first few Saturdays, once they knew the Americano was bringing his wife. "Sometimes, I had more fun visiting than watching the game!" she said.

I got up and retrieved my hat from my suitcase, thinking now about the many heated arguments, and the ball gloves flying in the air, and the bats waving over heads. At such times, I would go to the sidelines, put on my windbreaker and wait for them to settle it. The Dominicans were very quick-tempered and emotional, but they could also forgive and forget easily. The same players would soon be giving each other bear hugs and then the umpire would be yelling, "Play ball!"

"What's the story on tonight's game?" Fran asked.

"I really don't know, but it must be important, as we are playing under the lights. Only really important games were ever played with the lights on. "It must be because we are playing the champions of the league across town," I continued. "The boys have been talking about it for weeks, and wanted to be sure that I would still be here to play."

"Then let's get going, you don't want to be late for your last game!"

As we entered the stadium, the lights were already on and a few players were already starting to warm up.

"This is a perfect night," I told Fran, stopping to take a deep breath. "It makes me want to jump 10 feet and yell — what a beautiful night and then run around and give everyone a big hug and say I love you!"

Fran looked at me and said, "If you do that, you better start with me."

I hesitated a moment, "I don't think I can jump 10 feet. Will it be all right if I just say, 'I love you?' "

"A 10 foot leap would be more impressive," Fran said, "however, if you pitch a shut-out tonight, I will be satisfied."

"Just for you, I'll do that tonight."

We parted as Fran headed toward the stands and I to the ballfield. But then Fran did something that neither one of us would have done two years ago — she stopped and yelled above the crowd for all to hear, "Lew, I forgot something, I love you!" I turned around but couldn't see her, but I raised my hand to acknowledge that I heard her.

When I joined my teammates, I found they had only one thing on their minds tonight — to win the game. By now a large crowd had gathered and the tension and the enthusiasm kept building as the players gave each other pep talks. We huddled for last minute signals and planning, and then I started to stroll toward the mound, my thoughts going back to the Saturday afternoon when I headed out here for my first time. Then I did not have a uniform and played the game in my heavy work shoes, thinking, "If my buddies at home could see me now!"

How things had changed. Now I was a full-fledged, fully-uniformed member of the team. When I reached the mound and picked up the rosin bag, the loudspeakers blared and introduced me. "Starting pitcher, Peace Corps volunteer, Americano — Lew Gottfried!"

I moved on the pitching rubber, my heart pounding as the adrenalin was starting to flow. Sweat running down on my forehead, I was warm and loose, ready to pitch my last game for the D.R. and maybe forever, but I remembered to give a broad smile before throwing my first pitch. It had become my trademark. The final thought running through my mind was a familiar one, "If my buddies back home could only see me now . . ."

The game started out right, with the first three batters all hitting easy pop-ups into the infield. I grew stronger and gained confidence as the game progressed, helped by the right fielder yelling at the top of his voice, "Strike him out, Lewie," with each batter that came to the plate.

The game reached the last inning and not one player for the opposition had reached first base. Then the last batter came to the plate and I soon had two strikes against him. The crowd had been quiet and neutral throughout the game, but now they were all on their feet, yelling for the Americano to finish off the batter. I could not hear the right fielder any longer, but

I knew he was still out there yelling for me to "strike him out, Lewie!" with a voice that was probably by now hoarse. I reached for the rosin bag for the last time, banking on my 30-plus years of experience to keep from choking. I leaned forward and gave the pitch my total effort.

It was probably the best pitch of the best game I had ever pitched in my entire life. The batter missed the ball by a foot. Pandemonium broke out, as suddenly, all my teammates jubilantly swarmed around me and picked me up in the air and began carrying me around the ball diamond. Everyone was cheering, "Lewie, Lewie, Lewie!"

At first I did not know how to react — this had never happened to me before in all my years of pitching. But then I realized it would probably never happen to me again — this was my moment of glory — and I raised my arms in the air in recognition of the moment and the crowd's cheers. As we rounded second base I thought, my teammates expected great things from me tonight and I responded far above my natural ability. It was a little like all of Peace Corps. The people expected much from Fran and me, and because they did, we found unrealized capabilities within ourselves.

After the game, the players insisted that I go with them to a tavern owned by one of them for a little farewell party. They were still excited over the victory — whether it was for money or pride, I wasn't sure — but right then, that victory was the most important thing in the world.

The celebration was quite a party. No doubt, it cost someone a lot of money, or shall I say, a lot of rum. Somewhere in the middle of it all, the players pulled out a new ball and everyone signed it and gave it to me as something to remember them by. I stared at it amid all the noise and realized that I also wanted to give something to all of them, as they had all become special to me during my two years here. But what?

I had little with me, but I knew it would be enough. I took off my hat and looking around, found the elderly gentlemen who had come nearly every Saturday just to see us play. He was standing almost unnoticed by the door, but I walked over and placed the hat on his head. Next, I picked up my ball glove and handed it to the right fielder, the one who always borrowed a glove from the right fielder of the other team. After both times, the men cheered, so I continued. I looked at the skinny lad who had just joined the team, the one who played the first game barefooted and sat on the bench tonight because he did not have any spikes. I took off mine and gave them to him. They were way too large, but I knew he would work something out. I stripped off my ball shirt and tossed it to my friend Tonio, who had caught my first Dominican pitch at Fernando's party so long ago. Again the men cheered.

Finally, I had only one more thing to give away. It was the prize of them all, my blue windbreaker that I used for a warm-up jacket. I knew it was something that many players wanted, and as I picked it up I knew that it would cause a problem if I gave it to the wrong one. I slowly looked over the crowd and then spotted the perfect person, the man who least expected anything — Felix, our faithful umpire. I placed the jacket into his arms and said, "Es por tu, Amigo (This is for you, my friend)."

Every week, Felix was the subject of dirty looks, fists shaken in front of his nose and ball bats swung at him, but now, he smiled from ear to ear, missing front teeth and all, as he looked down at the jacket and clutched it tightly with both hands. Though all the players wanted the jacket, they all stood up and cheered him, even those who abused him the most, and I knew I had made the right choice.

Felix said nothing, but finally looked up at me with tears rolling down his cheeks. I smiled at him and wiped a tear from my cheek too, as the players continued to clap and cheer, and at that moment I felt I had become something I'd never dreamed of — a true Dominican. I stood among them with no shoes and no shirt, having just performed a perfectly spontaneous Dominican act, and was proud.

I returned home to find Fran sitting on the front porch, waiting to congratulate me. It was very late when I came in, a very tired, weary old man, dragging my feet up the steps, wearing only my pants, but clutching a softball in my raised hand like a trophy.

Fran had to laugh when she saw me. "I knew it Lew. I knew you were going to lose your shirt before we got out of the Peace Corps."

I threw my arms around her. "Oh, no," I said, "we have lost nothing. We have gained everything!"

Chapter 38
Journey's End

During our entire time in the D.R., the closest neighbors to us were Theresa and Alberto, who lived only a few feet beyond the hibiscus hedge that marked the edge of our property. They were an elderly couple, both badly crippled and so unable to work. They lived in an old house with dirt floors and weathered palm-frond sides.

They had four sons who would bring food for them to eat each day, but we were sure there were days when they had nothing to eat at all. During the entire time we lived there, however, they never once came over to our side of the hedge to ask us for anything, even though we often observed them digging in the fields for edible roots, struggling with a long cane and a well-worn machete.

One day Fran made doughnuts and I took a few over to them. As I placed the doughnuts in Alberto's hands, he closed his grip firmly, and nodding his head, looked me straight in the eye. He didn't say a word, but I sensed a slight quiver in his body, and I could tell he was both grateful and embarrassed, for he had never asked for a handout and had nothing to give in return.

We wanted the day before we left the D.R. to be very special, so after making final arrangements for leaving we stopped for a last dinner in the capital at one of our favorite restaurants by the sea, and then took a sentimental walk by the shore with the sounds of the waves of the Caribbean and the reflections of the moon dancing on the water.

Upon our return home, we immediately noticed oil lamps flickering in and around the home of Alberto and Theresa. People were milling around the house and we could hear the sounds of mourning and wailing. During our last few days, we had been saying our goodbyes to our neighbors. It was now obvious our goodbye to Alberto and Theresa would be different.

As we stood on our porch, Fran asked, "What are we going to do?"

"I think we should do what a good neighbor would do, go and join them," I answered.

Fran agreed, but we still hesitated. The custom was to keep an all-night wake with the body, but we had many things to do tomorrow and we needed our rest. But, they were our neighbors, and so we went.

The mourners paid little attention to us as we emerged out of the darkness of the hibiscus hedge into the dim light of the oil lamps. To them, we were no longer foreigners, we were neighbors. Our presence was expected.

Theresa had died early in the day. The house had a fresh awning of palm fronds over the door for protection from the sun. There were some old church benches outside, which we recognized from many wakes and bancos. We had arrived too late for the ceremonies, but now inside the home Theresa's body lay in a wooden casket which was placed on two wooden chairs laid sideways. The family had picked flowers from our hibiscus hedge, entwined them in a circle and placed them over the body, which was totally wrapped in a white sheet, except for the head. Lit candles stuck in rum bottles burned on the floor at the head and feet. Since the body is not embalmed, another neighbor, Alicia's mother, sat by the body to chase the flies and insects away. She also placed lime slices over Theresa's nose and around the body to keep the odor away and would on occasion wipe any excretions from the nose.

It was a Dominican law that a body must be buried within 24 hours after death, and the custom to stay up throughout the night until daybreak mourning the dead. Theresa's sons stood silently side by side next to the body, each holding a rum bottle with a lit candle in it. The son closest to me broke the silence and asked if I would take photos of their mother and the mourners for them. I accepted and hurried home for my

271

Journey's end for our neighbor.

camera. Not only would this help pass the time, but it would relax the tension of the brothers.

At the break of day, Alicia's mother started the preparation of the body, washing Theresa's face and then slicing more fresh limes to place over her nose and around the body. She then pulled the sheet from under Theresa and tore it into strips about a foot wide and placed one over the face and body. The remaining strips she twisted and tied onto pieces of wood at each end of the casket. These were used to help carry it to the burial.

A few minutes later four men came in and lifted the casket to take it to the cemetery. They were in their work clothes, one was barefooted and another had a rum bottle in his hip pocket.

The male mourners followed the casket out onto the road, while the women remained behind in the home, wailing, as was the custom. They had begun it during the body preparation, but now it became very loud.

One of the neighbor ladies approached Fran and asked, "Are you not going to wail?"

Fran thought for a moment and replied, "No."

Placing her hand over Fran's she said, "You should do this because it shows you are sorry for the loss of a friend."

Fran squeezed her hand. "I'm sorry, the custom where I live is different. We have never wailed. However, I loved Theresa and will miss her. There are many other ways to show love and that's why I am here."

This seemed to satisfy the lady as she squeezed Fran's hand and replied, "Thank you for being here." Fran squeezed the lady's hand in return, very glad to have had the opportunity to share in both the joys and sorrows of life in the Dominican Republic.

Chapter 39
Common Ground

Just as in the first days of our service, our last trip to the capital was for the purpose of completing paperwork. And, like our first trip, it was one filled with many adventures.

On our way, we passed the home of the three brothers who had invited us to their home that first Christmas Day. One of them was standing by the roadside waiting for a publico, and we stopped to offer him a ride as he was going our way.

He was happy for the opportunity to ride with us and very polite and courteous as he jumped in. As we drove, however, he soon removed some papers from his briefcase and began making corrections and adding notes to the pages. When he paused, tapping his pencil on the paper, Fran observed, "You seem to be very serious today."

"Yes," he replied, "I am making a very important speech at the National Cemetery today."

We both thought that was an odd place for a speech, and asked him why he was speaking there. He folded his papers and gave us his full attention. "Many important political speeches are made there. Today, my party is having a big rally." He paused before continuing in an apologetic tone. "Since my party is anti-American, I will not be saying anything nice about your country."

This came as a shock to both of us. All of our past associations with him had been as good neighbors and friends. Though we knew he was politically active, we had never discussed it with him since as Peace Corps volunteers we were supposed to avoid involvement in such matters. But since he seemed eager to talk I asked him, "Am I right in saying that you do not like Americans?"

"That's right. Please understand, I like you two very much. You are different than other Americans."

I was quick to correct him. "That's not true. Although we have all kinds of people in our country, Fran and I consider ourselves to be very average Americans."

By that time, we were approaching the gate to the cemetery, and he gathered his belongings to leave. Smiling he thanked us and added, "I still think you are different and if I am elected president, you both shall be invited to my inauguration. You may be the only two Americans invited, but I hope you will come." There was no time to debate on the subject, so we both reached out to embrace him and I said, "We would be honored."

He then hurriedly left the car, but when he was about 10 feet away, he turned around and smiled, shouting, "Hasta Luego. Si Dios quiere (See you later, God willing).

We sat in the car and watched with mixed emotions as he disappeared into the crowd that was assembling. We were sad that he would soon be delivering a speech against our country and people, but glad that he at least had met two Americans that he liked enough to invite to his inauguration. We considered this a great compliment.

On our return trip through Villa Mella, we made a special effort to say goodbye to special friends. First we knocked on the door of Andre Royes, the schoolmaster, where we found his lovely wife sitting in a rocker, holding their newborn child.

Fran, as always, was a soft touch for a baby, so we lingered awhile until I finally interrupted the ladies to ask if Andre was home.

"No," said his wife. "He is with his girlfriend celebrating the birth of his first son." She looked down at her son and up to me with a smile. "He will be very sorry to hear he missed you."

When we left, we drove over to the church, hoping to have better luck finding Padre Miguel. We were surprised to find him carrying boxes from his office behind the church. He leaned over to set them down on the ground when he saw us coming.

"I'm so happy to see you," he said. "I was hoping to say goodbye. You see, I am also leaving Villa Mella."

This was another complete surprise. It seemed our last Sunday to attend Mass was also his last Sunday, and we realized now why it was such a special service.

The Padre explained that he was being transferred to Canada. "My apologies, I wanted to visit with you more, but the transfer was very sudden."

Fran placed her hand on his shoulder. "The people of Villa Mella will miss you very much. You have been good for them and for the village."

The Padre gave his usual smile. "I hope when I leave my sheep, they will find new leaders. I am very thankful you two have been here these past two years. Your influence has been greater than you realize."

By that time a publico was waiting for Padre Miguel and we watched as he picked up his luggage and took a last long look at his church, the new recreation area he had helped to build, the park and then finally scanned the village. Smiling, he once again turned to us.

"The sun is setting on a part of my life and yours," he said, "Tomorrow will be the dawn of a new day for us all."

We watched as the car carrying the Padre bumped its way to the main road, with the Padre in the back waving goodbye to some friends along the way. We recalled his crazy driving, the house-hunting trip he'd taken Fran on, his unusual services and the friends he had introduced us to. It hardly seemed like an appropriate exit for someone that had given so much of himself. And then it was our turn to take a last look at the village and head for home for a final time.

When we passed the home of Fernando, he was standing by the road waiting for us, waving his hands wildly for us to stop. "Please come in for a cup of coffee!" he cried.

The family was all there, as they had been waiting most of the day for us. Fernando, as always, was wearing the hat I had purchased for him at the Miami airport, though it was now out of shape and frayed with loose straws and had a large hole on top where he'd grabbed it to remove it many times. But this time, he did not take it off as we entered the house.

Marie greeted us with two cups of coffee on one tray, one for me and one for Fran, as was the custom. But when we removed the cups, I said, "This time we will not drink until everyone has a cup. We're all equal and we will all drink at the same time."

Marie hurriedly poured a cup for everyone and we all raised them together, and then silently drank the coffee. Then Fernando left the room and returned with a nearly empty wine bottle. "I've been saving this special wine for this day," he said, and we filled our cups once more and we again raised them in another toast.

"To our friends," I said.

"Si," added Fernando and Marie.

Everyone followed us to the car and then followed the car to the road. Fran continued to wave as we drove away. As I glanced in the mirror to see Fernando, the last glimpse of him I saw was him raising his hat high in the air as a farewell gesture to us.

When we arrived home, it was not long before our neighbors began to gather in our yard to say goodbye. While most of them thought we were leaving for a short time, as we had done twice before, Kiki knew and understood the meaning of this departure.

This time she had no song for us, but instead carried a shallow metal soup plate. It had been used very much, and the software figure painting was starting to wear off in spots. She placed it on our hands and was silent for a few moments before she turned and ran home.

Fran looked at the dish and then at me. "We cannot accept this. This is her only dish. She uses this everyday."

I took the dish from Fran, and rubbed my hand across the bottom of the bowl, recalling, "the coconuts and eggplants the compensinos had given me, even though they needed them more than me."

"She will be hurt if we refuse," I said. And so, we kept Kiki's dish and have it in our home today. On the market, it would be worthless, but to Kiki, it was valuable — the only bowl she had — and to us it was priceless because of the treasured memories it continues to hold of our friend Kiki and the people of the Dominican Republic.

Very early the next morning we drove out of our lane for the last time. Like Padre Miguel, we left the D.R. without much fanfare, just waving at a few friends as we passed.

As the wheels of our Pan-Am jet left the runway, we both glued our noses to the window, and watched the D.R. disappear from view. There were the same familiar sights from the very first time we landed — the blue Caribbean Sea and the green rolling hills — but this time we no longer wondered what was hiding below the palm trees. We knew now that down there were Kiki's singing, Padre's teaching of love for one another, Antonio and his baseball team, sweaty laborers, noisy donkeys, crowing roosters, cock fights, fiestas, dancing and hunger, wailing, poverty, sadness, joy and love. At that moment, babies were being born all over the island, to join it all and add to the over-population problem that already existed. Yes, we knew more about this country and its people and the long road that lay ahead of them.

The island disappeared and we leaned back in our seats, clutching each other, sitting silently, each with a lump in our throats and tears in our eyes — grateful for the opportunity of having lived with the Dominican people, and happy for we were going home!

Afterthoughts

Now that time has passed and we are no longer traveling "Uncharted Paths" we can look back to our two years in Peace Corps with some perspective.

It is difficult to know how much we influenced the people and the country. We do know the years we lived and worked among the Dominicans influenced us much more than we realized. We have mellowed greatly to the faults of our country, as so many wonderful things overshadow them.

Kiki taught us that there is music and laughter in life, regardless of our environment.

Padre Miguel taught us that regardless of how serious the situation, "It's no problem."

Fernando set the example of serving and helping, even though it was not required as a part of his job.

The other volunteers taught us there really is little difference from one generation to the next. The people demonstrated to us the strength in faith, for regardless of the handicaps, they continue to struggle.

The New England group brought to light that understanding brings love, and love brings peace and happiness.

However, it was the right fielder on my softball team that made me realize the greatest thing that happened to us during those two years. He shouted until he was hoarse, and then continued to yell, "Strike him out, Louie!"

There was no doubt in his mind that I could do it, and I was not about to disappoint him. It was what happened to us in all of Peace Corps — the people expected more from us than we thought it possible to do, and because they did, we were able to do things far above our natural ability. Even today, when we are asked if we would do it all over again, I think of that voice, and I say, "Si."

In 1987 we returned to Santo Domingo to help celebrate the 25th anniversary of Peace Corps in the Dominican

Republic. One of the subjects discussed was "What can we, as former volunteers, do to help today's people?" It was agreed they needed more basic education, especially among the poor. Sometimes only a few dollars to a deserving youth would do it.

As a result, a special fund was established to be supervised by current Peace Corps volunteers, past PCVs and Dominican leaders. The fund will provide financial help towards the educational needs of the Dominican people.

Fran and I heartily support this effort. For if we give them fish, we feed them for a day. If we teach them to fish, we feed them for life. A percent from each sale of this book is being donated to this project.

In closing, we wish to thank you for reading our book, and encourage you to take your own journey down "Uncharted Paths."